The Curtain Rises

To our friends in eastern Europe.
You have truly enriched our lives.
How lucky we are!

The Curtain Rises

Oral Histories of the Fall of Communism in Eastern Europe

Susan G. Shapiro
with Ronald Shapiro

FOREWORD BY ELIZABETH LORANT

McFarland & Company, Inc., Publishers
Jefferson, North Carolina, and London

LIBRARY OF CONGRESS CATALOGUING-IN-PUBLICATION DATA

Shapiro, Susan, 1947–
     The curtain rises : oral histories of the fall of communism in
Eastern Europe / Susan Shapiro with Ronald Shapiro ; foreword by
Elizabeth Lorant.
          p.   cm.
     Includes index.

     ISBN 0-7864-1672-6 (softcover : 50# alkaline paper)

     1. Europe, Eastern — Social conditions — 1989– 2. Post-commu-
nism — Europe, Eastern — History. 3. Europe, Eastern — Social conditions — 20th century. 4. Communism — Europe, Eastern — History. 5.
Oral history. I. Shapiro, Ronald. II. Title.
     HN380.7.A8S5   2004
     306'.0947'0904 — dc22   2003020602

British Library cataloguing data are available

Cover photograph: Gap in the Berlin Wall *(Corel)*

Manufactured in the United States of America

*McFarland & Company, Inc., Publishers
   Box 611, Jefferson, North Carolina 28640
   www.mcfarlandpub.com*

Acknowledgments

Susan Shapiro

The stories at the core of this book are the result of friendships made over the past sixteen years. All the families gave their time and opened up their lives so that their stories could be told.

The research and writing could not have been done without my husband, Ron, who worked tirelessly by my side. His skill, determination and devotion were essential to the book's quality and authenticity. Ron wrote parts of the text, edited, reviewed, and added important information about the history, the present situation in the various countries and the people.

Thank you to my children, Dan, Steven, and Madelyn, for valuing my work in Eastern and Central Europe. Dan developed a peer counseling program and a curriculum on conflict management, *Conflict and Communication: A Guide Through the Labyrinth of Conflict Management*, which has been translated into twenty languages. Madelyn worked with Bosnian refugees, learned to speak Serbo-Croatian and helped hundreds of people during the Bosnian war. Steve listened to all the details and gave sound advice.

Thank you to my sisters, Margaret Gold and Elizabeth Rue, my best friends. Elizabeth's editing was outstanding. Special thanks to my mother, who continually said, "Hillary Clinton wrote her book in a few months, so can you!" And to Janie Rue, who listened carefully when I talked about the stories.

A special thank you to my niece, Katie Rue, who drew all the maps. The maps are painstakingly accurate, but more importantly, they are artistic and, I hope, add a dimension that enables the reader to understand where the families depicted in the stories actually live and where the countries are located relative to each other.

My access to the families initially came through my work at the Soros Foundation or Open Society Institute. Special thanks to Elizabeth Lorant for her belief in the Health Education Program and for her overall support; to George Soros for providing the funding and trusting in my work; to Viktor Osiatynski for his persistence; and to Carol Flaherty-Zonis, my co-trainer, for all the lessons we learned traveling back and forth across the ocean, and for her patience when mine wore thin.

Thank you to those who assisted in the book's development: Ruth Mathewson, editor and dear friend; Andy Boutcher, editor; and Jenny Row, who helped me find a publisher.

To my friends at home in Harrisburg, Pennsylvania: Lisa Pilsitz, my confidante and administrator of the Soros Health Education Program, for her constant encouragement and faith in me; Joan Myhre, my friend, who co-facilitated workshops in Lithuania and Macedonia; Jared Beitman, graduate student, Eastern European studies, University of Toronto, who assisted in the research; Vaughn Heym, filmmaker, who developed the photographs; and Arne Taksen, our driver during "Soros" days. To everyone at St. Thomas Roaster, my favorite café, especially Geoff and Pam Smith.

To Denise Moffatt, who worked with me in Macedonia. To my wonderful mother-in-law, Frances Shapiro, the first to believe the book would be published. And last but not least, to my six-year-old godchild, Frosina, in Skopje, Macedonia.

Thank you all.

Contents

Foreword

I met Susan Shapiro before the fall of the Berlin Wall. I was working at the Soros Foundation in New York, as the director responsible for our activities in Hungary. We had opened our office in Hungary in 1984 and were already well established as the one nonprofit organization able to deliver services and provide contacts in all of Central and Eastern Europe. Our days and nights were filled with frantic activity, as suddenly anything and everything became possible. We were fielding hundreds of calls every day, from the media, from government agencies, from universities and other foundations, all asking for information, contacts, and opportunities in the region.

In walked Susan Shapiro, who introduced herself as an expert on health education in the United States, with dogged determination to do something in Hungary. I listened as she told me that she had hosted an exchange student from Hungary and had become very concerned with his eating habits as his visit progressed. She wanted me to support her in visiting Hungary to determine if there was interest among teachers to bring health education, especially nutrition, into the school system. The Hungarian diet is notorious for its high fat and sugar content, and the health effects of smoking were not acknowledged by the Communist state. Nevertheless, I was highly skeptical that this was just what was needed at this time, when almost everything was suddenly needed. With a zeal comparable to that of a missionary, Susan would not give up on me — she called, she visited, she pleaded, she tried to convince me. Finally, her perseverance overcame my equally strong resistance to this idea and off she went, but with more anxiety than enthusiasm from my end. I also paid a huge airfreight bill, since she took mountains of supplies and educational materials with her.

Two weeks after her return from Hungary, I was subjected to a loud clamor emanating from teachers and schools in Hungary, pleading that I send Susan back to provide a full health education program. The reasons for this outcry became obvious later: for the first time ever, these tired, underpaid, isolated teachers had the opportunity to learn about something that was of great personal importance to their own lives, and most important, Susan had introduced them to a dramatically different way to teach and to learn. The methods that Susan used to communicate with her audience became a basis for teachers to change the old, authoritarian style expected under the Communist system to one where teachers and students communicated and exchanged ideas in innovative and interesting ways.

Two years later, the Romanian Soros Foundation somehow found out about the Hungarian Health Education Program, and asked George Soros to make it available to them as well. The reply was that we should make it available to all countries where we had offices. We did. From that point on, and for the next five years, Susan spent her life on airplanes, traveling to more than 20 countries, leaving fans everywhere she went. To date, the Health Education Program has been one of the most successful ever implemented in the Soros Foundation network.

This book profiles the lives of the people whom Susan met during these dramatic transition years, whose lives were undoubtedly influenced by her work and her unique spirit.

Elizabeth Lorant
Open Society Institute

Preface

Nineteen eighty-nine: The fall of the Berlin Wall signals the demise of Communism in Eastern and Central Europe and the Balkans. What initially was seen as a symbolic gesture of destroying the chasm between East and West has given rise to widespread reforms in political, educational, cultural, economic, and religious thinking. Who could have predicted the sweeping breadth of change that was created out of this simple act of demolition?

As governments change, the landscape of the whole continent is being transformed. Individuals are given new freedoms to express and explore. Leaders grapple with the market economy and political uncertainty. Capitalism has crashed uncomfortably into the formerly Marxist states, leaving a trail of unrest while paving a path for possible future prosperity.

Daily newspaper headlines help us to know and better understand the key individuals and governments who have set the wheels of change in motion. Many of us can recognize the names of those who enable, foster, and apply a philosophical change unprecedented in the history of the region. They are the leaders who pass the legislation, who develop new economic policies, and who exercise new controls on their militaries.

Lost in the popular perception, however, is a whole group of lesser-known individuals, the everyday men and women. These people are the ones who implement the changes about which we read. These are the people who struggle with the philosophical, political, educational, cultural, and spiritual adjustments. These are the people who wrestle with the mandate to find ways to integrate these new principles into their lives and those of the people around them.

Our focus will be on these people. As the New World Order races into the twenty-first century, it is these grass-roots leaders — entrepreneurs, artists, political activists, writers, teachers, thinkers and others — who are working among the people in the towns, who are implementing reforms in the schools, and who are assuming leadership posts in local government. Now, more than a decade after the fall of the Berlin Wall, you will meet and get a close look at the lives of these people and discover how they are effecting change in Eastern Europe.

— 1 —

Behind the Curtain

I grew up in the 1960s when our world was politically and economically aligned: East vs. West; Communism vs. Democracy; Socialism vs. Capitalism; Evil vs. Good. In 1960 Nikita Khrushchev, Communist Party Chairman, in a speech before the United Nations General Assembly, pounded his shoe on the podium shouting that our grandchildren (in the West) would live under Communism. In 1961 the twenty-eight mile long Berlin Wall, which became a symbol of the schism between East and West, was erected by Communist East Germany, effectively dividing Berlin into two cities. In 1963, the Cuban Missile Crisis threatened us, with possible war averted only at the last minute. Needless to say, our government and our media portrayed all Communists (except for a few dissident writers and artists) as a threat to "our way of life." It was war—"Cold War." We constructed public underground bomb shelters; we conducted mock air raids in our schools; we engineered civil defense plans to expedite evacuations of metropolitan areas; we built up our military forces and armaments.

With all these things happening, how could I possibly have realized that beneath the divisive rhetoric and displays of power by Communist leaders there existed people? People just like you and me, who wanted nothing more than to get a high quality education, to secure a good job, and to provide for their families. In the summer of 1984 my husband, Ron, and I took a journey behind the Iron Curtain to experience firsthand what life was like there. How could I ever have imagined this trip would lead me into a completely unexpected career and would introduce me to extraordinary people in twenty-five countries of the former Soviet Union?

It was a steamy night in the summer of 1984 when our Austrian Air flight landed in Vienna. The following day Ron and I rented an Opel Kadet with German license plates and drove to Budapest, Hungary. We encountered no problems crossing the Austrian border, but at the Hungarian border the guard motioned for us to steer our auto to an area that separated us from the other cars. He looked at my passport, and in broken English, questioned me about the origin of my maiden name, Gondleman. I replied that I was of Russian descent. A moment of silence followed. He continued, "What is your affiliation to our country?" Before I could answer, three guards approached and searched our suitcases, my purse, and Ron's wallet. They interrogated us as they placed a mirror under the car to see if we were trying to smuggle anything into the country. How long were we staying, where were we staying, and did we have relatives in Hungary? Were we traveling outside of Budapest? We were quite polite, but nervous with the manner of the interrogation.

Finally the guards waved us on and for the next two miles we drove through a "no-man's-land" of tall barbed wire fences and wooden watchtowers manned by heavily armed soldiers. Soon we were on a four-lane highway to Budapest. As we continued we could not help but notice from a distance the chilling grayness of the towns and factories. Unfamiliar signs (to us) were posted at certain spots along the road with an X over the picture of a camera — which we assumed meant that no pictures should be taken of these areas, such as railroad stations and military bases. Encountering little traffic, we soon arrived at the outskirts of Budapest. As we followed the directions to our hotel we got our first glimpse of life behind the Iron Curtain.

Matchbox, Russian-made Ladas swerved in and out of the lanes on Karl Marx Boulevard. Soon we stopped the car to get our bearings. At that moment a military officer walked by and saw us. Our expressions gave away the fact that we were simply lost and he immediately approached our car. My mind flashed back to my elementary school days when we practiced hiding quickly under our desks in case of nuclear attack. "Sir, can you please direct us to the Hilton Hotel in the Buda Hills?" He looked at us, uncomprehendingly. "Sir, the Hilton?" Suddenly the officer smiled at me, yes, actually smiled. He used sign language to show us the way. We arrived at the Hilton about ten minutes later.

At the registration desk the clerk asked for our passports. He said he had to take them to the local police station to be recorded and we could pick them up the next day. Surrendering our passports concerned

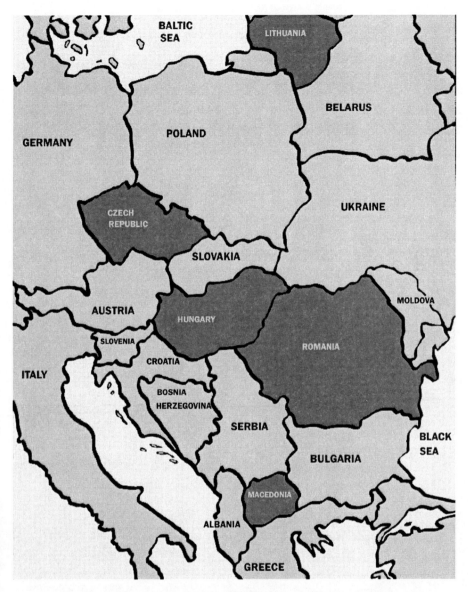

Map of entire region (see Appendix for individual maps). (Map by Katie Rue.)

us, but it seemed to be our only option. After registering we were escorted to our room, which overlooked the Danube River and Pest, the other half of the city. Anxious to explore, we unpacked and set out on foot.

The Danube River separates the city into two sections, Buda and Pest. The Hilton is situated on a high cliff on the Buda side of the city overlooking Pest. We descended 257 steps (I counted) to the river, walked across the famous Chain Bridge and crossed into Pest. What a study in contrasts; the architecture of the pre–Communist structures was impressive. It didn't seem to fit with the nearby concrete Stalinist buildings. The littered sidewalks were almost void of commercial activity. The few shops, whose windows were sparsely decorated with merchandise, had little inventory inside. The atmosphere was somber and an eerie, oppressive quiet prevailed. People — all of them — were dressed in simple brown and gray clothes, subdued colors.

On Friday night, the Jewish Sabbath, we decided to attend services at one of the most famous synagogues in Eastern Europe, Dohány Synagogue, located just blocks from the center of the downtown area of Pest. When we arrived, after a short taxi ride, we were saddened by what we saw. The synagogue was in disrepair with peeling walls, broken tiles, and wooden pews that were chipped and cracked in places. There were only a few elderly men and women worshipping — remnants of a once large and prosperous congregation. The men were doing most of the chanting to the same melodies I had learned as a child. The women sat whispering, not paying much attention to the service, just as my mother and her sisters would do when I went to synagogue with them. This Sabbath was quite an experience for us — never to be forgotten.

The following day we decided to tour the city. The hotel manager suggested that his friend, a guide, show us the sights. An hour or so later Falus Gábor (pronounced Falush Gaa´ bor) walked into the Hilton lobby (and into our lives) with an air of confidence. He told us that, although he was a psychologist by profession, he offered tours to supplement his income. Of average height and of slim build, he could have been a marathon runner. His gestures were quick and nervous, but when he smiled, his face softened, appearing childlike. I guessed that he was in his late 40s.

Gábor drove us around Budapest in his compact red Lada pointing out the major sights of the city while explaining their historical significance. He gave us the background of just about every statue we passed. When we happened to pass the Dohány Synagogue, Ron reminded me that we had attended services in this synagogue the night before. Gábor looked at us and asked if we were Jewish. We nodded and then there was a moment of silence. Did we say something that could get us into trouble with the government? But his face broke into a smile as he held out his hand and said, "Shalom. I too am a Jew." It would be months later before Gábor told us that this was the first time he had ever divulged to a stranger that he was Jewish.

Gábor spoke more freely with us the rest of the afternoon now that we had something in common. He talked about the denial of human rights, low salaries, and the black market. Then he described to us what he called the home personality and the work personality. "At home we talk freely, yet in a quiet voice, because the walls are thin. There is a code of trust that exists within the family. But this code of trust ends at our front door. Nothing is discussed outside our home. For most people the conversation we are having would never happen. In fact, I am breaking that code by speaking honestly with you. Once outside the door, we put on a different face. We learn to speak in circles. We don't make definite statements because they could incriminate us. And we learn never to trust anyone."

This lack of trust was unfamiliar to me. I explained to Gábor that I was used to expressing my opinion among friends and strangers alike, without fear of any kind. If I didn't like a politician, even the president of the U.S., I wouldn't hesitate to say so and state my reasons. It was my inalienable right. Gábor's confession exposed a new world to me.

Gábor revealed that he had never become a member of the Communist Party and in reality, most Hungarians were not members of the party. As we navigated the city, we shared stories about our lives and our children. This trip was taking on new meaning for me. I looked at the women in the streets and wondered what their lives were like, how they raised their children, and how they coped with the limits they had to place on expressing their feelings.

We decided to give Gábor some extra money for his services, so I took a twenty dollar bill out of my purse. Gábor quickly shook his head and motioned for me to hide the money. I slipped it into a bag in his car. I later discovered that it was illegal for Hungarian citizens to have American dollars. I simply hadn't realized how dangerous our simple gesture of appreciation was for us as well as for Gábor. Fortunately, no one saw us and Gábor was able to keep the money.

Upon returning to the United States, Ron and I became involved in our daily routines, but thoughts of our trip lingered. A year and a half later, in January 1986, Gábor surprised us with a phone call. He was coming to the United States for a psychology conference in Colorado and asked if he could visit us on his way. We welcomed him, and he arrived in Harrisburg in mid–February. While he was here, we talked about life in Hungary. By now, I had time to think of an endless stream of questions; Gábor graciously answered all of them. The state of health education, my area of expertise, in Hungary, intrigued me the most. Gábor told us of his wife's battle with alcoholism. There was no available treatment in Hungary; no clinics, no Alcoholics Anonymous, no support groups for spouses. He worried about his two children — especially Andy, his oldest child. For reasons that remain a mystery to me to this day, Ron and I proposed to Gábor the possibility of having Andy come to the U.S. and live with us for a year. In this way, Andy would be removed from the dysfunction in his family, and our children would learn about a "closed" society, firsthand, not from a textbook. Gábor thought about it for a while and decided to accept our offer.

The next year brought about dramatic changes for me. I spent months arranging for Andy's arrival. I had to go before our local school board to request special permission for Andy to come since our district only accepted foreign students from accredited exchange programs. Naturally, most Communist countries, Hungary included, had no exchange programs, since students from those countries rarely came to the United States. I struggled and persisted and finally succeeded in obtaining the necessary permissions.

Getting the necessary documents on Gábor's end was no easier. Gábor already had a visa, but it wasn't until he paid a police officer US$35.00 (about half a month's salary), twenty-four hours before their scheduled departure, that Andy was able to secure his visa.

On August 14, 1987, Andy landed at New York's JFK Airport. After a few days of settling in, the first thing I wanted to do was to find a violin teacher for Andy. He had been admitted to the prestigious Music Conservatory of Budapest for his skill in playing the violin, but had relinquished his spot so that he could come to the United States. I promised Gábor that Andy would continue violin lessons. Gábor wanted Andy to become a musician because he would have status and more freedom than that allowed the general public. For example, musicians could travel freely to their performances even if on the other side of the Iron Curtain.

It was important that the quality of lessons and practice in Harrisburg be equal to the superb caliber of teaching he would have had in Hungary. After a week of searching I found a well-known violin teacher, John Eaken, at Dickinson College in Carlisle, a forty-five minute drive from our home. In making my promise to Gábor, I hadn't realized that I was committing to long days of driving each week.

The first time Andy accompanied me to the supermarket, he went racing up and down the aisles with the cart creating quite a scene. He was utterly amazed at the quantity and variety of canned goods, fruits and vegetables available to us. He was accustomed to government owned "state" stores with limited selection. "One day there would be beef in our corner market, the next day it was gone," he told us, "and if there were beans or tomatoes in the store on a particular day, and we didn't need them, my dad still bought them because the next day they probably wouldn't be there."

On one visit to the supermarket, I bought bananas and put them on top of our refrigerator. Two hours later I noticed that they were gone and Andy was doubled over with stomach cramps. He explained that in Hungary bananas were available only at Christmas time. Parents waited in lines for hours to get a few brown bananas as a special Christmas treat for their children. It would take a while for Andy to learn that he could eat a banana every day in America, and there would still be plenty of them at the supermarket the next day. Andy recovered quickly and bananas became a staple of his diet. To this day, bananas are a part of the holiday season in most post–Communist countries and a symbol of the difficulties of the past.

Working in the health education field, I was especially intrigued by Andy's eating habits. He had never tasted broccoli, cauliflower, or asparagus; they were not available in Hungary. His selection of vegetables at home was limited to carrots, potatoes, onions and cabbage. But even with the wide variety available to him here, Andy chose a Mars bar rather than any vegetable. The universality of teenagers! I used to joke with him that one day I would teach nutrition to his class in Hungary, and then he would have to listen to what I said. He always said that nutrition had never been taught in his schools, and he doubted that anyone would ever care about it. Little did we know what lay ahead.

Gábor phoned us toward the end of Andy's stay and told me that Sashma Palmer, wife of the American ambassador to Hungary, had spoken to a group of psychologists about the need for Hungarians to examine their eating habits. I sent Mrs. Palmer a letter, included my curriculum (written for students, teachers and cafeteria staff in the Central Dauphin School District in Harrisburg), and asked for her assistance in locating funding for me to teach nutrition education in Hungarian schools. She wrote back that she had knowledge of a small, new foundation, the Soros Foundation, and that I should contact them.

Five months after Andy returned to Hungary, I walked into his class-

Andy Falus, holding his new guitar, returning to Hungary in 1988.

room in Budapest to teach my first lesson in nutrition, sponsored by the Soros Foundation. Neither Andy nor I could hold back our smiles. My topic was: *You Are What You Eat.* With an interpreter by my side, I lectured for the first ten minutes about Hungarian foods and the importance of making healthy choices, drawing on my observations of Andy. He and his friends told me they were bored eating the same foods over and over again. I divided the students into groups of six and asked them to write down the ingredients and recipes of two meals they loved. It turned out that small discussion groups were a completely new experience for the students. Questions and ideas began to flow as they were exposed to interactive education for the first time.

Now relaxed, the students overwhelmed me with questions. "What foods do American kids our age like? Does everyone eat at McDonald's all the time? What do you teach American kids?" Our discussion continued well past the allotted time. As I was leaving the room, the principal asked if I would offer more programs. I eagerly agreed. The next week I initiated a full health education program in the Egry József School in the 11th district of Budapest. It was a program that I would replicate hundreds of times over during the next several years, not only with high school students, but with teachers, psychologists, and doctors throughout the Eastern Bloc countries.

The Communist governments began to crumble in 1989, and I was there to experience some of the changes. One event in particular occurred on June 16, 1989, as I stood with several friends in Heroes' Square in the center of Budapest. The event was the reburying of Imre Nagy, one of the leaders of the 1956 Hungarian Revolution. Soviet flags hung from the columns. The hammer and sickle had been torn from the center of each flag. A crowd of 200,000 had gathered demanding freedom.

A former law student spoke. "If we can trust our souls and strength," he said, standing on a platform and addressing the people, "we can put an end to the Communist dictatorship; if we are determined enough we can force the Party to submit itself to free elections...." He continued, "Then we will be able to elect a government that will start immediate negotiations about the swift withdrawal of Russian troops." The crowd cheered. The mood in the country was changing.

By October 1989, politicians seeking democratization had challenged the Communist system, and a number of changes had begun to occur. Throughout the country, the old laws were no longer being enforced, so new laws were being legislated. Which laws still existed? Was a speed limit still in effect? What about the laws prohibiting drug use? Were they still upheld? Groups of concerned citizens began to make policy on a grass-roots level and new leaders emerged on the national level. Education reform was of primary importance. There was great need for change in the schools, so parents gathered together to initiate new programs. Several teachers invited me to their schools to speak about health education, a subject that the Communists had neglected. My program was expanding.

Early in November 1989, a Hungarian journalist and friend of mine, Éva Monspart (pronounced Ee'va Monsh'part), came to Egry József School to interview me for an article in the weekly women's magazine *Nok Lapja* and to tape a TV program about my work in the schools. We had met when she attended a Soros-sponsored health education conference in Harrisburg several months prior to this visit, and we had kept in touch. Even though she interviewed me about health education, the most interesting part of the conversation was about our personal lives. We talked for hours. Hearing that I was staying alone in a hotel, she invited me to her home. I accepted.

The restrictions placed on Hungarian families became apparent to me when I arrived at her house with my luggage. Before unpacking, we had to go to police headquarters so that I could record my passport and register as a foreigner. I became frustrated because it took three hours to

Ronald and Susan Shapiro in Heroes' Square, Budapest.

complete the forms, but Éva assured me that life wasn't so bad in Hungary. She was thankful that she lived in Budapest. After all, many of the Communist laws were disappearing, and the government continued to change. We walked along the city streets and Éva explained why she was so grateful.

She was born on January 2, 1944, in Nagyvárad, Hungary. But when she was eight months old, she and her family moved to Budapest because their city was no longer part of Hungary. The Russian front had closed in on the territory around Romania and Hungary and their city now belonged to Romania. Even the name was changed, from Nagyvárad, Hungary, to Oradea, Romania. Éva explained the confusion this area had suffered for hundreds of years.

"The region, called Transylvania, is a part of the world that has changed hands several times and has been a cause of tremendous tension for our people as well as for the Romanians. In 1918 it was given to Romania as a reward for entering World War I on the Allied side. During World War II, Hungary reclaimed Transylvania, but in 1945, it was occupied by the Soviets. In 1947 according to the peace negotiations, Transylvania was given back to Romania. My parents decided to move to Budapest, and once again live in Hungary. They were sad to leave our friends and neighbors, but they wanted me to grow up in Hungary. My parents never went back to their hometown. It was not possible to visit friends and relatives, only correspond with them. The first time we saw my aunt was in the '60s, so many years later.

"Life for us in Communist Hungary has been so much easier than life for the people of Romania. If I had stayed in Romania, especially in the Transylvanian region, their dictator, Nicolae Ceauşescu, would have controlled my life. People suffer terribly under his regime. It is illegal for foreigners to stay in Romanian homes. There is hardly any food for the people; they have to use newspapers for toilet paper. And electricity is limited. Here in Hungary, for example, we had to wait only six years to have our telephone installed. My friends in Romania wait up to twenty-five years. Life is more of a struggle for them. We have not had the same restrictions placed on us here in Hungary. We have always had some food. And jobs. We did not often have to wait in lines. Sometimes it is hard for us, as you can see, and we hate the Communist laws, but we can do most of what we want. At least here in Hungary you can stay in our house, even though we still have to fill out a lot of paper work and spend the afternoon at the police station."

As Éva and I boarded the crowded streetcar leaving police headquarters, she explained that she traveled several times a year from Budapest to Oradea to visit some of her friends and bring them supplies unavailable in Romania. Her closest friends, Márta and Miklós (Miki) Jakobovits (Ya'kobovich), husband and wife, were well-known artists living in Oradea. Miki had painted works that showed the atrocities of the Ceauşescu regime; Márta's creations were in ceramics. They were known throughout the Romanian underground for their efforts to expose the horrors of the Ceauşescu government. Their exhibits were shown only under the most secure conditions. Éva and her daughter Fanni intended to visit the couple that weekend. Would I like to join them and travel to Oradea to meet Márta and Miki?

We discussed the possibility at the dinner table with Éva's husband,

Rudi. He assured me that the trip would be safe and quite interesting. He criticized Ceauşescu and the Romanian government for oppressing over two million ethnic Hungarians who lived in Transylvania and repeated what Éva had told me — that Communism in Hungary looked good compared to the severity of life in Romania. I would be safe, but at the same time, I would see queues of people waiting for food and be witness to extreme poverty and despair. I decided yes, I would go. We would travel by train. I should wear simple clothes, no make-up, and bring $100 in cash. And I should trust Éva.

On Friday we boarded the 3 P.M. train for Oradea. Éva instructed me to sit far away from them and under no circumstances should I acknowledge even knowing them. We sat in a second-class coach that could comfortably fit eight people, but there were sixteen of us — mostly Romanian citizens, middle-aged men. No foreigners other than the three of us. Certainly I was the only American. Everyone smoked. The air was hot and stuffy.

At 5 P.M. the train stopped at the Romanian border and the border guard asked for our passports. Fifteen minutes later he came back into our car and shouted, "Amerikana, Up!" He motioned with his stick for me to rise. Four guards approached me, machine guns in hand and sniffing dogs by their sides. One guard took a small screwdriver from his belt and unscrewed my seat to see if I had hidden anything underneath. They pushed me outside to a dirty platform and demanded $30 to cover a charge of $10 a day to stay in Romania. My visa was stamped for Friday, Saturday, and Sunday. As I took out my money, a particularly aggressive guard snatched my visa from me and in broken English said that the head office in Bucharest would have to "check me out." I stood for the next four hours, until 11 P.M., alone on the dark platform, without my passport. I was scared; Éva and Fanni stayed inside the coach in silence. Finally, the guards returned my passport and gave me the correct change. I walked quietly back to my seat and the train sped on. They had been detaining the train because of me and the passengers seemed agitated. I sat with my head down and ignored their frustration. We arrived in Oradea at 3 A.M.

All I remember as I stepped down from that train was total darkness. There were no lights, darkness all around, policemen everywhere. Miki and Márta Jakobovits were waiting to greet us, standing next to their rusty old bicycles. Éva introduced me in a soft voice so that we would not be noticed. Márta spoke English and translated for Miki. As we walked away from the station, Éva handed them the packages. Éva and Fanni had successfully smuggled medicine, paints and food into the country. The Romanian government did not allow foreigners to bring any products into the country, presumably because it would expose their citizens to goods that were unavailable there. Ceauşescu preferred to have his people starve and deprived of medicine than to admit the lack of goods.

It suddenly occurred to me that I had been Éva's distraction at the border. "Don't wear make-up. Dress simply. Don't bring more than $100." Those words reverberated in my mind, but only for a moment. I didn't have time to dwell on the risks I had averted because we had to find a place to sleep. We were not permitted to stay at Miki and Márta's, and it was forbidden to walk the streets at night, so we ran from one hotel to another, looking over our shoulders, on the alert for the police. We entered several hotels; one manager said they were full; another just shook his head no and pointed to the door. At the third hotel, we were told that we needed business visas, so we left immediately.

We entered our fourth hotel. Éva motioned for me to be silent while she paid an old woman under the table (black market) and we finally got a room. We walked up four flights to a dirty, tiny room that lacked hot water and had worn, yellow-stained sheets on the bed. It probably would have been condemned in the United States, but at least there were beds for our weary bodies. We did not speak a word to one another. Éva knew that the room was bugged and I was learning quickly to do exactly as I was told. Here was yet another new chapter. Since so many of my preconceptions had already been erased by my experiences with people in Hungary, I was curious to see what I would learn about those living under far worse conditions in Romania. I had seen Márta and Miki only briefly at the train station, but my sense was that they were exceptional, universally so; they probably would be considered exceptional in any country, under any conditions. My thoughts raced almost as fast as my heart, and I was so absorbed in making sure I was ready for this new adventure, I forgot all about my squalid surroundings. Needless to say, I didn't get much sleep that night.

We ate lunch Saturday with Márta and Miki in their two-room flat. It was difficult for them to make a full course meal because of the limited food supply, but they served rabbit obtained through their black market connections. We had potatoes, cabbage, dark bread, and delicious, dry red wine. The meal was a treat for all of us.

After lunch, Márta showed me two hidden shelves of books — poetry, art books, classics, and an old Bible. If these were discovered, the repercussions could be disastrous. Their paintings and art supplies would be confiscated, and they would face a possible prison sentence. "Safe" artwork hung on the walls, and pottery and oil paintings covered the floor of their tiny bedroom where we congregated after lunch. The couple wanted to hear about everything happening in the United States. They never received any information from the outside world and they were desperate for information. They wanted to know what life was like for my family and for me, what books I read, and how democracy really worked. And then they asked a question that startled me: was the United States really as poor a nation as the Romanian government claimed?

At that time, in November 1989, I was practicing transcendental meditation, known as TM. I found that, for me, this technique relieved stress. Márta and Miki had heard about it and asked me about it. When I told them that I could teach them a simple meditation procedure, they were thrilled. So we closed the blinds in their apartment, and I whispered them through a meditation. Why the need to whisper? TM might have seemed strange to some, if not many, in America in the '80s, but it was hardly considered a danger to our society. In Romania, on the other hand, meditating was the number one crime, a particular fetish of Ceauşescu's, and more incriminating even than directly criticizing him. TM came from "outside" and its underlying philosophy is that through meditation, the individual can control his thought process. An experienced meditator can resist psychological pressures from the outside. I came to understand that this kind of thinking was threatening to Ceauşescu. Furthermore, TM was considered by many to be a spiritual endeavor. Any kind of spiritual or alternative lifestyle was banned under the Ceauşescu regime. It was forbidden for writers to express radical ideas or painters to exhibit works that showed independent thinking. These were major offenses with major consequences. But if caught practicing TM, one was condemned to life imprisonment.

Naturally, at this point in time, I had no idea of the possible consequences of this quiet, simple meditation. But retrospectively, I'm glad I taught them (particularly since there were no repercussions!), and it helped create a relationship with my new friends that simply could not have been achieved in any other way. Márta and Miki obviously were skilled at learning whom to trust; they instinctively knew that I was not a spy.

The ceramic box broken by the guard at the Romanian border.

It was suddenly Sunday, and time to say goodbye. After many hugs, we said that we would try to keep in touch. As I was about to board the train, I noticed that Márta was wearing only a heavy sweater, no coat, so I gave her my full-length, red wool coat that I had just bought before I left the States. Years later, Márta told me that she never wore the coat in public because it was too colorful. No one wanted to attract attention, and people would notice her on the streets if she had worn it. So she used it as a blanket and continued to wear her sweater in public.

Éva, Fanni, and I returned on the same train back to Budapest. Márta had given me a piece of her pottery, a clay box, which was permanently sealed closed. She said that inside this box lay hidden all her hopes and dreams for Romania, and that is why she had sealed it shut. I cherished the gift and held onto it tightly at the border. Reminiscent of our train ride just days earlier, a stocky guard approached me and asked for my passport and visa. Seeing the ceramic box, she grabbed it and asked what was inside. She shook it but heard no sound; she banged it against the wall but still heard nothing. Éva told her, in Hungarian, that it was only a piece of junk, an empty piece of worthless pottery. But she slammed it down on the floor to crack it open, certain to find something. But she found nothing inside. I thought to myself that she lacked the wisdom to see all the hopes and dreams for Romania inside. Satisfied that it was indeed an empty piece of worthless pottery, she permitted me to pick up the broken pieces. I still have the broken box, sitting on a counter in my home in Harrisburg. I often look at it, remembering the hatred in the guard's eyes, and Márta's sad yet hopeful words.

On my return to the States, my memories of Oradea lingered. It was a difficult time in my life. When I was in Hungary and Romania, I missed my family and the comforts of home. But when I was in Harrisburg, I missed my friends and my work abroad. And the situation in Romania haunted me. I wanted to do something to help my Romanian friends who suffered under smothering government controls. Márta and Miki had shared their story with me; perhaps I could share their story here. I told my colleagues about the atrocities in Romania and the problems in Hungary. I wrote the Harrisburg newspaper. I talked with professors at our local universities. People seemed mildly interested, but nobody really responded. It wasn't relevant to their lives. They simply couldn't understand.

Three weeks later I was back in Harrisburg when the revolution broke out in Romania. A dissident group, the National Salvation Front (NSF), proclaimed itself the provisional government. On December 22, 1989, the dictator, Nicolae Ceauşescu, and his wife, Elena, were captured and immediately put on trial by a military tribunal. On Christmas day, the tribunal reached a verdict and Nicolae and Elena Ceauşescu were executed by firing squad a short time later, ending the reign of terror in Romania. All across Eastern Europe people began to fight for constitutional governments. Márta might one day be able to realize some of her hopes and dreams.

As the lives of my friends and colleagues changed, my work expanded. Through Éva, Márta and Miki, my teaching methods spread into schools across Hungary and Romania. My style of teaching was welcomed; I could not keep up with the requests for workshops. I had to think about my next step.

Initially, I had received nominal funding from the Soros Foundation (named after its founder, George Soros). Mr. Soros was interested in helping Eastern European countries move from closed societies to open ones, and my program fit his goals. He had a personal interest in the region because he was born in Budapest, Hungary, and suffered under both the Nazi regime and the Communist government. He left Hungary after World War II and studied at the London School of Economics before he emigrated to the United States, where he became a highly successful financier and money manager. He has made significant contributions to programs in Eastern Europe from his foundation.

My contact at the Soros Foundation was with the executive director of their Hungarian foundation, Elizabeth (Liz) Lorant. She had agreed to pay for some of my early work, but I covered most of the costs. As schools continued to request my services, however, I could not continue to underwrite my travel expenses. I must admit I was relentless in calling Liz to explain the importance of my work and the fit with the goal of the Soros Foundation. Finally, Liz consented to give token funding for a health education program in Hungary. She was aware of the success of my work, but when she asked the Soros Hungarian Foundation to fund the program, its director scoffed at the idea. Liz suspected that his lack of interest in a prevention program was because he smoked three packs of cigarettes a day and didn't want his lifestyle challenged. Since she couldn't get money from the Hungarian budget, Liz funded my work from the foundation's U.S. budget.

In the meantime I met Viktor Osiatynski. Viktor, a well-known author and constitutional lawyer from Warsaw, Poland, was working directly with George Soros on a strategy to effect change in several Eastern European countries. He became interested in developing a health education program in Poland. As a result of our meetings, he went directly to Mr. Soros and asked him to fund my health education program there.

In September 1991, Viktor told me to write a major grant proposal to the foundation. At his request, I wrote the grant to develop health education in three countries — Hungary, Romania and Poland. Mr. Soros' response was astounding: the foundation wanted me to develop a major health education program, not in three, but in ten countries. I was charged with writing curricula that would be appropriate to Eastern Europe on nutrition, smoking prevention, alcohol and other drugs, human sexuality, and AIDS education. The curricula were to be ready for print by early February 1992. I was to present the first workshop in Budapest in April 1992. Countries participating would be Estonia, Hungary, Poland, Romania, Bulgaria, Russia, Czechoslovakia, Yugoslavia (and the newly formed Croatia), Lithuania and Ukraine. I knew I needed a co-worker and contacted a woman in Harrisburg, Carol Flaherty-Zonis, an expert in sexuality education, teacher training and AIDS education. We became a team — co-trainers, co-inspirers and co-energizers.

The first training in Budapest was called a "regional training." Liz actually attended it. She was skeptical prior to the training, even to the point of telling me not to wear "those long earrings. You must wear a conservative suit, and please, Susan, no meditation!"

Of course, I didn't listen. I taught the participants relaxation techniques; we had early morning yoga sessions; we played Enya tapes and the participants communicated with one another in ways that were revolutionary for them. At first, it seemed that nothing met Liz's approval, but later I came to realize that she was astonished to see the way the people reacted to the activities. The workshop provided an extraordinary vehicle for the assemblage of attendees from ten Eastern European countries.

Liz took pride in the results. She reported back to the foundation: "Not only was the subject matter well received but the participants had a very positive reaction to the way the material was presented. The participants from all ten countries loved every minute of the workshop. I knew this style of teaching was accepted in the West, but I took a chance despite the negative attitude of the Hungarian Foundation and my own skepticism." This program was the first exposure the Soros Foundation had to bring democracy into schools and to change the relationship that Communist-style teachers had with their students. The foundation has grown considerably since 1993 and now has thousands of employees with a worldwide network of foundations established to foster the development of open societies. They base many of their programs on the methodology and style of teaching we used at this first "regional training."

So our first training was a success, in spite of the issues that we faced. Like the "tablecloth lady" who didn't work on Sundays, so we couldn't get additional tables or tablecloths from the hotel until she returned Monday morning, or the manager who did not have authority to turn the heat higher.

On the final day of this workshop, Liz told the participants that if they translated the curricula and selected 50 people to attend a workshop, Carol and I would present the same seminar in their country. Darko Tot and his colleagues from the newly formed (the transformation occurred during our workshop) Croatia became the first to do the required translation and preparation for a workshop, so Carol and I flew to Zagreb, Croatia, in June 1992. It was at the beginning of the Croatian War (with fighting a mere 20 minutes from our hotel). The other countries came on board that year, and so Carol and I gave workshops in all the other nine countries.

The program's achievements gave the foundation the incentive to continue to expand it. By the beginning of 1993, eleven more coun-

Top: Taking a break at an H.E. workshop, Elizabeth Lorant, Susan Shapiro, Vera Janíkova. *Bottom:* Participants in the Soros Foundation Health Education Coordinators' Meeting, representing the countries of Albania, Belarus, Bulgaria, Croatia, Czech Republic, Estonia, Latvia, Lithuania, Moldova, Macedonia, Poland, Romania, Russia, Ukraine, Serbia, Slovenia, Slovakia, and the United States.

Carol Flaherty-Zonis, George Soros and Susan Shapiro in the Hungarian Foundation. Budapest, Hungary, April 1992.

tries were added: Albania, Bosnia-Herzegovina, Latvia, Moldova, Slovakia, Slovenia, Macedonia, Belarus, Mongolia, Kazakhstan, and Kyrgyzstan. Carol and I spent the next five years flying back and forth to twenty countries doing workshops. The curricula we developed have been translated into 22 languages. The ministries of education in all of the countries officially approved each program. Since the program began in 1992, it has reached over 200,000 teachers and at least 5 million students. The program still thrives today.

The Health Education Program introduced elementary and secondary school teachers and health professionals to innovative ways to instruct their students on nutrition, alcohol and other drugs, smoking prevention, human sexuality, AIDS, environment issues, and conflict management. The overall goals of the program were to help transform educational methodology in the participating countries and to teach basic health education, a subject neglected under Communism. The real strength of the program was changing people's way of thinking.

Through my work and travels I have developed meaningful relationships with people from various backgrounds; from Lithuanian businessmen to Hungarian underground leaders, Romanian dissidents to Czech schoolteachers, from Macedonian peace activists to "Roma" Gypsies. For me, these friends are not "faceless victims of Communism" but rather people, just like you and me, with families, jobs, hopes and dreams about the world.

Since I stepped on that Austrian Air flight back in 1984, my life has been blessed with a whirlwind of new people, new places and new experiences. Had a fortuneteller revealed to me the course my life was to take, I would have said: "Impossible! That could never happen to me!" But indeed it did. And now I have the good fortune of being able to present to you some of my many friends whose fate placed them in controlled societies. These are their remarkable stories.

— 2 —

Romãnia (Romania)

Apart from Russia and Ukraine, Romania is the largest Eastern European country, covering an area of approximately 92,000 square miles. Romania lies in southeastern Europe bordered by Moldova, Ukraine, Hungary, Serbia and Bulgaria. It is approximately the size of the state of Oregon. Bucharest is its capital and largest city, while other key cities include Iaşi, Constanţa, and Cluj-Napoca. The population is close to 23 million people. Romanian is a romance language with similarities to French, Italian and Spanish.

History

Two thousand years ago, the geography approximating modern Romania was conquered by the Romans. Over the centuries, the evolving Romanian people formed three principalities that still exist today: Moldavia, Wallachia and Transylvania. There were revolutions over the decades in one or more of the principalities, but the region that bore the greatest political upheaval was Transylvania, being shunted back and forth between Romania and the country at its northwestern border, Hungary. At the beginning of the 20th century, Transylvania was under the control of Hungary.

With Austria-Hungary's defeat in World War I, however, Transylvania was reunited with Romania. At the end of World War I, Romania had more than doubled its territory and its population.

In 1940, a weak Romania was forced to cede Transylvania back to Hungary, but four years later, Romanian and Soviet armies drove the Hungarian forces out of Transylvania. By the end of World War II, Transylvania was again reunited with Romania and remains there today.

After World War II, the Communist Party began to grow both in popularity and membership. In 1946, the power of the Communist Party was established; a year later a constitution based on the USSR model was introduced.

In 1952, Gheorghe Gheorghiu-Dej was elected general secretary and the country became a puppet regime of Moscow. Over the next several decades, Romania struggled through different leadership, different styles of government, loss of personal freedoms, and scarcities of food, fuel and drugs. Dej died in 1965 and was succeeded by Nicolae Ceauşescu.

At first Ceauşescu appeared benign and endeared himself to Western leaders. However, his domestic mismanagement led to severe economic problems by the early 1980s. Paying off Romania's mounting foreign debt became one of his main obsessions. He began exporting food, fuel and drugs and rationed bread, potatoes, eggs, salt, sugar, and oil. Lines for food became synonymous with everyday life. Personal liberties were breached. Fear became pervasive.

In the late 1980s there were strikes to protest the economic conditions. In late December 1989, Ceauşescu tried to garner public support but was met with hostility and spreading protests. He was forced to declare a state of emergency. Ceauşescu and his wife escaped by helicopter but were captured on December 22, 1989, and executed by firing squad on Christmas Day.

A provisional government was established and an end to Ceauşescu's monopoly was decreed. By early 1990, the army had restored order and the securitate had been abolished. In 1991 a new constitution was approved and a republic created based upon private property rights and a free market economy.

Faces from a Unique Land

There actually was a real Dracula who lived 600 years ago in the region of Eastern Europe called Transylvania. In western countries, Dracula is portrayed as a cruel character, a vampire, the prince of darkness. My friends in Romania, however, learned about the real Dracula in school. He was Vlad Ţepes Dracula, son of Vlad the Devil. At the age of seventeen, young Dracula seized power from the Turks and later built a dynasty in the Wallachia region. By using extreme measures, including severing limbs and decapitation, King Dracula eliminated thievery and corruption. Although considered by some to be cruel, he brought order to the country. He advanced the economy by encouraging trade and making credits available to local business people. He improved the welfare of the people and was admired for his political acumen.

The ruins of Dracula's castle stand near the town of Braşov in the Carpathian Mountains, but the People's Palace that stands today in the center of Bucharest is a reminder of a much more recent ruler of Romania, Nicolae Ceauşescu (pronounced Chow chess' cue), who led his country from 1965 to 1989.

Nicolae Ceauşescu was considered by most to be a cruel dictator. While he advanced Romania's world standing and relationships with the West, and while he retained an unusual degree of independence from Russia, his management of domestic affairs was disastrous. The victim of his mismanagement, however, was not the economy but rather the people of Romania. In the stories that follow, you will meet some of these people and hear how Ceauşescu's regime affected their lives.

I share the stories of three families, who, like Dracula, were all born in Transylvania. Their lives have gone in different directions since Ceauşescu's regime ended in 1989. The first story is about the Baciu family: Dan, Simona and their two children, Ruxandra and Tudor. They live in Cluj-Napoca, the largest city in Transylvania. Despite opportunities to move to Germany and the U.S., they choose to stay in Romania. They are committed to rebuilding the country. Since 1989, Dan and Simona have worked to change Romania — the country, the region, and their city. They feel it is their responsibility to create a new and healthy future for Romania.

The second family is Márta and Miki Jakobovits, artists who live as Hungarian nationals in Oradea, a city in Transylvania close to the Hungarian border. They were nonconformists, part of the artistic underground. They refused to live the prescribed life under Ceauşescu. Artists were not considered a threat to society and were usually left alone. Under a more democratic political system, they continue to be nonconformists, still struggling for artistic survival.

Finally there is Marius Mateş, a young man disillusioned by the poverty and hopelessness in his country. He was raised in Baia Mare, a city in northwest Transylvania. His mother is a nurse and his father is an X-ray operator. They provided Marius with an abundance of love and security but, as a teenager, Marius became angry with the Ceauşescu and successive governments (he believes that Communism still exists). He enrolled at Illinois State University in Normal, Illinois, and received two master's degrees, the first in counseling psychology, the second in computer science. He now works in Chicago for Hewitt Associates. Marius loves his homeland and misses his family dearly, but he prefers to live in America.

Dan and Simona Baciu
Cluj-Napoca, România

I met the Bacius (pronounced Bah´chu) in 1992, a middle-aged couple, born and raised in Romania. Dan describes his wife: "Simona is quite unusual. She is optimistic, aggressive, and quite talkative. It's best for me because I can absorb a lot through her eyes. She sorts out the news and I follow through. I'm the detail man."

Simona describes Dan: "There are thousands of talented people here, but only one Dan. He is ambitious and quite decisive. He developed the first health education program in all of Romania, the first elderly day care center, and also the first hospice center here in Cluj-Napoca. These are amazing accomplishments. He looks at every aspect of something. If you want to accomplish a task, ask him. He will see every obstacle — convenient for me because then I am aware of what I face when I begin a project. Together we have a full brain — both hemispheres complete. Dan is the left-brain in our family; structured, organized. Not me. I am the right-brain in the family; creative. Don't give me too many details. But I can think out of the box."

If opposites attract, Dan and Simona are a perfect fit. She is usually on a diet, an optimist under the most difficult conditions, and she bubbles with life. Her hair is henna red, the henna found only in Romania, with auburn and red highlights over a brown base. Anyone who has lived under a dictatorship filled with fear could be angry, but not Simona. Whoever she works with picks up her energy; everyone adores her.

In 1998, Simona created the first private English speaking kindergarten and primary school in Romania; now more than 250 children attend. She personally supervised the construction of the school and also acts as director, administrator, teacher, and teacher-trainer. The school's modern building and distinctive teaching methods make it one of a kind. In 2000 she added an elementary school in an adjacent building; she intends to build a private gymnasium and boarding school with classrooms, laboratories, chapel, dormitories and cafeteria. There are few limits to what Simona intends to do. Her dreams bear reality.

The Baciu Family: Simona, Ruxy, Dan, and Tudy.

In contrast to Simona's outward energy, Dan is contemplative. He is tall and handsome, with a solid body and a strong mind. He has dark brown hair, blue eyes, and a self-assured personality. He is a man of few words, but a sharp wit, and is comfortable in silence. A doctor by profession, Dan does not practice medicine today because of the scarcity of equipment and medicines. Instead, he works to help build the community in Cluj-Napoca. He administered the health education program for the Soros Foundation and trained thousands of teachers to integrate the information into their classrooms. Dan established an elderly day care center because the elderly have been neglected both during the Ceauşescu regime and now. He also started one of the first home palliative care services to assist the terminally ill in Romania. He is one of the few Romanian doctors working with cancer patients, although it is usually as a volunteer.

The success of Dan and Simona is not built on money earned during the Ceauşescu regime. Professionals like Dan had the same salary as janitors and secretaries; everyone was paid about $100 a month. Looking at their lives, I see qualities that enabled them to survive and actually thrive in their society. They do not succumb to pessimism or hopelessness; rather they become role models for their children and everyone around them.

Dan and Simona have two children; Ruxandra, 17, and Tudor, 15. Ruxy, as she is called, is almost five feet tall with shoulder length, light brown hair and big blue eyes. She is slender and self-assured. Her friends are always stopping by or calling on the phone. Tudor, nicknamed Tudy, is long and lanky, still growing and will be over six feet tall. He has dark brown hair and dark eyes. He is shy and spends much of his time alone, creating art designs and listening to his music. He makes airplanes, Romanian and American bombers, using plastic bottles and Q-tips. Ruxy and Tudy have been raised to know that they are expected to make change and help others. But they also live as normal kids.

The other important person in the house is Tante Maria, the cleaning lady who bustles around the kitchen making stuffed cabbage, chicken soup with noodles, and other Romanian dishes. She is part of the family. Everyone who visits the Bacius more than once looks forward to seeing Tante Maria again. She talks constantly to herself and has the kind of wrinkled face that shows all the secrets of old age. She wears the same dress every day. The top third is red and green plaid, the middle, a solid light orange, and the bottom third, blue and orange flowered print. The Bacius pay her $5 a week. She is old, slow, and not able to do much work, so Ruxy and Tudy do their share of the housework.

The Baciu house sits on Bacau Street, a fifteen-minute walk from downtown. It is a small house with a hospital across the street and a family of 25 Gypsies living next door. (I asked several Gypsy families what they would prefer to be called — Gypsy or Roma. They all preferred "Gypsy.") The houses on the street vary in sizes and condition but are all connected. Directly inside the Bacius' small house is a long, narrow foyer with pegs lining the walls for hanging coats. Shoes, boots, high heels, old sneakers, and dusty torn slippers are scattered about the floor. The foyer leads to a hall with a mirror and a shelf that has several spray cans. I thought one was hair spray, which I used for ten days and was very pleased with the results. I asked Simona where I could purchase it and discovered it was spray for the inside of shoes, to make the odor go away. I never asked what the other cans contained.

To the right is the living and dining room. Two worn sofas, with a cocktail table between them, take up most of one side of the room. One is a sofa bed and used almost nightly. A dining room table is on the other side of the room and is usually filled with papers and school supplies. An old gas stove sits in the corner and is used for heat in wintertime.

The one bathroom in the house is next to Dan and Simona's bedroom. It has an old tub with a long shower hose, but without hooks to hang it on, and no shower curtain. The fixtures are old and worn. The paint on the door is chipped, and the wallpaper spotted with watermarks.

The kitchen has a table in the center that can seat four comfortably but rarely has fewer than seven or eight. There are three bedrooms in the house — Dan and Simona's, and one for each of the children. In this household, guests get preference, so Ruxy and Tudy often sleep in the living room.

The house at one time had doors separating small rooms, typical of apartments in Communist times. People usually kept the doors shut to give themselves some privacy. When Simona came to the U.S. and stayed with us, she loved the openness of our house. She went home and made Dan knock down most of their walls.

Their house acts as storage space for Simona's school. The hall is filled with supplies; crayons, paper, scissors. The doors intended for the school were laid against the wall of Ruxy's bedroom, because there was no room for them in the school until the workmen were ready to install them.

I could share many of my visits to the Baciu home, but the summer of 2000 was exceptional because that was the year Dan and Simona told me the story of their lives. Dan and Simona met me at the train station, with Ruxy and Tudy. I had flown to Budapest, Hungary, with my niece, Katie, age 19. I was going to Cluj to interview Dan and Simona for this book and to introduce Katie to the Baciu family. Katie wanted to work at Simona's school for a few months before attending college in the fall.

THE STORY THAT UNFOLDED THAT WEEK

We arrived late in the evening on Sunday, July 7, 2000, and squeezed into two taxicabs. Dan and Simona were without a car since they had loaned their 1980 automobile, a Romanian manufactured Dacia, to a Belgium friend, Rinilda. We walked into the house and were greeted by their German friends who were also staying with the family. Other local friends stopped by. We introduced Katie, talked for awhile, drank some tea and went to bed around midnight. I was given Ruxy's bed.

When I awoke at 9 A.M. Monday it was already hot and hazy. The reality that I was back in this unusual home hit me immediately. Dan and Simona's German friends were leaving, saying a million good-byes. They had brought playground equipment and bricks for the school from Munich. They were loading their belongings into their old blue van which seemed to have a 50–50 chance of making it back to Germany. I listened to their conversation as I walked into the kitchen to make a cup of espresso.

"Take the goodie bag that Tante Maria made for you. You have a long trip — several borders. The Romanian border for sure will have you wait. Give the border guard Tante Maria's food and they'll let you through sooner," Dan said as he hugged Gertrude, the tall blonde German.

"Dan, we've done this so many times before. At least now we don't have the clothes, toys, and playground equipment that we did when we came here. It should be okay. Don't worry," Gertrude said.

Ruxy shouted from the kitchen, "Each time you leave here you stock up on Tante Maria's food. Does it taste good after you leave?"

"Ruxy, don't start trouble! Our choice is limited. I think we won't find a food store until we reach Hungary," Gertrude replied.

At that moment, Simona dashed into the house. She had forgotten some supplies that the teachers needed and wanted to check on the workmen. It was a two minute stay, and then she ran off to the school again. Tante Maria was folding the laundry she had ironed for the Germans and stuffing it into their bags. Two workmen walked into the house with more boards and equipment for the school. They talked with Dan, but he was distracted by three phone calls, the Germans' good-byes, and my need for some attention.

I dressed quickly and told Dan about my plans. "I must be at the school by 9:30 A.M. I have to leave now or else I will be late. I have a class to teach." I had been waiting for Dan because he thought we would have time to talk about his new project.

"Go ahead," he motioned to me, holding the phone away from his ear. "I could be in a crazy house and it would be more sane."

I answered, "Simona and I will stop at the store to buy some food for dinner. I think the Germans wiped you out." We laughed, and I left.

I went out into the street to walk the four blocks to the school, and with my first breath was hit by the smell of diesel fuel. Several Gypsy children joined me in my walk.

I entered the school. Simona was working with the builders who were finishing up the new structure. I taught a class of 15 six-year-olds on the harmful effects of smoking. Later Simona and I discussed the curricula for the school as we walked to the neighborhood store. I took the food home, and Simona went back to school. When I returned to their house it was full of activity. The television was blasting an English program with Romanian subtitles. The workmen were there with more doors to put in Ruxy's room. The phone was ringing.

I sat down with Tante Maria to drink some coffee. Then the Bacius' "Belgian Friends" phoned. Rinilda and her son Brendan had car problems and needed to talk with Dan. They had gone to a village town about four hours away (driving Dan's car) to visit some friends. When they stopped for gas, a mechanic, or so he described himself, put bad diesel fuel into Dan's car. They were stranded outside of Cluj. Dan calmed Rinilda, who was crying, and took a cab to meet them. I told Dan I'd stay at the house while he helped Rinilda and Brendan try to get the car fixed.

These "Belgian Friends" (as Dan calls them) come to Cluj about three times a year to help Dan and Simona in their various projects. They had met in 1990 when Rinilda and her friend Eric traveled from Geel, Belgium, to Cluj to donate supplies to orphanages across Romania as part of the organization "Doctors Without Borders." They had brought an entire truckload of chocolate Easter bunnies for the children and arrived on Easter Sunday to find the administrative office closed. The office faces Dan and Simona's house and Simona was outside hanging laundry when she heard Rinilda banging on the door of the office. Simona invited them in. Tante Maria made one of her specialty dishes, noodles with cabbage, and Dan and Simona convinced them to stay the night. They gave them their bedroom. Rinilda and Eric stayed for three days, and a longstanding relationship was off to a good start.

As a friend of the Baciu family, my stay was typical. I don't need structure, so their household has always suited me just fine. That afternoon, I decided to take the black belt karate class that Ovidiu, a third degree instructor, was teaching at Simona's school. We went there Monday evening practicing our forms. I returned to the Bacius hungry for one of Tante Maria's specialties.

I walked in to meet Florin and Cristina, former classmates of Simona, who were visiting from a nearby village, so I sat down with them. They had just become engaged and it is a Romanian custom to visit friends' homes to inform them in person of their intent to marry. They

described the wedding they would have, typical of most village ceremonies: Florin said, "A village wedding in Romania is very special — three
days of feasts. Half of the people in our village are invited. Everyone
helps to make the tent, bring the chairs and make the food. People dance
in the street. Early in the morning we start with the music and it doesn't
stop. We drink Ţuica, which is a prune liqueur. The entire family goes
to the church and after the service the children throw money at the bride
and groom." They talked with Dan and me until Simona arrived from
school. When she heard they were engaged, she brought out the wine,
and the family toasted them. When they left, I took a quick shower. Hot
water — a pleasant surprise!

Dinner was at 9:00 P.M. We all sat around the kitchen table eating
Tante Maria's chicken noodle soup. After a rich dessert of orange cake
topped with berries, Dan, Simona and I walked to the school to check
on the night watchman and to see what the construction workers had
completed. We talked with the neighborhood children who followed us.
It didn't matter that it was almost 10 o'clock at night, there were dozens
of young children walking the street, including some of the Gypsy children from next door.

The school is painted yellow, with white trim around the windows
and planters with vibrantly colored flowers on the window sills. Several
pictures of Big Bird and other Sesame Street characters are seen from the
street. The bright colors radiate from the school in contrast to the stark
neighborhood surrounding it. Dan and Simona talked a moment with
their full-time night guard. They told me that the playground equipment could easily be stolen and delinquents could carry away the windows and doors. They feel a sense of accomplishment, yet are very
concerned by the crime that surrounds them.

When we got home, Dan brought out the wine and we sat at the
kitchen table nibbling on sheep's cheese and dark bread. "Tell me your
story," I said to Simona. "Let's begin with your childhood."

Simona began. "For Dan and me, our childhood and early adult
years were typical of most people living in Romania. I was born in 1962
when things were already difficult. You see, between the late '60s and the
early '80s, Ccauşescu made life hard on us because he was obsessed with
paying off our foreign debt. In the early '70s our food was rationed, and
there were always shortages of fuel and medicine. There were also human
rights violations carried out by the Secret Police. Everyone was forced to
be strict and untrusting. I remember how scared I was in nursery school

when my teachers forced me to hold my hands straight out so they could roll yarn around my wrists. Then they would use this yarn to knit for hours during class while we sat in silence. They did this to make additional income. I was five and I learned to do as I was told. I knew I shouldn't complain or tell anyone about my fears."

"Was your life similar to everyone else's?" I asked.

"Yes, I was raised in an ordinary home in Cluj-Napoca. My mother was a dentist, still is, and my father was an engineer. I have one sister, Roxanna. For fourteen years we lived in one room on a small street around the corner from here. When a neighbor died we were able to rent that room so our own home expanded. Two rooms, a hall and kitchen. Everybody shared quarters with everyone else. The furniture was sparse — all dark wood. There was an old sofa bed, a large armoire, and two chairs in the main room. My sister and I slept in one bed. The kitchen was narrow with no windows, very little light. On one side was a counter with two wooden stools. There was a tiny refrigerator that held only enough food for one or two days. We had a sink, and gas stove; sometimes it worked, but often it did not. The government permitted each family to have two light bulbs in their flat. Just two! So I remember it was always dark. We lit candles when we could get them. More often than not we had water, although the state regularly turned off the hot water pipes — they said to clean them, but actually it was just to show the people that the government had absolute power over their lives. There were always problems with water. We used to joke (ha, ha!) that you don't get cold water in the winter because the pipes freeze. And in the spring, no cold water because the snow melts so quickly and they can't manage to clean the filters. In autumn there is too much rain so they can't clean the filters, and in summer, there is a drought so no water!

"And you might ask about hot water? We can tell you why no hot water. In winter, there is not enough gas pressure to heat the water so they scheduled water for morning and evenings only. In spring, filter problems again. And the pipes get rusty and full of mud. The water is brown. Always some crazy excuse.

"Ceauşescu took houses away from people and put families together in apartments. My grandparents' house was transformed into quarters for three families because the government claimed one family did not have the right to live in more than one room. My grandfather built a kitchen and bathroom in the hall, which they shared with their neighbors."

I asked, "What about the stores? Was there food?"

Simona continued, "It wasn't only in homes that problems existed. The stores had limited supplies. Families had to eat the things that Ceauşescu decided they should have. If he decided that a family should have half a package of butter a month, or one kilo sugar, and a half kilo of pork, then that is what we would receive. My mother walked back and forth to the shops to see if the food had arrived. Once it did, she had to wait in line for hours before she could purchase it. Her life was centered on work and making sure there was enough food. If the grocer said the food would start coming at 7 P.M., I remember we began to stand in line often by 4 A.M. the day before so that we could buy the product. Some days there was milk; some days there was cabbage. Nothing was predictable. When something was available, you grabbed it. The conversation between my mother and father was always about how to get something. How to get substitute coffee (regular coffee was unavailable). How to bribe the butcher for meat. How to pay off the farmer for fresh milk. Bribes were a part of our lives. A bribe to get a can of beans. I remember when my mother couldn't find shoes for me; she could only find jackets in the stores. But I needed shoes. It wasn't exactly that she couldn't find any shoes. There was one type, but not in my size. So she bribed the salesman by offering him beef that she had just bought and then I had new shoes. They weren't the right size, of course, but I didn't know any better. So that was the essence of my childhood.

"As for my future, I wanted to be an elementary school teacher, but my father vehemently opposed my choice. Let me explain why; it will help you to better understand the times.

"I always wanted to go to university to get an elementary school teaching degree. My grades were high enough for me to enter the pedagogical university, but my father forbade me to even apply. If I had become a teacher, he told me, I would have to work in a remote village for three years where there was no running water, no gas, and no transportation. The government decided where people should live, the government even separated married couples. My father knew that I would meet someone, want to get married and start a family. Many young couples had to live a great distance apart and only saw each other a few times a year.

"Engineers, on the other hand, were not needed in the villages and were in higher demand in the cities. In that profession, the chance that I could stay in Cluj was far greater, even though I had no desire to become an engineer. My father's word was final. I knew he was right, but you can imagine, I was frustrated. My grades were excellent, and I hadn't even cheated once during all of my high school years. Cheating, you see, was quite common in school during the Ceauşescu regime, because grades were the key to one's success in life.

"People had to cheat. There is a famous tale regarding grades that circulated among the students: The students with the A's would work in the cities where the train stops. The students with the B's would work where the train goes through, and the students with the C's would work in the places where people only heard about the train! I was fortunate to have a photographic memory, so I never had to cheat, but many students cheated to survive. So I became an engineer and taught technical drawing and design. It was odd, I think, during Ceauşescu to teach design, since there was no design in any clothes then.

"Dan and I met in 1981 and married two years later. Dan's salary was 1500 lei, paid by the state, less than $80 a month. The same wages as any other occupation, including janitors, engineers, teachers, and bus drivers. It was impossible to live on such a paycheck. I had graduated from Cluj University with a degree in engineering, but I still needed to tutor in math and physics at night for the additional income. Our rent was 256 lei a month (about $15 a month), one-fifth of our earnings.

"It was the early '80s and during these early years," Simona continued, "we ate all of our meals with my parents, who lived around the corner. My mother had contacts to get food, because she was a dentist. When people are in pain, she would say to me, they are more vulnerable, and give more away. My mother would stand at her dentist's chair, drill a little, then stop, and that's when she got what she wanted. It sounds barbaric but when your family is hungry, you do many strange things.

"We had a typical flat when we married. Two rooms on the bottom floor of our house where we still live, can you believe it! An architect lived in the bedroom right next to our living room. He shared the kitchen and bath with us. Another room was used for storage space for our neighbors and we weren't permitted to use that space. Imagine not being able to use your own rooms! And a general in the Romanian Communist Army lived right above us in a spacious apartment. Ruxy was born in 1984 and Tudy in 1986. Even with four people, we still only had two rooms; the four of us shared one bedroom and the living room.

"During winter it was so cold," Simona shivered as she recalled, "we all slept in one room close to the fire stove. When the gas pressure was low we huddled together next to the stove to gain warmth from each other. When there was no pressure, and we couldn't get gas, Dan had to go into the forest and gather wood. He had no car, so he took several buses to the forest, and a taxi home."

Dan interjected, "Let me tell you, it was a crazy time. The general upstairs would drive us crazy. He would play loud music and even spy on us. He's still our neighbor. We weren't afraid of him, just very much annoyed. We joked about him. One of our favorite jokes went like this: Three presidents sat together, an American, a Russian, and a Romanian, boasting about the loyalty of their armies. The American president says, 'I will demonstrate true loyalty; General John, take your gun and shoot yourself in the leg.' So John takes the gun and shoots himself in the leg. He winces but says nothing. The men are impressed. So the Russian president says, 'Oh! General Ivan is far more loyal and brave. Ivan, take a machine gun and shoot yourself in the leg.' Ivan riddles his right leg with bullets as he says, 'For this my kids will go to the university, so it was worth it.' Not to be outdone, the Romanian president says to his general, take your gun, and shoot yourself in both feet. The general says no problem, and blows a bullet into each boot and doesn't even flinch. They are all amazed; no one can figure it out. But, you see, his boot is five sizes bigger than his foot, since in the Romanian army you get shoes that rarely fit."

Dan went on, "Actually, the general never really bothered us. We ignored him but we hated his loud music." We laughed.

At 1:30 A.M. we decided to get some sleep. The next day we were going to Dan's parents' house in a village nearby Cluj. I went into Ruxy's room (she was fast asleep on the sofa bed in the living room). I fell asleep to the continuous sound of howling dogs.

Tuesday I awoke early. Katie was sleeping in Ruxy's room with me; still teenagers, she and Ruxy had agreed not to get up before 11 A.M. I left for the school with Simona at 7:30 A.M. and spent several hours working with her and ten of her teachers developing a strategic plan that laid out their goals and objectives for the next year. In the afternoon we went back to the house, had Tante Maria's chicken noodle soup and pancakes for lunch and sat around the kitchen table talking and laughing with the kids.

In the late afternoon we all squeezed into Dan's road-weary Dacia and drove to his parents' village twenty-five minutes from Cluj. We parked a short distance from the village because it had rained and the dirt road leading to their cottage was impassable. The cottage itself is

Spartan — only two rooms. They live there only in spring and summer since there is no heat and only outdoor plumbing. The house was Dan's grandfather's. There are about seven other homes close by, all inhabited with people and their livestock; there were the sounds of screeching chickens, mooing cows, and snorting pigs. A church, which Dan's grandfather helped to build, can be seen from their porch. His parents have a large hillside garden that produces enough food; bread is the only thing they must buy at the store.

We were welcomed with many hugs, kisses and "so good to have you back," spoken in Romanian. A trip to Cluj must always include a visit to this village. We sat around their kitchen table, eight of us; Dan, Simona, Dan's parents, his aunt, Ruxy, Tudy, Katie and me. I heard about their life as we ate an assortment of fresh vegetables, sheep's cheese, olives, and heavy black bread and drank homemade plum brandy and delicious Romanian wine.

Dan's family suffered in much the same way as Simona's except that he came from a religious family and in the late '60s and through the '80s, some of their problems stemmed from their religious practices. Simona's family followed the Orthodox religion, acceptable to Ceauşescu, but Dan's family was Greek Catholic, which was forbidden.

Dan started telling their story. "My father, Octavian, had no major problems with the state until he married my mother, Otilia, in 1954. He had been employed in the army, one of the selected ones chosen for his high achievement. But when the authorities learned that my maternal grandfather was a Greek Catholic priest, my father had to leave the army. My grandfather tried to make it easier on my parents and gave up preaching as a Greek Catholic and became an Orthodox priest. When my parents had us [meaning Dan and his siblings], they raised us as Greek Catholics in the quiet of our home.

"Around the same time, my Aunt Maria [who sat at the table with us] married a Greek Catholic priest. They had four children. He knew the possible harm the family could face, yet he just couldn't give up his Greek Catholic beliefs. Throughout the '60s he led his church in the traditional Greek Catholic manner. But the Secret Police had spies who came to his sermons and heard his liturgy. One night they barged into his house and dragged him away. For three years no one knew where he was. Then one night someone knocked on their door and handed my aunt his wedding band, a symbolic statement that her husband was dead. She went into mourning and wore black for the next year. We all grieved for him. Then two years after he was presumed dead, he appeared at my aunt's door. The Secret Police had tricked her; he was very much alive."

Dan talked about his parents' strong religious convictions. "Praying was dangerous. But my parents believed that God had a plan for them and their responsibility was to emphasize the good in their lives. When we could get meat, or bread and butter, or cheese, even though almost everything was bought on the black market, my mother would say that things were good.

"When Ceaușescu came to power, Romania had taken a relatively independent stand from the Soviet Union. The people were generally pleased with this independence even though many, like my parents, didn't like Ceaușescu's personality. Ceaușescu tried to make us feel proud to be Romanians. In the early '70s he seemed to favor some forms of individual rights and freedoms. He allowed people to write editorials, he wanted the peasants to have more material goods and he even promised the 'intelligentsia' that they would have privileges to write without restrictions. Scientists had freedom to do their research. Ceaușescu acknowledged that private businessmen should be permitted to lease state restaurants. So there was the possibility that people could make a profit. My parents were encouraged by the times. However, it soon became apparent that this was just, as I believe you call it, 'window dressing.'

"I was admitted to medical school and graduated with top honors. I was young and full of dreams, and I fantasized about helping my patients. There were few supplies because of Ceaușescu's program exporting food and medicine to pay the national debt. During the '80s, I worked in a family doctor's office in downtown Cluj. But the supplies were so limited; I only had a stethoscope, thermometer and sometimes gauze. Little could be accomplished. You couldn't help somebody with nothing to give to them. If I wanted to try to get medicine, I had to get it illegally. And I had to be very careful. When I got hold of some medicine, I could not have the patient come to my office. I would have to pay a house call so no one would see that I had the medicine. And for sure I could never telephone them. I didn't think the lines were tapped, but one never knew for sure. I would joke with my friend, Marius, who of course I trusted, and I'd say in the middle of a conversation, 'Okay, dear friend, wait just a second, they have to change the tape.'

"In spite of the shortages, I longed to continue practicing medicine. But I suffered as I watched so many people die waiting for an ambulance that never arrived. The elderly, especially, were mistreated. The hospital would ask how old the patient was, and if they were in their sixties, they would wait forever. You weren't important when you were older since you couldn't help the state. They didn't care about you. A bare office, no car, no supplies, no sterilization turned my fantasy into a nightmare."

"How did your children cope with these times?" I asked.

"They were okay. But Simona and I suffered."

Simona added: "My daily routine was exhausting. In the late '80s when the children were in kindergarten and primary school I would take them to school, work as a technical teacher, tutor classes after school, then pick the children up and go back home to tutor more students. Then late at night I would sew clothes, and make stuffed elephants. Let me tell you about the stuffed elephants. Kids in Romania had no toys, you couldn't buy them in the stores. So I decided to make stuffed animals using a picture of an elephant that Ruxy had drawn. From the pattern, I created these stuffed elephants. I just thought that would be something neat. Then I would try to sell them as toys. But I had to invent ways to get the cloth and the stuffing for the elephants. I took old pajamas, cut them up and made elephants out of them. Once my mother bought a new housedress and she asked me to shorten it for her. I made it really short and with the extra material I made seven elephants. But then I had to figure out how to stuff the animals. You couldn't find cotton anywhere so I went to a shoe factory where they threw out the torn linings from inside the shoes. I stuffed my elephants with this. It took me weeks to figure out how to manage this because there were never any supplies. I had to use every bit of creative energy to make my stuffed animals. With the money from selling them, I bought clothes for my kids. And I only got about 10 cents for each elephant so I had to make and sell a lot.

"But that wasn't my main problem — clothes, I mean. It was finding food and medicine for my children. I will never forget the time that Tudy was sick. He was an infant with a high fever and a bad ear infection. His father is a doctor, yet we had no access to antibiotics. I went to the pharmacy, but they had none. I walked several miles to three other pharmacies, but I was still unsuccessful. I even brought soap for the pharmacist as a gift, but that didn't work. I was frantic. Tudy was just a baby. I hurried home, grabbed some perfume I had received from someone on the black market, and headed for the vet. This vet was an acquaintance of mine. I had gone to school with him. I asked him for an antibiotic for "our very sick dog" and gave him the bottle of perfume for his wife. I paid four times the value of the antibiotic, but Tudy took the antibiotic that was meant for animals, and his fever broke. I have never forgotten this episode."

Dan stood up from the table and refilled our wineglasses. We had been sitting for hours. His mother was hovering over me as she continued to fill my plate with tomatoes, a number of cabbage dishes, and homemade raspberry juice. Much better for you than Coke, I was told; and it had bubbles in it. She poured me another glass of plum brandy too. I needed to use the bathroom, but it was getting dark outside; it seemed too complicated. Anyhow, Dan began talking again.

"It was Ceauşescu's view on birth control that really made us furious. You see, Simona's life, along with that of all child-bearing Romanian women, was a public spectacle. Ceauşescu and his wife did not believe in abortion, and contraceptives were not available. In 1957, before Ceauşescu rose to power, abortions were the only means of birth control. By 1965 the number of abortions had steadily increased to over one million a year. Ceauşescu wanted the population to increase, so in 1966, he abolished abortions. By the mid–70s, the ratio of illegal abortions to live births was one to one. This was so intolerable to Ceauşescu that he decreed mandatory pelvic exams of all women."

Simona recalls, "I was so embarrassed. Imagine, I was subjected to a pelvic exam at my workplace to check on whether I was pregnant. The exams were random; you never knew when they would call you in for one." If a woman was found to be pregnant, then the doctor examined her weekly to make sure that she didn't try to abort.

Because of this, many women had unwanted children. And out of that came the horrors that we have seen on TV — the infamous Romanian orphanages. Parents, with children they neither wanted nor could feed, would leave them stranded in dirty orphanages. Thousands of children were abandoned. Many of these children had AIDS.

"So much sadness," Dan said, "Abortion, AIDS, Anxiety. When we were miserable, what did I do? Tell a joke! That's how I coped. This one was from the '80s: God had a meeting and called together the three great presidents on Earth: Gorbachev, from Russia; Reagan, from the United States; and Ceauşescu from Romania. God told them that in three days there would be a great flood that would destroy the earth. They must go back to their countries and share this horrible news with their people.

"President Reagan goes on CNN, and says to the American people that there is good news and bad news. 'The good news is that I had the honor to see God, and He is, as we expected, an all-powerful God. The bad news is that in three days a huge flood will destroy the earth. We must prepare to die with our heads held high, proud of our American heritage.'

"Gorbachev said, 'Well, dear Russian comrades, I have two things to tell you tonight and they are both very bad. First of all, Marx said that God does not exist, and this is not true, because I saw God, and that is quite annoying. The other bad news is that there is going to be a flood in three days, and it will be the end of the earth. So prepare yourselves, dear Comrades, for your death.'"

"Now Ceauşescu goes back to Romania and says, 'My fellow countrymen, I have two very important things to tell you, both excellent. You know the Russians said there is no God, well, we proved them wrong, because we were together at a conference and God was there. Gorbachev had to face God and admit he was wrong. The second good thing that I have to tell you is that in about three days I assure you, there will be neither glasnost nor *perestroika* in our country. Russia will not have their way!'

"On a more serious note," Dan continued, "I hated Elena, Ceauşescu's wife, even more than the dictator himself. It was bad enough to see Ceauşescu's picture plastered across the country, but to have to hear Elena, who didn't even rise to power on her own, was too much for me to bear. I despised her. She claimed to be an engineer, an educated woman, but we knew that she had never finished school. She forced the party to present her as a great scientist as well as an 'activist,' a politician of the highest level. It was such a mockery." His face twisted with anger. "But say one word against either one of them in public, and you could be thrown in prison — taken away in the middle of the night."

Dan and Simona's suffering continued, but as the years wore on, the people's patience grew thin. In 1987, several thousand angry workers from a factory called the Red Truck Factory in Braşov marched in the streets protesting for better conditions. Dan explained that this was never publicized over TV or the radio, but word spread quietly that this had occurred. "We heard about it through relatives in Braşov," said Dan.

Then in 1988 numerous international organizations (Amnesty International, the Conference on Security and Cooperation in Europe [CSCE], and the U.S. Department of State) began to protest that Romania was not the wonderful country that Ceauşescu claimed it to be. Dan explained that he found this out years later. Even so, Ceauşescu continued as a ruthless dictator and the people became more and more oppressed.

In 1989 when the Berlin Wall fell, still Ceauşescu had control. He made his famous six-hour speech to the 14th Party Congress and was again elected president, by "unanimous consent." "A farce," exclaimed Dan. "It seemed that Romania would not follow the other Eastern European countries. But as history now shows, the people were about to explode. We were so weary of our conditions. We were suffering and very tired.

"An incident that started in May of 1989 is what really led to the demonstrations and the overthrow of Ceauşescu. There was a Hungarian minister living in Timişoara, in Transylvania (about five hours from Cluj) who resisted the authorities. The authorities were forcing a resettlement of many of the Hungarians from their remote village to the city. Ceauşescu was trying to rid the country of the ethnic Hungarians. This minister resisted the authorities and wouldn't leave the city. On December 10th, he told his congregation that he had received the final order to leave. His parishioners set up a nightly vigil at his church and the crowd grew to about 1,000 people. Timişoara is an ethnically mixed city and Serbs joined with the Hungarians demonstrating against the regime. The demonstrations grew in number and strength. Soon the demonstrations spread to other cities, and it became obvious that the army did not want to support Ceauşescu. But the fighting was fierce. It spread to Cluj."

Simona spoke, "That day and night Dan was out in the streets working as a doctor, helping our friends and neighbors. I, of course, didn't want him to go. I was scared but I knew he had to do it. He needed to bandage the wounded and care for the dying. All of us were tired of waiting in lines and living in fear."

Dan continued. "When I first heard about the demonstrations in the streets of Cluj, I left the house. Simona stayed home with the children. I was scared that I would die but I knew I had to go. Simona tried to convince me not to go, that I had a family to care for, but as a doctor, I felt the allegiance to those brave students outside getting shot. I had to go. It was dreadful. I saw my good friend Mihai die, fighting for freedom, and I couldn't take time to cry because I had to care for the sick. Bullets whizzed by me but I focused on helping the injured. What else could I do? When I came back home late at night Simona was sitting on the sofa, crying, I should say she was hysterical. I think she had been there for hours. She was so afraid, but I know that she was proud of me. It was such an emotional time for all of us." Simona nodded.

"We all wanted the repression to end. It had been several decades of harassment and torture, led by a man who was evil to all of us. Ceau-şescu continued to believe that we would listen to him. But his destiny was not what he had hoped. He was captured by the new government on December 22, and three days later, put to death, along with his wife. We had our day, that Christmas day in December 1989, killing the man who brought such suffering into our lives. The revolution was violent with thousands of deaths, and that is horrible beyond description, but the Communist leadership was overthrown. Both he and Elena were found guilty of genocide and shot to death by a firing squad."

It was after midnight and we were all tired. Dan's mother had even stopped feeding me. Dan said it was time to go. We left and walked in the pitch black to the car. It was cloudy with light drizzle so there were no moon and stars to guide us. The people and the animals of the village were asleep. There was a serenity that made me feel very close to God. We clung to each other each step of the way until we arrived at the car. Twice the car failed to start, then Dan succeeded and we cheered, as usual, and drove home. That night I dreamed of lines — people waiting in lines, so many lines — and bullets flying overhead.

AFTER THE FALL OF COMMUNISM

On Wednesday morning I was again at the school before 8 A.M. I observed the teachers and offered suggestions to improve their teaching skills. In the afternoon I sat with Dan and Simona in their kitchen eating Tante Maria's chicken noodle soup. We talked about their lives after the fall of the wall. How did they adjust? Did life improve? Could Dan practice medicine now? What kind of life did they have now, what did they want?

Dan recalled the times immediately after the revolution. "There was chaos. Some would say there is still chaos. There was so much insecurity. You were free to talk and travel, but most people didn't have, and still don't have, the money to travel. More goods were brought into the stores, but the salaries didn't change much, if at all, so no one could afford to buy the products. The dictator died, but the problems did not die with him. There are many changes that needed to be made, and that still need to be made — economic, political, social. But, as you know, change takes a very long time.

"On the other hand, there were some dramatic changes that had an immediate effect on our lives. For example, before the fall, many Communist governments allowed their citizens to travel to other Soviet bloc countries, although with strict monetary and lodging restrictions. But Romanians were not allowed to travel anywhere.

"However after the revolution, I got my first passport and traveled outside of Romania. This was amazing to me. I have always thought of that day as Day One of my new life. You remember, of course, it was April 1992. I traveled to Budapest, Hungary, to attend your health education workshop, offered by the Soros Foundation. My medical practice had not improved much since the revolution, so participating in the Soros workshop gave me the opportunity to positively impact the health of the people in my country, but in a completely different way."

Dan would never forget that week. I told Dan, "I remember when you first entered the room. You sat in the first row, center. You put your folder down, I nodded and welcomed you. The workshop was to begin at 9:00 A.M., but you were an hour early."

"I walked up to you," Dan said, "and reached out my hand to introduce myself. I was so nervous; I still recall what I said. 'I am Dan Baciu from Cluj-Napoca, Romania, located in the hills of Transylvania; you know, where Dracula lives! I am a medical doctor. I want to live in freedom, and make changes in my country. It is a sad time for my people, and yet a happy time. Life is hard now, but it always has been. But we adjust.'"

I added my own recollections of the meeting: "You told me that you were chosen from many other applicants because you were well known for your medical role here in Cluj. Yes, you said, you were interested in health education, and the information in Romania was very sparse. We spoke briefly, and you did most of the talking.

"We began the workshop with introductions and you spoke louder than the other forty-nine participants. Do you remember that you were friendly and turned to your neighbor and introduced yourself? You were the only one who did that."

It was unusual for people to talk with strangers in Eastern Europe. Even in a seminar, people would sit next to each other and never communicate. Communism had ended in 1989, but the Communist leaders had been highly effective, instilling fear and distrust in everyone. "Was it hard for you to ask those questions?" I asked.

"Just because the wall fell, behaviors did not easily change," Dan explained. "It was a scary time for me, but I knew that I had this one chance and if I didn't take advantage of it, all could be lost for me. So I shared information. I knew that this workshop was my ticket to the free world."

I reminisced: "Remember how your group designed makeshift costumes and arranged the room to look like an ordinary Communist flat? Simona, you should have seen Dan role-play a grandmother in an alcoholic family. He was all dressed up, wearing a babushka, stuffing his shirt with a pillow to show a big bosom. He (as she) tried to change her son-in-law's drinking habits. He was boisterously entertaining as his group depicted the difficulties of living with an alcoholic. Everyone was relaxed as he led a discussion on alcoholism and its effects in the different countries."

"I told them," he continued, "that if we join hands, and don't allow negative views to enter our minds, we can make a better life for our children. I still believe strongly in what I said." Dan was happy as he spoke, and Simona gave him a long, reassuring smile.

I continued. "I recall that that year we at the Soros Foundation chose you to become the project director of the Soros Foundation Health Education Program in Romania. We knew that you would do a good job, but we were surprised at how much you accomplished. You organized the first workshop and I went with you to present the training. It was a two-hour drive from Bucharest to the mountain town Sinaia. We offered a five-day seminar to sixty teachers, doctors and social workers from all regions of the country."

Dan explained to me, "When I returned home from the workshop in Budapest, I was determined to promote healthier lifestyles for the children of Romania but I needed to learn so much. If I had been given a job description for the Health Education Program director before accepting the position, it would have included management experience; budget, accounting experience; and of course, teacher-training experience. It also would have included a working knowledge of English, a basic understanding of democracy, and naturally, the fundamentals of health education. And finally it would have included a strong dose of determination.

"I had plenty of determination but few of the other skills needed for the job because, under the Communist system, people were not trained in these areas. No one but top Communist officials had experience in organization and administration. I had to learn quickly and become a jack of all trades. Even organizing the workshop in Sinaia was a task, but I believed in the need for the program.

"My intent was to place health education as a mandatory subject into every school in the country. There were so many details to work out. What does a budget look like? Will the government allow me to include sexuality education in my program? How many teachers must I train? How will I make decisions on my own? How can I gather support from colleagues? I had a major assignment ahead of me and many obstacles to overcome. But I had purpose, I had a goal; and it was among the happiest times of my life."

I added, "You did a great job organizing that first workshop. I hadn't been to Romania since my train ride to visit Márta and Miki Jakobovits. I remember stepping off the plane at the Bucharest airport and seeing you waving to me, but I was distracted by the German shepherds, the military personnel with pointed guns and the soldiers on the runway. I felt that same tension that I had experienced back in 1989. Once we left for Sinaia, accompanied by Soros staff, I felt safe. When I saw my accommodations in Sinaia I realized that the conditions in the country really had not improved." We stayed in a sanatorium, the typical former vacation spa for Romanian workers and their families, and it was in shambles. "I had no hot water, often no water at all and very little heat."

"I thought that the place was great," Dan piped in.

"I didn't," I said. "The bed was smaller than a cot, the mattress worn, and there were no sheets. I was given one lightweight blanket, and the temperature in the room did not go above 40 degrees Fahrenheit. I covered myself with my coat and two sweaters. I didn't tell you that. The sanatorium provided one towel that didn't absorb water, and there was no soap, TV, or radio."

"I know. I know," Dan said. "But remember that the seminar began on November 1, 1992, the week of the U.S. presidential election between Clinton and Bush. That added flavor!" Dan reminisced, "The moment you and Carol [Flaherty-Zonis, my co-trainer from Harrisburg] walked into the seminar room, people approached you, excited to meet their first Americans. They asked about the upcoming U.S. election. 'How could you be here and not vote for your president? And if you were at home, who would you vote for?' You were calm and told them about absentee ballots and every American's right to vote. That night we held our own election, and Clinton won by a large majority."

As a humanitarian, nonsectarian organization, the Soros Foundation did not want politics or religion to enter into the discussions at our workshop. It was a challenge to honor that request because the participants kept asking questions about the U.S. system. They wanted information about Clinton, Bush and American politics. They needed to know about democracy, and frankly, health education took a back seat.

"The participants loved the workshop. I called Darko [a colleague from Croatia] and told him about how well it went. Then Solvita [a colleague from Latvia] called me." Dan was talking about the other project directors. The Soros Foundation had hired nine project directors from other countries, all of whom participated in the workshop in Budapest. These directors developed a network of support. They talked with each other about their country workshops and found that they were often faced with similar challenges. Dan talked about their problems.

"The phone systems in our countries worked only about forty percent of the time," Dan continued. "We couldn't get the supplies we needed. We all thought that such items such as colored paper, scissors, magic markers, easel paper, easel stands were important, but they were simply unavailable. Then we had other problems. The copy machines were old and made copies so slowly that it took hours to prepare a simple handout. The heat didn't work in the buildings, and the buses didn't run on schedule. Nothing was predictable.

"We had communication problems among ourselves too. The coordinators spoke different languages since we came from many different countries. Communicating with other directors from the other countries was so vital to success; often, these were the only people who really understood the challenges, the goals. Although almost everyone spoke fluent Russian, our common language was broken English. You see, it was mandatory to know Russian during Soviet times, but few of us wanted to speak it. Do you remember when Zina tried to describe Lithuania's attitude toward homosexuality, but no one understood her English? Svetlana suggested she speak in Russian, but the group vehemently opposed it. So we ended the discussion.

"To try to improve my English, I watched American cartoons on television with my kids. My English improved as I continued to work with Americans, but we couldn't predict or prevent all the language problems. I remember when I invited Darko [from Zagreb, Croatia] to come to Cluj to take part in my workshop and collaborate on projects. I called him and said, 'Take a train to Cluj on Tuesday.' But Darko confused the word 'Tuesday' with the word 'Thursday' so I was waiting at the train station for him on Tuesday, and he didn't arrive until Thursday."

In spite of the obstacles, Dan succeeded and introduced a major health education program into schools across Romania. He used his connections, his survival skills and his determination developed during the Ceauşescu regime to his advantage. He trained Romanian colleagues to become trainers and paid them higher wages than those available elsewhere. With his dry sense of humor, Dan broke traditions and told his personal story, shared his feelings, his fears, and his goals.

"The Ministry of Education approved my program despite the opposition of several former Communist officials who were still in power. It was early in 1993, and the outside world perceived Romania as a country moving toward democracy, but there continued to be tremendous struggle here. The bureaucracy was awful. One time I walked into the Ministry of Education to get the endorsement for my program and was told to leave. The government official said, 'Your papers are not completed correctly.' I told them I had been informed by mail that my papers were certified and that I needed to come in person to get an official stamp. But they sent me home with new papers to complete. This happened to me four times. The challenge was that each trip to the ministry took ten hours by night train. It cost the foundation hundreds of dollars and consumed endless hours of my time. The staff at the ministry intimidated many people because they were authoritative and threatening, a remnant of the old Communist system. But I did not give up. I finally got what I needed."

Dan marketed his health education program so that professionals, ordinary citizens and students knew about it. The major bus company in Cluj-Napoca allowed him to put anti-smoking designs on the sides of city buses. He printed pamphlets and carried them to doctors' offices. He provided physicians with official papers proving the authenticity of the project. Mailing the pamphlets was not an option. As a secondary project he developed a public health program. To tackle so many programs was unheard of in Romania.

"I facilitated hundreds of workshops to teachers in dozens of cities. If I didn't have enough money from the Soros Foundation to pay for some of their expenses, I asked for contributions from people within the community. Owners of newly privatized restaurants supplied leftover food. Businesses donated paper. Sanitoriums offered rooms at a discount. Friends made desserts for the participants, and colleagues translated the curricula. I stretched the monies to render as many services as possible. And I presented the participants with materials that they could not get anywhere else.

"Simona was a great help. She's a natural businesswoman. She kept the budget and assisted me in the administration of the program. I worked eighteen-hour days and Simona often did as well. Together we wrote

Local Romanian bus advertising the Health Education Smoking Prevention Project.

health education scripts for television and radio, designed newsletters for teachers that circulated across the country, and began a peer-counseling program, training thousands of teenage students."

Dan looked gratified when I said that he had accomplished the impossible. It was a marvelous irony that the Communist system had created exactly the kind of person who would make the health education program so successful. The perseverance to survive, and the resourcefulness to find food and clothing for his family were all skills acquired during a dictatorship; these were precisely the skills that enabled Dan to overcome the countless obstacles to the creation of the largest health education program in Romania.

We finished Tante Maria's chicken noodle soup and took a break from talking so that I could accompany Dan to his elderly center. Dan initiated the first senior center in Romania in 1998, choosing a building in a poor Gypsy neighborhood. Many older citizens had lost their pensions, and life was terribly difficult for them. While resources for the center were limited, Dan used leverage with his contacts in Western nations to acquire necessary articles and equipment and to build a haven for those he believed were the forgotten ones. Over a hundred people were treated daily at the center. Dan also instituted a program of home visits to assist the terminally ill and in-home visits for others unable to get to the center. We spent about four hours there and Dan talked about his frustrations living in Romania and about how he ran for mayor because he wanted to make change.

"While Simona directed the school program, I continued trying to make changes for the country. It was early 1999. My friends started a campaign for me to run for mayor of Cluj on an independent ticket. Their motto — 'Dan, The Man with a Plan.' I decided to pursue this position because I believed that I could instill democratic principles into our society.

"So on February 26, 1999, I, Dr. Dan Baciu, officially announced that I was running for mayor of Cluj, Romania, before a crowd of over 300 people. I ran on a new party ticket, the Union of the Right Wing Forces, stating that nationalism must be abolished and capitalism expanded in Romania. My platform incorporated several programs for the elderly. I targeted reform for laws related to people with special needs, something unheard of before.

Dan Baciu, mayoral candidate for Cluj-Napoca.

"I was forced to publicize my program without money because my party had few funds. I got free television publicity when I organized a blood drive and talked about its importance. This is something uncommon in Romania. The newspapers covered a community dinner at this elderly center, right where we are now. The radio station covered my talks to student groups about welfare reform.

"My platform was based upon two fundamentals. First, if people can work, they should work to make money; but for those who are old or sick, the state must assist them. Second, I believe in an anti-discrimination policy. The anti-discrimination policy was a particularly sensitive issue in Cluj. You see, Transylvania has many Hungarians. In addition, 20 percent of Cluj is Hungarian. Some Romanians are afraid of ethnic conflicts if minorities, especially the Hungarians, get too many rights.

"I not only came out against discriminating against Hungarians, but I openly challenged the incumbent on this issue. You see, there are two statues in the center of Cluj. The first statue is of a famous Hungarian king. The incumbent decided to dig a huge, ugly hole directly in front of this statue, supposedly to search for Roman ruins. The digging stopped long ago, but the huge hole remains.

"At the same time, the incumbent approved the construction of a statue of a Romanian leader just a few hundred meters away. The first statue stands in darkness with a huge, black hole and construction signs around it, while the second statue is surrounded by flowers and light. It is quite a sore issue for the Hungarians living in Cluj. So this was a major issue in the campaign.

"Unfortunately I lost the election," Dan said sadly. "The incumbent had a strong party, more connections, and more money. But I am proud that I was sixth out of 25 candidates. I think it shows that Romania is changing. Just for me to be sixth says something, don't you think?"

I nodded my head yes as the children from the neighborhood came into the center and wanted candy from Dan. He often brought little treats for them. We left the center and went back to the house where we dined on Tante Maria's cabbage soup. We ate about two loaves of bread covered with sheep's cheese that Dan bought from a farm near his parents' house. Friends came to visit, the phone rang continuously, there was nonstop action. I went to sleep, once again, to the sound of howling dogs.

THE SCHOOL

Thursday morning Simona and I decided to have our chat in the kindergarten room of the school about her life after the Revolution. We left the house to take the short walk to the school. On the way, Simona pointed out a run-down house next door and told me that its occupants are Gypsies. Gypsies, Simona explained, suffered through extremely difficult conditions under Ceaușescu, and the truth is that not much has changed for them since. Simona told me that their houses were formerly homes of professionals; a doctor owned the house next door to them, but the Communists took it and put a Gypsy family of 25 in it. The Communists allowed the son of the doctor to rent one room from the state and live there. Even today they have no heat, no electricity, and no indoor plumbing. They have little money to pay their bills and get very little help from the government. The situation for most Gypsies is the same. I had candy in my pocket and gave it to the children.

Simona continued, "There, across the street, a family of ten lives in one room. It was once the hallway of an apartment. We gave them mattresses, some old furniture, and as much equipment as I could, you know like brooms, dust pans, old bicycles for the kids. But their lives do not seem to improve. The rain pours into their homes. They have no money at all to pay for their medical care and there is tremendous discrimination in the country toward them. One neighbor was killed in the revolution and the family had to sell everything in their house to pay for the funeral. The government doesn't know what to do with them. Their culture is so different." Simona added, "The older children often work in bars for minimal wage. They don't get social security. But they pride themselves on their musical ability." As we passed the neighbors' house, a woman came out to greet us.

"Hello, I am Greta Maria," she said as she shook Simona's hand and smiled at me.

"I am Susan," I said. "Is this your child? She is beautiful. How many do you have?" I asked as I patted the young one in her arms.

"I have six," she replied. Immediately she began talking about her life as Simona quickly translated. "Life is so difficult for me. I worked for 23 years at a shoe factory and now I still have to live in a hallway. I sleep on the floor. Imagine, I am a 50 year old woman [she looked 70], but I sleep on the floor.

"Our music is the best in the world, but we are looked down upon; rejected by society," she told me, hungry to share her story. "My son worked in Russia in a construction company, and made $1,000. An Italian man came and said that if he gave him the money, he would give him a place in the circus, so he did. He worked there for one week, and then the Italian kicked him out. He wouldn't give him his money back. He then beat him up, kidnapped him and took him to a hotel, where another person attacked him until he lost consciousness. He finally ended up in the hospital but it took several months for him to recover. It was all over the news. It happened in 1998. The discrimination toward us is awful." Simona nodded her head in agreement.

Greta Maria was overweight, her clothes shabby, and her shoes dirty, but she was so happy to talk with us. She asked us into her home. I knew that Dan and Simona wanted to get to the school but they both consented. "Only for a few minutes." They knew it meant a lot to me. I had talked with her children, using sign language, giving them candy, and I wanted to see how the family really lived. I couldn't imagine.

I was the first American guest they had ever had. Greta Maria made us wait outside for about ten minutes, I assume so she could straighten up. She apologized when we entered, "So many people come and go. There are twelve of us that live here, in this tiny space." It was a hallway just as Greta Maria had said and poverty that I had never seen before. Old bicycles resting against a dirty wall (probably the ones that Dan and Simona had given them), one gray, dusty rug, bottles strewn across the floor, mattresses piled one on top of the other. Dirty cups and saucers. No sink. Greta Maria wants her children to live a better life than she has. "We are so frustrated, and angry. Life was better during Ceauşescu. Yes, then everyone suffered. Not just us."

Greta Maria kept talking. "My 19-year-old son was killed in the Revolution, back in 1991." This is actually the wrong date, because the Revolution occurred in 1989. "I had to sell everything in my house to get money to bury him. They first burnt his ear, then they beat him to death, tied him to a tree. My children are my soul and my son is dead."

"Who killed him?" I asked.

"Those who are the real problem," she replied.

"Who is that?"

"The Hungarians — they are evil, and Hungarians are Jews."

I wondered whether she had any idea that I was Jewish. No, I'm sure she didn't. I considered telling her, but Katie was going to stay in Cluj to work at Simona's school. I didn't think they would hurt her, but my maternal instinct was aroused and I kept silent.

Greta Maria didn't stop talking about Jews. "There are two families of Hungarian Jews. They live over there." She pointed in the opposite direction of Dan and Simona's house. "They are big liars. They don't fear God. They are very bad. If you go to them with your problems, they lie."

I asked, "Have you met many Jews?"

"Just these two Jews," she replied.

After we left, Simona said it seemed ironic that Greta Maria was so happy to have me in her home, yet I was a Jew, and to her they are the worst. But Simona added: "You also are an American and that is the most important thing."

We walked on to the school handing candy to the many Gypsy children we passed. We arrived moments later and settled in with a cup of coffee to talk about Simona's life after the Revolution. The kindergarten seemed the ideal place to have this conversation.

In 1992, the same year Dan ventured outside of Romania for the first time, Simona opened a private kindergarten in their home, using her children's bedroom as the classroom. Twelve students attended. Four years later she was continuing to build her reputation as an educator, but she needed to learn more about early childhood education. I arranged for her to come to Harrisburg, stay with my family, and become trained as a Montessori teacher. It was very difficult to get a visa. Though the Communists were no longer in power, changes in the bureaucracy were slow. Simona had to travel ten hours by train to Bucharest to the embassy to apply. She was denied three times, but on the fourth trip, was lucky enough to find a sympathetic officer. Finally, she arrived.

I reminisced with her. "Remember the culture shock you suffered when you saw the materials at Brookside Montessori School and when you saw how the teachers respected their students? Nothing like this existed in Romania."

"Yes," she agreed, "I remember the special training I received. I also vividly recall that they gave me ten boxes filled with materials. I still use them in my classes today. I also remember when we visited a teacher's library in Harrisburg [a Resource Center] where teachers can borrow materials for their classrooms. There were 6,000 films on every subject and they were about to be thrown away and replaced with videos. Those films were on reels and the teachers were not using them because they no longer had the projectors. I remember saying that I would give anything to have just six of them in Romania. We begged the director not to throw the films away. We said that we would find the means to transport at least some of them to Romania."

I told Simona, "After you left, I spent weeks searching for companies that would transport these films free of charge and finally succeeded."

"So 6,000 films, over one-half a container load, ended up in Cluj — and our house. Dan found two old film projectors. Dan is so resourceful. He met with three Romanian TV stations and gave them several of the films to show on TV. Then he distributed many of them to schools across the country. He even gave some to the downtown movie theater. Imagine, the local downtown movie theater showed Lincoln's Gettysburg Address and a nutrition movie about American's eating habits! Dan had Romanian subtitles put on many of them. He did all of this work without pay. There are still about 2,000 in our bedroom. We use them as nightstands, at least until we can figure out what to do with them all.

"By 1998 I had moved my classroom into a two-room apartment, increasing the enrollment to 25 students. More parents continued to hear about my school. I used so much of what I had learned in Harrisburg. The philosophy was new to Romania and many people liked it and wanted their children in my school."

The school continued to grow. Finally, in 1999 Dan and Simona decided to build their own school. Simona's technical training gave her the skills to design the building. Dan's work in the health education program provided teacher training and administrative, budget and people skills.

"In April 1999, Dan and I began to construct the first English speaking kindergarten in Romania. It was two months after Dan decided to run for mayor. We hired the workers, developed the plan, and conjured up the many skills we had developed in surviving under Ceauşescu. You see, in Romania, you don't just go out and hire a contractor like you do in the United States. Here, you have to get different people to do different

Simona Baciu, surrounded by donated educational materials.

things. I had to find the bricks for the building, the stones for the pave-
ment — every little nut and bolt needed to build the school. And then
we had to find the people to do the work. Our neighbors, the Gypsy family of twenty-five who live next door, worked for us. Dan transported
them to and from the school each day, in between campaigning. We had
to oversee their work. We had to teach them what to do, how to do it,
and make sure it was all done correctly. We also, of course, had to be
sure the building would be safe. We had to find the right people to do
the electricity, the plumbing, and on and on.

"Also, once the construction was complete, we had to be resourceful to stock the school with the many things we needed. For example,
when I was visiting my sister in Germany, I was introduced to a friend
of the family who happened to be the head administrator of the Edin-
burgh Prison in Scotland. One afternoon, he was bemoaning the waste
that sometimes happens in the prison. For example, he explained that
prison mats were about to be thrown away because the inmates mistak-
enly had placed them on a newly painted floor. I asked if he would possibly consider giving them to me. After he overcame his surprise and was
assured that I would transport them to Cluj at no cost to the prison, he
agreed. My 'German' friends, the ones that were at the house the other
day, rented a truck and brought the mats to Cluj. We spent days remov-
ing the paint. The children now take their naps on them."

Simona talked about the school with pride. "The school, Copii
Fericiţi [Happy Kids], is named appropriately because the philosophy is
that when children are happy, feel loved and secure, they learn more and
become productive members of society. Construction of the kindergarten
was completed in September 1999 and school began with 125 students.
Shortly thereafter, an unforeseen problem arose — the parents did not
want their children to go to the state school for first grade. So, in 2000,
we built a primary school." It is three stories high and connects to the
kindergarten. Painted white on the outside with yellow trim, it is the first
English-speaking school in Romania.

"We believe that speaking English is key to success and to finding
employment," Simona continued. "Also, I have trained our teachers to
treat the children as individuals and, of course, to focus on helping them
learn to be happy. Today, we have a waiting list through the year 2004.
We offer after-school programs to an additional 150 students, teaching
computer skills, karate, and dance."

Simona has been very selective in choosing her staff. Simona explained why this selection is so vital: "I would interview 80 teachers to find one who could be trained for our school. It may sound arrogant but, you see, the university teacher training is slow to change. It is difficult to find teachers who can be innovative and creative. The State schools retain the old mentality. The pedagogical training has not developed new methods yet, so I must train those who are, in my opinion, born teachers. My staff are all young, in their twenties. They are open to new methods, but they still have much to learn.

"A family recently approached me and asked if I would admit their son who is afflicted with Down's Syndrome. The staff discussed the situation; they were hesitant because they didn't feel their training was sufficient. We invited the parents to the school with their son, Miklós, so we could observe him. Miklós entered a kindergarten class and became disruptive and nasty to a student sitting next to him. The student rudely asked him to leave the room and said that he didn't want him in his school. The teacher scolded him and said: 'If you don't stop behaving like that, you will begin to look like him.' She did not realize how hurtful her remark was to Miklós and how unhealthy it was for the other students to hear."

Simona continued, "I ultimately decided not to admit the child or other special needs students without specialized training for the teachers. The special education training in our pedagogical institutes does not yet meet the standards my school requires. It was an awful situation. The parents of the boy left dejected because there are no accommodations in Cluj suitable for their child. But I had to say no, at least now, because no one in the school was trained to assist this youngster."

Simona says, "Today, 'Happy Kids' stands as a symbol of hope for the children, and a symbol of perseverance and success for our people. The school has received donations from sources in the United States, Germany, Scotland, and Belgium. The Ministry of Education recently evaluated the educational program and facilities. He gave us the highest grade and designated 'Happy Kids' as a model school for Romania."

We finished our talk and walked home. Everyone was starving, so we decided to drive to the Pizza Hut and share a pizza. We piled into Dan's car; Dan and me in front; Simona, Ruxy, Tudy and Katie squashed in the back. Dan tried to start the Dacia, and we sighed a hungry sigh when the car finally started on the third attempt.

I spent my last day, Friday, relaxing. Ruxy, Katie and I went shopping and bought some henna for my hair, the red henna found only in

Romania. Ruxy surprised me with a wooden mask of Dracula, a gift for Ron. That night friends came to say goodbye. Several of us sat around the table eating Tante Maria's specialties. "Tomorrow, I will take the train back to Budapest. Katie will stay with the family for three months," I said to Tibor, Dan's best friend. At that moment Katie walked into the kitchen. I looked at her. She was learning so much, I could hardly believe that she had been in Cluj less than a week. She sat down next to me. I spoke softly to her, "Katie, some people find difficulty here. Others try to see the positive, which can be very challenging. Look at the surroundings here in this kitchen and outside the Baciu house. Do you see cramped living quarters and poverty right outside their front door? What do you think Dan and Simona see? I believe that they see adventure and hope. And they see that they can make a difference. So can you, Katie."

I left on Saturday. It was a tearful goodbye. I boarded the train thinking about Dan and Simona and the remarkable experience that Katie was about to have. Dan and Simona live a hectic but challenging life. They are surrounded by people who are committed to their values. They continue to raise their children with the expectation that they, too, will contribute to their society. Dan and Simona have chosen to take the road less traveled, and because of that, their lives are filled with hope and promise for themselves, their children, and for the people of Romania.

Márta and Miklós Jakobovits
Oradea, România

This is the story of Miklós (pronounced Mee´klosh) and Márta Jakobovits (pronounced Ya´kobovich), husband and wife. Their story is similar to the stories of many Romanians living during the Ceauşescu regime. They suffered the same shortages of food and medicine; they stood in the same lines; they shivered through the same winters; they were subjected to the same indignities and repressions.

But in other ways, their story is quite different. While Miklós (affectionately called Miki) and Márta have lived in Transylvania all their lives, they consider themselves Hungarian Magyars who happen to be living in Romania. If you ask them, "What is your nationality?" they will say: "We happen to be Romanian citizens, but that is because of politics and bureaucracy. We have learned that citizenship changes with the times, but what doesn't change is that we are, and always will be, Hungarian."

Their statement has significance because their region, called Transylvania, has been a political football, passed back and forth between Hungary and Romania. It is located on the northwest border between the two countries.

For hundreds of years, Transylvania actually was part of the Ottoman Empire. But in the mid–1800s, some Hungarians in Transylvania were seeking independence. Simultaneously, some revolutionaries in Hungary were seeking independence from Austria-Hungary. Both revolutions failed and Austria-Hungary gained control over Transylvania. The official language of the region became Hungarian, and for many, the Hungarian roots grew deep into the soil and psyche of the people.

During World War I, Austria-Hungary was defeated and Transylvania became part of Romania. The cities, towns and villages changed from Hungarian names to Romanian names; the Hungarian street signs were replaced with Romanian street signs; Hungarian officials were pushed aside by Romanian officials; and the official language changed from Hungarian to Romanian. The children stopped speaking Hungarian at school and began speaking Romanian. The people whose allegiance was with Hungary developed what they called a "public Romanian" facade but retained their "private Hungarian" face.

This was the world into which Miki Jakobovits was born on August 9, 1936. His family called the city where he was born Kolozsvár, the Hungarian name. The official name was Cluj-Napoca, Romania. When Miki was four years old, Romania was forced to cede northern Transylvania and its two and a half million people back to Hungary. For his family, this was a welcomed relief. And so the people in charge changed from Romanian back to Hungarian; the cities, towns and villages were renamed their (proper) Hungarian names. Up went the Hungarian street signs. The old Hungarian schoolbooks were dusted off, and the children, once again, spoke Hungarian at school. And now Miki, who had not moved an inch, lived in Hungary.

But before his family got accustomed to this Hungarian life, in the fall of 1944 as World War II was coming to a close, Romania drove the Hungarian forces from Transylvania, and Transylvania was once again united with Romania. And, of course, the same changes happened once again. The officials, the signs, the names of the towns, the language all changed.

In 1948 his family moved to another town in Transylvania, Sepsiszentgyörgy/Sf. Gheorghe, where his father, Mihály Jakobovits, directed the painting workshop in the local theater. They lived as Hungarian

Magyars in Romania. Miki began his painting career. He studied fine arts in the secondary school and attended the College of Fine Arts in Kolozsvár/Cluj. As a young man Miki already was in the inner circle of artists, and his friends were important Transylvanian artists: Sándor Mohi, Albert Nagy and Andor Antal Fülöp. He married Márta (a ceramic artist) in 1967. He was surrounded by Hungarian culture and art, yet he lived in Romania.

Márta was born September 22, 1944, in Santău, Satu Mare County, Romania. That was the year that the country had changed hands from Hungary back to Romania, so Márta was actually born in Romania. She was raised as a Hungarian Magyar. As a young child she lived a traditional Hungarian lifestyle, eating Hungarian foods, playing with Hungarian friends and reading Hungarian books. But Márta had an interest separate from her Hungarian identity. She loved the earth and always wanted to play with stones and rocks; she was fascinated by their shapes and texture. Her parents helped her pursue a career in the arts. When she was 17 years old, she went to the Technical School of Architecture in Oradea, Romania. From there she studied at the "Ion Andreescu" Institute of Fine Arts in Cluj-Napoca, Romania.

While control of the country changed back and forth, what remained stable in Miki and Márta's world was their Hungarian culture. They learned that their nationality was their ethnicity. It is not who runs the government or what the name of their town is or what the official language is. Those things could and did change with the wind. So when asked their nationality, Miki and Márta say, "We live in Romania, but we are Hungarian nationalists or Transylvanian Magyars."

During the Communist years Márta and Miki, as Hungarians, were under more pressure than the Romanian citizens. Ceaușescu had imposed terrible restraints on the Romanian people and used his securitate to instill great fear in the population at large, but he reserved particular discrimination for the Hungarian nationalists. It was widely known that Ceaușescu wanted to rid the country of all Hungarian nationalists. His greatest achievement in this regard was a broad scale "resettlement plan" forcing Hungarian Magyars from their remote villages to military-like barracks in city developments. It was grey and dismal for those who were victim to "resettlement."

Fortunately for Márta and Miki, they were not forced from their homes, but they watched as their parents' farms were converted to raise industrial crops for export to pay Romania's mounting debt. So Márta

Márta and Miki Jakobovits at their kitchen table.

and Miki learned to live in a society that was not only repressive and full of fear, but that wished to expel the very culture they held dear.

Márta and Miki turned inside themselves; they turned to their innate artistic talent as their vehicle to survive. They became artists extraordinaire. They also became quite famous. Much has been written about them describing their personalities and their works. They each have their own "Jakobovits" style. They study the world from an aesthetic point of view and try to find the "special and changeable" in the picturesque image.

A colleague of theirs, Găină Dorel, says of Miki: "Miklós Jakobovits the man can be confused with the painter. Miklós Jakobovits the painter can be confused with the man." Through his entire artistic career, Miki has illustrated an understanding that the intellectual aspects of life can only take place through a multitude of manifestations — colors, shapes, surfaces and design. Through color, he shows the changes of the times. All of his works are subjects for study. His resume is impressive with individual exhibits in national museums and galleries across Romania during the Communist era, and now throughout Europe since the fall of Communism. His works are shown in domestic and foreign museums and public collections. Miki teaches art history in several universities in Transylvania and is an active member of the Arts Committee of the Ministry of Culture in Romania. Films have been produced about him: *In the Workshop of Miklós Jakobovits*, by Emil Lungu for the Hungarian broadcast of Romanian television (1979); *The Paintings of Miklós Jakobovits*, film by Stefan Fischer for German television; and *Miklós Jakobovits*, by Márgit Raduly and Marius Tabacu for Hungarian television.

Márta is equally well-known in her area of expertise. Her ceramics are in art museums across Romania, Germany, Holland, Italy, Croatia and, of course, Hungary. Several documentary films have been produced about her as well: *The Play with Clay, Water and Fire,* by Olga Buşneag; *Márta and Miklós Jakobovits,* by Gábor Xántus for Romanian TV; *Symbols and Signs,* by Kinga Papp for Romanian TV; and *Interview in the Paper Arts Exhibition,* by Kinga Papp. She has won numerous awards for her sculptures. Besides her artistic activity in the fields of ceramics, painting and graphics, Márta teaches art, publishes in newspapers and periodicals, and organizes exhibitions. She is cited in the *Encyclopedia of Romanian Contemporary Artists* and is acknowledged in the *World Encyclopedia of Contemporary Artists* (Bologna, Seledizione Publishing House, 1984). As Găină Dorel says of Márta, "Márta Jakobovits could at any time and above all act as an ambassador of the planet Earth. She feels what the earth, the rocks and waters of the planet feel; as a creature and a being, she's magically composed of earth, rock and water; she loves the earth, stones and water but this is not enough for her; she needs to also love, to meet, admire and respect the known and unknown fire of the cosmos and the strong air of the near and faraway skies."

What follows is a typical day in the lives of these two extraordinary people. You will see that they grapple with universal questions of art and of philosophy and the convergence of these two disciplines. They continually debate philosophical questions with one another; they continually debate the impact of philosophy on art and on the artist. Why am I here? What do I need to do to reach the innermost part of my soul? How do I interpret the difference between flesh and spirit? How genuine and honest is my soul, and how genuine and honest is my artwork? How do I stay true to my philosophy?

While spending time with Márta and Miki, I came to understand that because of the road these two people have chosen, it matters not whether they lived under Communism and now live under democracy — their quest is the universal quest of the artist.

A DAY IN THEIR LIVES: JULY 17, 2000

I sat with Márta at her dining room table as she nibbled on a rice and paprika dish. Two pieces of black bread were on her plate. It was 8:00 A.M. "I got up at 6:30 and I've done my one-hour yoga routine, followed by a Zen meditation," she told me. These techniques, unavailable in the Ceauşescu era, have fascinated her and added a dimension to her already busy life. "It was forbidden to meditate during Ceauşescu. The dictator considered it a spiritual cult; harmful to the mind and damaging to society. It is a necessity for me to meditate each morning, a full meditation including yoga." I had taught her how to meditate when I visited her with Éva Monspart in 1989 three weeks before the Revolution. Márta says, "Meditation allows me to feel a new freedom in my life. Now I am invigorated, but I must do my errands first. Miki and I take turns. Today's my day."

Márta, now in her mid–50s, has high cheekbones, a round, warm face, medium complexion and black hair streaked with gray. She cuts it herself and wears it short. Her height is average, but she appears taller because she carries herself head high with back straight. She wears baggy, hippie-style clothes, dyed green or pink.

Miki is in his mid–60s. He has a solid build, a full face with rosy, round cheeks, and hair that is receding and flies wildly, as if charged by electricity. He has the presence of a celebrity or a practiced politician and the looks of a serious professor. I can imagine him in the inner circle of Picasso or van Gogh.

Márta and Miki live in Oradea. This magnificent city is very close to the Hungarian border. Its downtown is replete with Gothic and Romanesque architecture. Unfortunately, virtually all the streets and structures are in poor condition because there is no money to repair them. Many of the side streets have potholes so large that only four-wheel-drive vehicles can make it across the road, and there are few of those in Oradea. Márta and Miki love their city, and because of the way they see the world, Márta and Miki see mostly Oradea's beauty and charm.

They have lived in the same apartment for over thirty years. Their street is not torn apart like many others, but that is simply luck. During the Ceauşescu regime, people were given apartments; the couple just happened to be given these living quarters. Their apartment complex is hidden from the street behind a huge cement wall. The entrance is an old wooden door.

At 8:30 A.M., Márta began to dust and tidy the apartment. Their flat is Spartan with a kitchen, bathroom, living room, and bedroom. But it is filled with Miki's paintings and Márta's ceramics. Books are everywhere — art books from other countries, Plato's *Republic*, and Romanian and Hungarian philosophy books. Papers are strewn over the shelf, and rumpled slippers are stuffed under the chair near the door. Márta said, "Miki's most recent painting [an abstract painted in shades of blue] has been hanging over our bed for about a month. He used the variety of one single color in this work as Bach does in his famous fugues. I reorganize his artwork often for variety." A wooden table covered with a red and white–checkered plastic tablecloth sits in the middle of the main room with light from a large window. There is a long, dark, wooden dresser resting against one wall where Miki's paintings lie.

Márta took one painting and carefully fussed with it, first glancing at it, then wiping the frame, and finally placing it gently back against the dresser. She described the emotions Miki expresses in his work. "You can see how intricate the lines are, and how the color is mixed perfectly. During our married years Miki has gone through many different stages, each one producing works of equal significance. As with many artists, I may criticize works that I come across, but with Miki's, I never do." She sees only his expression of love, self-identity, and soul.

Márta continued, "Most of the works [in their main room] were painted during the Ceauşescu era, and are political pictures depicting the situation at that particular time. Miki painted without too much fear of reprisal because we as artists were not usually considered a threat to the government. His works mirror the desperation that we all faced during the Communist era." Márta looked at her favorite, a black and white made with stencils, representing in symbols the dictator Ceauşescu, standing on a pedestal, surrounded by his men. "Don't the expressions on their faces show the self-serving loyalty of each man to his leader?" she asked me.

Márta went on, "It was illegal to criticize the dictator. If we were caught doing so, we could be sentenced to a long jail term." Márta showed me the allegorical pictures that Miki had painted during that time in history. "Usually artists didn't fear reprisal, but then on the other hand one never knew. We could have been imprisoned. Yes," Márta said, "Our world was just like that. Confusing — and we lived both with less fear than others, but possibly with as much. To you it probably doesn't make sense. To us it does."

"In the U.S.," I explained, "we don't experience those contradictions.

Political satire of Ceauşescu done in 1982 by Miklós Jakobovits.

An artist is not a threat to the government. People are free to paint what they want." I suggested that one of the most difficult things about life under Ceauşescu was the unpredictability.

Márta nodded her head in agreement and resumed dusting the works of history that lay covered in the apartment, unseen by the world. "Artists are more fortunate than others because we have a means of expression. Even during Ceauşescu, we were not really held back like other people were. Miki did risk painting political pictures but he only showed abstract works in public, paintings that expressed the same emotions as his more blatant symbolic ones, understood only by those who knew Miki."

Márta explained the importance of these works. "Miki and I have discussed what should become of our works after our death. We know that our art communicates valuable information about Romania under Communism, but for now, we leave them in our apartment. That is how we both want it." It is not the time to enmesh themselves in all the inter-pretations of whoever might see them. "We are content to lay them side by side, with cloth draped over them for protection, at least for now."

She carefully placed against the far end of the dresser an oil painting Miki was restoring for the museum in Oradea. "He takes pleasure in
this profession, which also adds income. The painting, a rare piece, and
one of the museum's finest, was done by a famous Romanian artist in
1711. Miki had placed it here so we could easily see it, and enjoy its serenity." Márta walked around the tubes of paints and tiny toothpicks that
were scattered across the floor. It was off limits for her dusting, and she
would leave the art materials where Miki had placed them.

We walked outside to run her errands. It is difficult to actually see
the apartment buildings in Oradea unless you know where to look. People live in these apartments concealed behind large cement walls. "For
me, this is familiar, my home, and I love it," Márta said.

I noticed that Márta scanned the street. I mentioned it, but she said,
"It is probably a remnant from my past life, one I can't seem to overcome. During Ceauşescu, I watched for anyone who may be unfamiliar.
When I saw a stranger, I reported it to Miki and we would be on guard
for at least the day, usually the week. Who knew what an unfamiliar face
meant? Suspicion and fear were always players in our lives."

We entered the market. It was a small store with all sorts of products,
and very different from stores in America. There were scarves, dresses,
food, silverware, one hammer, odds and ends. We bought soap powder,
milk, eggs and paprika, and hurried back to the apartment to unpack
them. Around 11:00 A.M., we left for her studio.

We walked briskly through the downtown with its magnificent old
and decorative architecture. "I love the bustle of the people in the streets,
the sounds of the tram bell, automobile horns and children laughing,"
Márta said. She stopped in a park to pick up stones and wooden chips
and put them in her coat pocket. "I will use them. You will see how I
will transform them into a work of art."

She stopped along the walking mall to give 100 lei to an old, blind
man, begging on the corner, then another 100 lei to a student playing
the flute in the square. "I can't walk past those in need without giving
them something." She stepped lightly on the curving, inlaid mosaic design of the mall walkway. "Its dramatic effect always fascinates me." The
colossal Orthodox Church directly in front of us, with its silver Byzan-
tine cupolas, reminded both of us of the one in Moscow's Red Square. I
noticed many red, yellow, and blue Romanian flags hanging from windows, but Márta seemed unaware of their presence. I commented, and
she shrugged her shoulders as if to say it was not important to her.

The air reeked of gasoline, the emissions of inefficient cars and trucks that pollute the city. "People joke and say the Dacia, the popular Romanian car, is not even a car," said Márta.

"But they don't jest about the smell?" I asked.

"We are accustomed to this odor, and, in a way, I would miss it if the country improved its controls," she answered.

We arrived at her studio, a building that had once been a Jewish synagogue. It had many religious ornaments on the outside, and although the Star of David had been removed, the pole still stood on the roof. The stained glass windows were cracked. We climbed three flights up a wide, marble staircase, and walked through a door that led us to a balcony that overlooked an outdoor courtyard. There was an unkempt garden and several apartments. An old hunchback woman waved to Márta, mumbling something to her. Márta waved back. We turned right, and Márta opened her studio door. It was 11:30 A.M., and I could see a sense of harmony take over her.

The studio has three rooms: an entrance area, one main room, where Márta does her work, and a large closet. "Miki sometimes paints in the closet, but it is mainly used for storage." The entrance is long and narrow and is filled with Miki's sculptures. It leads to Márta's workplace. "This large room was once an old sanctuary." It is now crowded with machinery for her ceramics, her artwork, and various wares. I noticed an outline where the Ten Commandments had been placed. There was much on which one could reflect on what once had taken place in this room, but Márta saw only her nature design, lying on the floor. The sun produced multicolored light as it shone through the stained glass windows, brightening her work and the wood chips that were scattered about.

Márta's ceramics occupied the space along the far wall. There were many shelves with hundreds of distinct pieces. An assortment of magnificent ceramic boxes lay in various groupings. Márta confided, "These boxes hide my dreams. During Ceauşescu, I made many of them believing the hopes and dreams for my people lay hidden inside. I prayed at one time they could be opened, of course symbolically. Today, in that way, they have been opened for me." But when she talked about all the dreams and hopes that she wanted from the boxes, she shuddered. "I was more optimistic about the character of mankind in general, before Ceauşescu's execution. I believed that Ceauşescu was evil, but that kind of evil did not exist in other places around the world. I have learned differently, since those days. But we don't have time to philosophize," she quickly added.

Marta Jakobovits' nature design, lying on the floor in her art studio.

She turned to her new and special piece of work, knelt on the floor, and began arranging and rearranging the small objects. Márta placed each piece into what seemed some preordained position, as she herself had moved into a creative consciousness. The light that shined on all the individual parts seemed to pull them together as if universally connected.

"I would say my philosophy is simple and deep. It produces a sense of serenity that surrounds me. Organized religion has its place for me, and I occasionally attend church, but there is a constant spiritual nature that directs my life and permeates my art." Immersed in her nature design, she credits her peace to the simplicity of each day. She seemed to use her senses of smell and sight. Time did not seem to exist for either of us, as I too became consumed in her work. Before we knew it, Anca, her student, arrived.

"Welcome," Márta said to Anca, and Márta introduced me to her. Anca shook my hand and then turned to Márta. Speaking in English, she said, "I know you are going to be disappointed but I am not going to attend art school at Cluj University. Instead I have decided to take a scholarship at Michigan State in computer science.

"I love my country, and feel secure here with my parents, but I don't see hope for my future. There is such insecurity here and I researched on the Internet that if I study in the U.S., life could change for me. I look at you, Márta, with such admiration, but I need more. I don't want to have to marry to get money, like so many of my friends."

Anca turned to me and explained, "Many young men and women in Romania today marry as an investment. Otherwise they can't live comfortably. Here's what happens. At their wedding it is now a custom for the guests to give them money. So if 300 people are invited, each guest who is not a relative gives about $30. Relatives customarily give as much as $500. The couple starts a life with that money." Anca spoke almost in a whisper. "Both parents pay for the wedding. Marriage is a business now because it gives the young couples an opportunity otherwise unavailable. It costs their parents about $3,000 or 50 to 80 million lei for the wedding, but the couple makes $6,000. Of course, you know there is a payback. They also are invited to other weddings." Anca explained the details to Márta and me, but she knew her teacher was not of that world.

"But I don't think this is a viable option for me," Anca continued. "I am 20 years old, and I feel a sense of hopelessness here in Romania. No matter what my profession is in Oradea, I will never earn enough money to travel anywhere or rent my own apartment. I don't want to live with my parents forever. Even when young couples marry they live with one set of parents."

How different Anca's life has been from that of my own daughter. Yet, Anca and her peers in Romania have now seen another world, with access to computers and information not available to their parents and grandparents.

"Yes, I love my country, but we are a poor people. If I can avoid struggling so much and if I can help my parents, it would make me happy, even though art is my passion."

Márta looked somber. She understood Anca's dilemma but she didn't want her to give up art. "I know there is chaos here now. This country has always had its problems. During Ceauşescu there were hard times too. I understand you want your dreams. I hope that you can achieve what you need to do." Anca nodded.

Márta continued, "You are young, with different dreams than I. The pragmatic world is grabbing you, dear Anca, and you must go. But who is to say that you won't come back. As long as I am here, you can come back to me, and I will be your teacher." They embraced goodbye, and

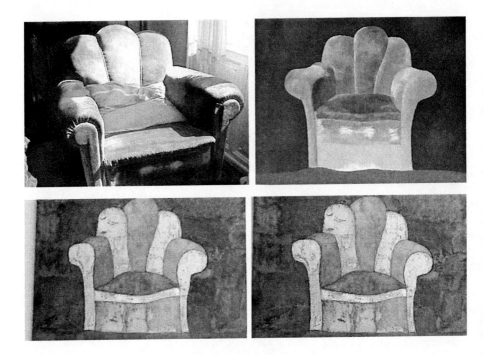

"The Chair" by Miklós Jakobovits.

Anca left the studio with a small box, hidden with her dreams, a gift from Márta. Saddened, Márta went back to work.

During the day, while Márta and I were together, Miki was working on his latest painting. His studio is directly across the courtyard from their flat in a building that once was a cereal factory. It has been his workplace for many years and it is where he painted his works that represent the contrasting periods of his life. Márta had arranged for me to go to Miki's studio and see him at work.

I entered the studio and saw Miki standing over his easel. "I am painting another version in a series of armchairs, patterned after the one that sits in the main room of our apartment. It has always been my favorite chair, where my father once sat, and probably my grandfather. You see, Susan, it is green. It was once a shiny velvet, but now it is quite worn. It is very ordinary, and that is what intrigues me. I decided that I wanted to develop a relationship with this undistinguished thing. I have completed about a half dozen different pictures of this same chair."

Many are scattered about the apartment. "We can show them all to you. I developed a relationship with the chair and now when I sit in it,

The Jakobovits' workshop.

I feel a wholeness to my life, a place in the universe. It depends on the soul of the artist, how much he can concentrate on the ordinary and transform it into the universe." Miki continued to focus on the chair.

Miki's artist friend, Gábor, entered the studio. They began one of their many philosophical debates. Miki started: "The soul of an artist is more complicated than the ordinary person. If an artist is thinking how to sell the art, the art cannot be pure. He is not genuine. Do you agree?" Gábor replied, "Probably it is true, but it is not so simple to create great art. One needs to have the genes. You are born with the talent."

Miki continued, "Yes, but there is much more to a good artist than heredity. A painter needs to be genuine and to have full concentration. The essence of art is gathering energy from nature and from within ourselves. The more genuine the energy, the greater the work. It is in visual art that the interrelation of these energies is seen, especially in painting, and the genuineness shows in the end product.

"In the great works of art you feel the energy of the artist; the cooler energy of the mind, the warmer energy of the heart, and different temperament of the sexual energy. When all those energies are not in balance, something is missing." He continued, "If you are working only with your mind, then you are too rational. If you only work with your heart, you are too instinctive. It is the character of a great artist that can balance the three energies," said Miki. "But the deepest part of the soul must be genuine. The more genuine a person can be within himself, the more truthful he is in his art. That is more important than the genetic pool."

Miki, his eyebrow raised, contemplated, "I learned love in my home, growing up, and I got balance from my parents. I got the sense of color from my father. I like the quiet surface of balance and color. The quality of the color is important. The quiet images show strength, but I cannot analyze how deep that comes from inside of me. I only know that color fascinates me, and all the time, I want to explore its significance. I pursue those secrets, glimmering towards us in their mysterious glow. It is as if I were querying for the past and for its enigmatic relations from within a magical dimension just as one seeks the frivolous, banal, and bizarre human symbols of our present age."

Gábor spoke: "You possess your own style. You are not interested in politics but you seem to be preoccupied by everlasting truths going beyond time and space."

Miki responded, "Yes, you are right. My paintings," he continued, "are not abstract works of art but rather approach the metaphysical, since I am decoding the secret signs arriving from distant layers of ages and spaces. I am like a medium receiving messages. I avoid bombastic symbols, which are tensing and provoking each other and I rather try to make space and time perceivable. To sanctify them. In this process even the most banal objects receive seriousness and predetermined significance."

Gábor asked, "But how does that fit into our world today, Miki?"

"Because it is not pragmatic. There is too much pragmatism in the world today. We, as artists, see beyond the pragmatic world, because when I am painting, it becomes an interior openness, like a medium. Sometimes I am surprised at the outcome. I cannot calculate the process. I begin a work and then it flows, and becomes a dialogue with the materials. I must be genuine inside. Yes, I keep thinking — being genuine and concentrating, those are my links."

Gábor interrupted, "Yes and I think because we need to search for that genuineness we, as artists, are not really part of society. Sometimes I laugh though at how naive we are. We thought we were genuine under Ceaușescu, but were we?"

Miki continued where Gábor left off. "Remember when we believed there was only one Ceauşescu, and if we could rid ourselves of him, then peace would beset us? Our outside world was limited, and we knew nothing, but we still searched inside ourselves. Now, we see there are many Ceauşescus, many evil people across the globe. During Ceauşescu, we just saw the problems here in our country. Sometimes I painted the problems, and other times I just carried the anguish into my soul. Now I see Ceauşescus all over the world; signs of anger, violence, materialism and too, too much technology. Under Ceauşescu, we idealized a lot. Yes, we believed that he was the cause of the problems. Now we know it is humanity itself. That is much harder for me to comprehend." Miki then turned to his "armchair," ignoring us while contemplating his work.

Later, Miki and I joined Márta at home, and the three of us sat at the dinner table. There have been changes in Romania, but Márta and Miki agreed that their life has not been altered very much.

"Life has changed considerably for most Hungarian Magyars, not always in ways we would have liked, but the important things for Márta and me have remained the same. Our apartment and studios have remained the same, except now we don't need to hide our books. We aren't afraid that our neighbors are listening to us. We can travel, although I prefer to stay at home and paint," Miki said.

Márta added, "The state of mind of the human being should be used for beautiful things, and we believed during Ceauşescu that the positive part of people's character is stronger than the negative. We believed appreciation and power of human values would rise, and not nationalistic attitudes and hatred. We believed everyone would come with good human values after Ceauşescu, because we were oppressed. We opposed the Ceauşescu government and the tyranny of the regime, but we did not allow anyone to shape our inner lives. We lived as artists and Hungarian Magyars."

This is the essential truth of Márta and Miki. They lived under subjugation, yet found peace inside themselves. Their view of the world, perhaps in spite of, or perhaps because of, Ceauşescu is captured by Márta's words: "We continue to believe that the ultimate cause of peace or conflict comes within the individual, not from the outside.

"Yes, I reminisce about those times," Márta said sadly, "but now Miki and I, we are disillusioned and disappointed with the world today. We still are idealists and can express that in our workshop, but in the pragmatic world, we are very naïve. The politicians and the churches have betrayed us. The only answer is to seek the peace within. Not to look outside ourselves. The answers are deep within each of us."

Miki nodded his head in agreement. Theirs was a mutual understanding brought about by the experience of many years of life in a country that was changing around them.

We sat in silence. Márta smiled at me. Miki walked over and sat down in his armchair.

Marius Mateş
Baia Mare, România
Chicago, Illinois

As Dan and Simona sacrifice to build their schools, and Márta and Miki continue to paint in their artists' world, Marius Mateş (pronounced Matesh´) is sitting at our kitchen table in Harrisburg, Pennsylvania, talking with my husband and me.

Marius is 27, born in Baia Mare, Romania, a city in Transylvania. He grew up in a typical working class family and is an only child. He is six feet tall with broad, massive shoulders; he could be a heavyweight boxer. Marius speaks English well and has great wit and intelligence.

I met Marius in the summer of 1995 when he picked me up at the train station in Budapest. Dan Baciu had told me to look for a rugged looking young man in his early 20s. He would be waiting for me at Track No. 6 in the main train station in downtown Budapest. I had been working in the Hungarian schools, and Dan had invited me to speak to a group of teachers in Cluj. I didn't want to travel alone, so Marius rode the train from Cluj to Budapest so that he could escort me back to Cluj. On the eight-hour ride from Budapest to Cluj, Marius talked about his life.

SUMMER 1995

"I was born in the city of Baia Mare in 1973," he began. "And as a kid, I think that my life was pretty normal. That is, as a young child. I remember the first time I went to the cinema to see a 3-D movie and my parents bought me some candies and fruit for the movie. I remember

Marius Mateş

people very nicely dressed and there was a pleasant atmosphere. In 1977 and '78 it didn't matter whether there was socialism or Communism because there was still food on the table; we had electricity and hot water, and our basic needs were very much fulfilled. There was a pretty active social and cultural life available even though it was a Communist society.

"Around 1978 my parents said that it was the beginning of the end of the good times. Ceauşescu was the leader of the country, and had been since the '60s. My parents liked him, as did most of the people, because as I said there really was nothing missing in their lives. There was stability and it wasn't really oppressive, so what wasn't to like?

"In 1978 Ceauşescu made a trip to China and probably saw that people didn't need much to survive and from that moment on he decided that we could live with less. In the years after that food was scarce."

"Did it happen all at once?" I asked.

"In the beginning the exotic things disappeared. There were no imported foods anymore; no oranges, no bananas, nothing extra. We had fruit during the season, mostly apples."

"Did you have enough money to buy food?"

"Yes, we did. That was one thing, we had money, but there was nothing to buy with it. So gradually a black market system developed. People continued to want what they had had and now these items weren't available. Fruits and vegetables at first, then toilet paper became scarce, then medicine.

"You have to understand that all of this happened during at least five or six years, so it wasn't that one day we had everything and the next nothing. In the beginning my parents were not scared because they said, 'Well, it's just one thing that happened. It's not that bad and we can really live without it.' That's how they talked but when they couldn't get what they wanted, it was a different story."

"What was the first thing they really missed?"

"Coffee. I remember when my mother came home from the store and said there was no coffee. You would have thought she had said someone had died. Then we could only get a pound every three months, which was not enough. So the black market developed for coffee.

"But in time, during the early '80s, the situation deteriorated. Half a pound of butter had to last one month. It was the same thing with meat. There were huge lines to buy meat. I remember waiting in line for two or three days to be able to get ten pounds of meat that we would then try to store. But we only had a tiny refrigerator so we had to put the meat in friends' homes. It was all so complicated.

"I can't forget waiting in line day and night. I mean 24 hours a day. Our family would take shifts. Sometimes we would stay in line for some of our friends and then they would stand in line for us the next time. By 1985 the situation was really bad and people started to feel a lot of pressure. We were afraid to speak, or say anything in public.

"My parents were gloomy because suddenly their focus of their everyday lives was to get food, to get enough food for me. My dad was an X-ray operator and my mom, a nurse. Employment was not a big problem because the state would give you a job. You couldn't choose the job. You got one automatically, which then gave you the money to rent an apartment or buy a car. Life in a way was predictable. But don't think it was easy. Does it sound confusing?"

"Yes, I don't understand how it could be predictable if you were searching for food all the time," I said.

"Well, my mom and dad had a job, and when they weren't working they were waiting in line. They didn't think about where to find a job, what kind of work they wanted. They didn't even have time to think about where to get the food. They just waited in line.

"The conversation at home was about how to get something — how to get coffee, how to get meat, how to get milk. My dad would say to my mom, 'Who do you know that we can give this piece of meat so we can get Marius some fruit?' Everything was about me, but I didn't realize it then. I remember when we wanted to go to the seaside. We only got to go away once a year, so this was always our special vacation. The whole year we would have to prepare for this trip because there was nothing to buy there. So we talked about whom to bribe to get canned meat to take with us on this vacation and what did we have to give them in return."

"Was your household tense?"

"I am going to give you one example because I remember it clearly. I was about 12 years old. I definitely was not a coffee drinker and I was angry at my parents for wanting to spend 400 units out of their 2,000 on coffee. I told them it wasn't worth it. I even screamed at them and said, 'Why can't I have that money or why don't you buy me something with it? You don't have to drink coffee.' I wanted toys instead."

"Could they have found a toy for you?"

"Probably, yes. But we couldn't find shoes. Maybe I shouldn't say that we couldn't find shoes, but getting my size was a real problem. We'd have to bribe someone in order to get shoes that fit me.

"Because of all of this there was a lot of depression. But depression was not recognized as a disease. My mom and dad spoke about everybody being so unhappy, but you would never label anyone with depression. That's because psychiatric help was, and still is, perceived as being for people who are 'nuts.' There were no services such as counseling available. So people didn't even think of looking for professional help. My mother was depressed for a long time. Exhausted and depressed. But she would never let anyone outside the house know that. And she definitely didn't use medication. First of all medication was so hard to get. The price would have been prohibitive, but there was just a lack of medicines altogether. Legal drugs were practically nonexistent. We had to bribe someone for medicine when there was an emergency. Or we would try to get it from friends. My mom being a nurse helped us. She sometimes went to the hospital and got some pills there. I never asked how."

As we talked, I noticed that the train had stopped. I started to perspire, remembering the last time I had taken this same train, back in 1989, with Éva Monspart and her daughter Fanni. When the border patrol questioned me again, Marius translated, but the old fear came back. I did not forget being dragged out onto the platform in the dark of night, and I wondered what would happen this time. Did they have a record of me? Did they find out that I helped Éva smuggle food and paint to our friends Márta and Miki, and would they accuse me now? If the country hasn't changed to a free democracy, could I be held on charges of transporting illegal goods in the past? I was only beginning to know Marius. The conversation we were having was personal, but could I trust him?

Two new border guards came and looked at our passports. I noticed one guard studying me. I sat there composed and tried to look secure. Marius seemed relaxed, but he didn't know what had happened to me the last time.

The guards demanded to search our boxes (we had seven of them). I had brought all sorts of materials for the workshop; pens, crayons, colored paper, easel pads, notebooks for the teachers, little gifts like scrunchy balls, etc. We said that they were materials for teachers. "Open them," he directed us. "Must I open each box?" I asked Marius.

"Don't ask him anything," he said to me. "Let me deal with him." Marius spoke in Romanian to the guard. Then the guard took a pocketknife and cut open one box. Marius took out some crayons, paper and small gifts and walked out of the compartment. The guard followed. Several minutes later Marius walked in, closed up the box, and smiled at me.

We thought the train would start, but then another guard entered our cabin. I looked at the other passengers, who now seemed annoyed. Another flashback of 1989, when the guards harassed me and the people on the train were furious at me. I remembered how, at that moment, they pointed their fingers at me and shook their heads. The guard looked at Marius, who was listening to music on my tape recorder. He approached him and asked, "What are you listening to?"

"Bach," Marius replied, now irritated.

"Let me hear." Disgusted, Marius took off the earphones and gave them to the guard. The Communist regime may have ended, but the old ways continued, and I wondered, does it matter what anyone is listening to and what right do the authorities have to invade one's privacy? But these are "democratic" thoughts. The guard gave the recorder back to Marius and walked out.

The train was rolling on, but it was two hours later when another guard came into our cabin and stamped our passports. I breathed a sigh of relief but also realized that we were now in Romania, and my voice dropped to a whisper as I asked Marius more questions.

"Did your mom and dad have many friends they could contact to get what they needed? I assume if they bribed someone it would have to be someone they knew."

"Well, one thing that has actually really changed since 1989 is the feeling between people. There was an extreme bond between friends. On a personal level people really cared about one another, and listened to each other. You really didn't bribe your friends. It was the person with the contacts, and the person you knew was not a spy, but had something that you needed that you bribed. I think also we were afraid of some things but we believed nothing would happen to us. It would happen to the next person.

"I often felt that they covered up their feelings for my sake. At night I would pretend I was asleep and that's when I heard the truth about their fears and pain. They whispered. My parents tried so hard to protect me."

"Tell me about them."

"My mom is 49 and the best definition of my relationship with her would be one given by a Romanian proverb that says that two swords cannot stay in one sheath. We are so very much alike and consequently we cannot stay together for a long time without having a conflict, whatever that might be.

"She was born in a village near the Hungarian border. If you ask anyone from that village, 'Are you Hungarian or Romanian,' they wouldn't really be able to say that they were definitely 100 percent one or the other. Everyone there speaks both languages. My mom speaks fluent Hungarian. My grandfather, her father, was deported by the Hungarians during World War II because he had a bitter tongue."

"What do you mean?"

"I mean that he didn't like being under Hungary and when the Ribbentrop-Molotov Pact gave Transylvania to Hungary he was taken into a war camp. He came back two years later but from that point on, I don't think that my mom really loved Hungarians very much. My grandfather began to distrust some of his neighbors and it affected her."

I said, "In the U.S. we have no idea what it feels like to be threatened by borders. We travel from Pennsylvania to Ohio and cross the border, and only the sign welcoming us from one state to the other shows us that we have entered another state. I realize it is all within the same country, but most Americans do not know what it means to have borders changed around and have our home placed in a different country."

I noticed that the six others in our compartment were staring at us. Perhaps it was that Marius was talking with his hands, which were flying in all directions, or it was because I was an American, or it was just out of boredom.

"How did your parents meet?"

"My dad is from a village that is probably only 100 yards from the Hungarian border. My mom and dad's villages are about six miles apart. My mother used to be a schoolteacher in my father's village. She actually walked each way to the school and she met my father in his village, through mutual friends. They married and then the state told my father that he had to take a job in Baia Mare."

"So you were born in Baia Mare. Who was in charge of running the house? In the U.S. it used to be that the woman was the one who did most of the housework, raised the children, and did the laundry and cleaning while the man had a job. It is different now with women's rights."

"Communism treated everybody equally so women had to be employed just as men were. There were very rare cases where the woman would stay at home and not have a job, but the man was not seen as the provider of the family. Sometimes the woman made more money. But men held the top positions and had more status in the job market. The man was the figurehead in the house. But in ours we joked that my dad had the final word in our house: 'yes dear.' Women really had more than one job, because they had all of the household responsibilities as well. My house was different because both of my parents did everything. But in my friends' homes, that was not the case."

Marius talked as the train chugged slowly on. We passed Oradea and headed toward Cluj. He described his teenage years when he smoked, drank, and rebelled against his parents. "It wasn't that I was a bad kid, but my drinking was out of control. It started when I was an adolescent and I wanted to go out more with my friends. And I also began to feel that something was completely wrong in my society. There was a pressure and I could see that people were really scared. It was around the time when there were big changes in Russia. It was the mid-eighties. My government did not want Russia to influence our thinking in any way at all. Ceauşescu hated the Russians. He did not want glasnost or *perestroika*. He wasn't about to give us any kind of freedom. But we had our own kind of stroika, which is what we called it. It was a real joke though, 'cause it wasn't freedom.

"Actually we called it ferestroika. It means 'windows stroika.' In all the restaurants they removed the drapes from the windows so you wouldn't be in a secluded area where people would be able to talk. It was like a huge window. So it was worse. There was always the fear of saying something wrong. Ferestroika was the way of saying it's worse here. We can't say or do anything."

"Were you ever a member of the Communist Party?"

"Actually, not me, but my dad was. I think it was in '88 that he decided to join the party. It wasn't a good thing or a bad thing. It was just that you had a red notebook, and you had to go to some meetings from time to time where everybody was bored. There was such a fear at that time. I was not able to understand why my parents were so afraid to say anything. I questioned them and accused them of being cowards, but they ignored me. I said it's all because of you guys, if you had done something we kids wouldn't have to suffer like we do."

"How did they react to that?" I asked, thinking as a parent, and knowing that if my children had accused me of doing something hurtful to them, I would have been defensive, but would explain my reasons.

"You can imagine, they were really bitter at the government and I was not able to understand the system. What were they trying to do to keep me safe? I didn't know. They told me that they didn't care about themselves, that they only cared about me. 'I would not forgive myself if anything would happen to you.' My mom must have said that to me one hundred times. Not only that. My father joined the Communist Party because he didn't want me to be denied the right to get into the university because he was not a member. I had been denied a visa to travel to Russia with my class because my parents were not Communist Party members, so my dad thought that probably some other repercussions would occur if one of them did not join."

I said, "Marius, I try to raise our children to have values that are consistent. Like cheating and stealing are wrong. I have heard stories that show that under the Communist system these values sometimes were not consistent."

"Absolutely. It was a good thing to steal from the state. If you stole anything, it was one way of rebelling and people would think that you were cool. It was a whole culture that you would steal whatever you could.

"Here's an example. My grandparents had a field of watermelons. It was where they worked. It supposedly was their field, that's what the state said. But at the end of the crop season the authorities would come and take half of the melons. My grandparents had no say, and of course the state would pick the best ones. So my friends and I would go into the field and pick watermelons and eat them until we were sick. When crop time came we would have less to give the state. So stealing was a national institution. But there was a moral separation of what was okay to steal and what wasn't. It was not okay to steal one cent from someone and it was not okay to steal the neighbor's watermelons. That would be his share of stealing."

I asked, "Could you cheat on a test in school?"

Marius responded, "Well, there was a lot of cheating, but for another reason. Grades were the one criterion on whether you got into university. And then once you got in, there was limited scholarship money for basic needs. You didn't pay to go to university, they were all state owned, but you needed money to pay the rent and to pay for food, and so everyone cheated. Your final grade would determine whether you went to university, and what happened to you for the rest of your life; where you would end up living, everything. So we all had to cheat."

"Were your grades good?"

"Yes, in high school they were always good. I didn't drink, well, only a glass of wine with my dad. So I got into Cluj University. It was hard to get into, but my parents made sure that I studied a lot, so I got in. I was an okay teenager. I guess no angrier than anyone else in our society. Yes, as angry as everyone else.

"I went to Cluj University and began to drink. I really was very messed up. I think it was my society. I felt no hope. I could study, get a degree, and what would that bring me? Communism was over but life was no better. You can't imagine what it was like for us as young adults, having nothing to look forward to. As a psychologist I could get $60 a month. As a beggar you could get $50 an hour. And I know that for a fact, 'cause I did an experiment one day and dressed up like a blind beggar. I sat with my cup on a street corner and my pockets got filled. I only stopped begging after two hours because I had nowhere to put the money.

It was an experiment at school, but it showed me how crazy our society was.

"The one good thing was I had a girlfriend, Andrada, who really cared for me. Fortunately she was against the constant drinking and smoking and tried to convince me that my habits were unacceptable. She even threatened to break up with me unless I stopped drinking. She decided to attend a workshop that was advertised in the Cluj newspaper. And that's when my life began to change."

Marius described the ad, which read:

FOR TEENAGERS; A WORKSHOP ON PEER COUNSELING: NO COST, HELD IN THE MOUNTAINS NEAR CLUJ, LED BY AMERICANS DAN SHAPIRO AND JEN DELLMUTH, ORGANIZED BY DAN BACIU. JUNE 15–19, 1994. CALL 555-555 TO RESERVE YOUR PLACE.

"It sounded intriguing to me," he went on, "but I would never have admitted that. Just that it was going to be held in the mountains and it wouldn't cost anything. Of course I was too stubborn to say that I would be interested in such a thing so I took Andrada to the bus station and stood at the gate ready for her to depart. I had my dog Donna with me."

Marius remembers that as he was kissing Andrada goodbye, Dan Baciu walked up to him and asked him why he wan't going to the workshop. When Marius answered that he wasn't invited and the workshop didn't interest him, Dan responded, "You are invited and you will have a good time." Marius argued that he had his dog with him. Dan replied, "Bring her." The bus was scheduled to depart in 15 minutes. Marius had to make a decision.

"I walked onto the bus," said Marius, "not knowing that my life was about to change. At first I just sat there, being a moody kid. I didn't participate. Daniel and Jen did the icebreakers and I didn't know what was going on."

As Marius spoke about the workshop, I was hearing for the first time about the program my son, Dan Shapiro, had created. As a psychology major at Johns Hopkins, he had developed this program because he wanted to help others. He asked his close friend Jen Dellmuth, a student at Princeton University, to co-facilitate, and he asked the Soros Foundation to sponsor them. Dan Baciu advertised for students. Although my son had conducted workshops for American students, this was his first time instructing abroad. He and Jen went from Romania to five other former Communist countries, doing the instructing.

After Dan and Jen left Romania, they did another workshop, this one in the former Yugoslavia, near the Hungarian border, a place called Subotica, very close to the fighting. It was during the Bosnian War and we had to get special permission for Dan and Jen to cross the border. Only through special contacts could they even enter the country. The workshop was for the refugee children and held in a zoo park. Although Dan called us and said they were all safe and the Soros Foundation promised that they were in good hands, I was still a nervous mother. But the workshop in Romania had been his first, and I was delighted to have the opportunity to hear about it first-hand from one of the participants. I asked Marius to tell me all about it.

"As a participant," said Marius, "I was brought into a world I didn't know existed. I remember one activity. Dan and Jen had bowls of M&Ms; I had never seen those candies before. They asked us to take as many as we wanted but not to eat them right away. They said for each M&M we had to tell our neighbor something about ourselves. It was so different from anything I had ever seen. We never talked about ourselves. And as a group we created our own rules. Then we did activities that were fun, but they also had an objective. Like we each had a partner and we tied a scarf around our partner's eyes. We took turns and walked around the fields together. Sometimes we even ran. We were learning to trust each other. You have to really trust someone if you let them lead you around.

"Everything was new and my emotions were stronger than I knew what to do with. We sang songs to Dan's guitar playing until 4 A.M. and the whole group made the most awful tasting vegetable soup. But we loved it and laughed. We used ketchup for the base. Even today every time I use ketchup I think of our ketchup soup.

"A lot of the time I felt threatened; almost in shock. Everything I learned was falling apart. The spoken language in the streets was so contradictory, and our government had made sure that we were under its authority. I knew nothing but the Ceaușescu way of thinking.

"I became intrigued with the process of communicating efficiently in ways never known in Romania and when I left the workshop I believed that there were ways to treat individuals without intimidating them, abusing their human rights, and destroying their egos. And I was resolved to change my society. Now, at this workshop I realized that the psychology studies, the ones they had in our schools, were awful.

"When I was making my choice of a career in high school, the country was still Communist, and psychology was not an option. I considered going to medical school, but in 1990 the psychology department was reinstated, so I decided to get a Bachelor's degree in psychology. The program was very limited in its information and the professors did not have enough knowledge of psychology to teach it, but I received my degree, and it was in my second year of graduate studies that I went to the workshop led by Dan and Jen.

"After those five days in the workshop I began teaching high school students in Cluj. I started with kids that I knew and soon word spread about my work. I got to that workshop by mistake, and I think it was the best mistake of my life, now that I am looking back. It changed my life, not as externally then, but it changed me internally. I wanted to help teenagers so I began to prepare workshops and taught hundreds of young persons, holding classes in my tiny studio apartment.

"I believe that these workshops are the best experiences of my life. I am talking about having a workshop where teenagers never had the option to learn how to communicate. Neither did I. We are learning things that are important for our lives and not for somebody else's."

"Describe one of your workshops and how they were different from Dan and Jen's. I am sure that you had to adapt them culturally." We had been talking by this time about six hours, and had at least one more hour before we arrived in Cluj.

"I work with my best friend Adrian. We start the workshop and every time it's amazing. We don't sit on a bench but in a circle on the floor. We hang paper on the walls and the kids draw on the paper and they speak whatever they feel. It is not important what I want, but what they want to get out of the workshop. This is a completely new concept for Romanians — that you are encouraged to speak about who you are and what you expect from life. I don't think that ever happened before, at least not to me and probably not to 90 percent of the kids who come. It is such satisfaction for me to see that with no money I am providing the participants with this opportunity. Adrian and I took it into our own hands and students kept coming back to help. In my university people walk up to me and say, 'Are you the guys who are doing those workshops?' and they all want to come.

"The most incredible thing for me is that many of these kids have started to do things on their own. I have just heard that kids from Timisoara, completely without me, and I am happy to say that, went into an orphanage and took kids to their own home and talked with them and did some activities with them. This is not very common in Romania; in fact, it's unheard of. That makes me feel very good. Many of my students involved started to teach other students. I developed a train the trainer program so that it wasn't only me and my few friends who were teaching."

Next we talked about Romania's teens. I asked Marius, "What were teenagers like under Ceaușescu and how are they different now, that is, if they are?" He responded, "Most teenagers did not rebel against the Communists. I would say that it was rebellion against our parents, just like me. Wouldn't you say that this is an intergenerational conflict the same as with teenagers in America?"

I nodded and said, "Yes, American teenagers rebel too."

He continued: "There was less rebellion against the system since as a teenager you felt a kind of powerlessness against the whole mechanism. The only rebellion against the Communists was that we wouldn't attend their meetings or we wouldn't perform the obligatory social duties. Like going to the fields to pick potatoes, something mandatory that had to be done every autumn. Or we would tell political jokes. That was pretty much the way we rebelled.

"The big question I think about is, do we rebel more or less now? I would say that teenagers rebel more now. During the Communist years we felt safe. After we graduated from high school, we had two paths to follow. On one path, we got admitted into the university, on the other, we got a job. Both ways, at the end you would get a job. The job might have been at the opposite end of the country; you didn't have the choice. But still the state assigned you the position and that meant a source of income. It meant an apartment, maybe even a car along the way and safety for us. When we rebelled, it was against our parents. Just like I did. But after '89 things changed radically, pretty much overnight. The security was gone. First, getting into the university no longer provided us with a certainty that afterwards we would get a job. There were thousands of engineers and they found themselves with no place to work. This field, once the most popular, became the most despised because people weren't able to find a job. So a lot of teenagers migrated from a very, let's say, industrial or technology-oriented profession, to jobs more oriented to social services. And so we had to start thinking in new ways.

"During Communism, kids tried to have fun. We didn't really think in terms of the future. We knew that after we finished high school or university all hell would break loose. I thought I would have to find a job and I would have to find a place to live, and everything would be a struggle. So this was the only time in my life where I had the chance to do a lot of things without being really required to work. And all the kids thought like this. So we drank, partied and had fun. Today it is so different. The teenagers are more desperate. I know that this does not sound very nice but I really do think that this is how things are today. There is ambivalence and a very hard life. We can't find jobs or make money.

"I have heard that teenagers in America can work. Is that true?" Marius asked.

"Yes, our children had summer jobs," I said. "Madelyn worked at an ice cream shop and Dan was a camp counselor. Steve, our oldest son, worked at McDonald's, part-time, even during the school year."

Marius responded, "Well, in Romania there is no way for teenagers to work. The adults pay high bribes to get a job in a fast food chain and so there are no jobs for teenagers. They are not allowed to work. They would like to be independent, just like American kids, but there is no way for that to happen here."

When Marius and I arrived in Cluj, I went to the Bacius' house and Marius went his own way. We emailed one another when I was back in the U.S., and in 1996, one year after we met, Marius asked me to help him find a school in the U.S. where he could receive what he would regard as a more legitimate degree in psychology. Dan, my son, helped him select Illinois State University. His life has changed a great deal since those days we spent together in Romania. He visited us several times, and now, on this spring day in March of 2001, we are talking at our kitchen table.

MARCH 2001

"I can't believe that you have been here in the U.S. for four years already," I said, looking tenderly at this young man who has added so much to our lives.

"I survived Ceauşescu and the years of turmoil that followed, and I came out whole. How? Why? When I look around, I don't believe I am here. After so much humiliation, stability is hard to comprehend. The Ceauşescu government harassed me, well, all of us. I didn't really know it until I was a teenager. But I had to recover and work very hard to release the anger pent up inside of me. A burning. And then life after

Ceauşescu was no better. There was even less food, and very stormy times. I came here to the U.S. almost four years ago, and I saw people laughing and having fun. I came from chaos — and I saw that something different existed.

"I do not feel that the USA is my home and Romania has painful memories. I miss my parents, but for now I don't want to go home."

"Where do you feel comfortable, Marius?' I asked.

"Around your kitchen table."

Questions whirled through my mind. Why does Marius feel so comfortable in our home? What binds us together? My husband and I live in the suburbs of Harrisburg, in a neighborhood, with trees and substantial space between homes, different from his environment in so many ways. But spread throughout our house are objects of Eastern Europe and especially Romania, brought back from our many trips. There is an eclectic combination of portraits, floor coverings, icons, Russian army hats, puppets, and more. Miki Jakobovits' artwork, smuggled out during Ceauşescu's time, decorates our foyer. Abstract artwork painted by mentally challenged Czech orphans from a school in Cechy pod Kostrem cover the walls in the family room. Letters from students in Sarajevo, composed during the Bosnian War, are framed and arranged near the piano. Marius says he is touched by a sense of home among these familiar objects, artifacts which also represent some shared experiences. He also knows the importance that Eastern Europe had and continues to have in our lives, and he asked, "What does it mean to be so immersed in the lives of people abroad?"

After careful thought, I said, "I know well that living in the moment is what I believe in but how do I accomplish that when my closest friends live thousands of miles from my home? It is rather melancholy for me to see you even though I love you. You bring out the need for me to be with all of my friends. Which, of course, is impossible because they all live in different countries. So instead I surround myself with things from each of their countries and duplicate some of their behavior. And having you sit at our kitchen table and talk about your country and sense the sadness you feel makes me understand, not only more about you, but more about us as human beings. It is hard to imagine any other life than the one I live. There are always foreigners staying here. You know that. If I counted the guests that have stayed with us, it would reach hundreds, from at least thirty countries. People come and go all of the time."

Ron, Marius, and I sat at the kitchen table talking for hours. My chair was closest to the refrigerator, Ron's faced the window, and Marius lounged, spread out on another chair, directly across from me. That was his spot, always has been, always will be. He had already consumed a quart of kefir (a yogurt based drink). The sun was shining through the window; we had dodged one more snowstorm. The trees were swaying to a light breeze, and the only sign of winter was the odd patch of snow on the ground. We talked about walking to the St. Thomas Roaster, a neighborhood café Marius and I both love, for a cappuccino, but we didn't budge. Marius spoke.

"Let me tell you a little about why I am more content here in the U.S. than in Romania. You know that during Communism, psychology was banned because the Communists felt it was too introspective, and 'nonsense.' After 1989 Cluj University developed a psychology program but with no information. I graduated from there and then got my master's degree in industrial psychology but I knew nothing. The one workshop with Daniel, your son, changed everything in my life, but I had to deal with the transformation. Even though I went to graduate school and received the degree, I couldn't let go of the fact that the professors were not trained properly, and that the degree was practically useless. I couldn't do what I wanted. I knew that I wanted to teach conflict management but I couldn't find the money to do it. Now I am doing what I want. I have the degrees, I studied psychology in the U.S. and now my work is my passion. I can say that I have the education I need to do what I want. Oh, how I miss home."

Ron and I have become Marius' surrogate parents. During school vacations, he often comes to stay with us, but we know that we can't replace his roots — the home where he grew up, the warm smells that he knows so well, the touch of his mother's hand. We love him dearly, as do our friends and relatives, but we can see in his face the sadness when he describes what he longs for from home.

Ron had been sitting long enough, and went out for a walk. Marius and I finally decided to have our special alone time. We took the phone off the hook and brought out the leftovers from last night's dinner — chicken noodle soup and apple pie. Now with only Marius and me at the kitchen table, I asked what I thought was a simple question.

"Marius, what do you miss most and least about home?" Marius looked at me. Sorrow appearing in his soft gray eyes and tears rolling down his cheeks, he thought back on the significant lessons that he learned from his parents and he began talking.

Marius' parents, Florica and Emil Mateş, with their dog Donna.

I Miss Home

I miss home. I am sitting here crying because I miss home. I miss my parents. I miss being able to speak what I mean; not being desperate to be looking for words that say what I mean.

I miss going to see my grandparents, in the village. I miss the smell of burnt wood, the strong smell. And it is the chicken with sour cream, my grandmother's. She makes the best chicken in the whole world. It's the smell of old things, but it doesn't smell like a museum.

I miss the blue color of the whole house. Every time when I am thinking of their house, it is a light blue house. It is not that they paint it blue for aesthetic reasons. It is calcium paint; the same paint that is on trees so the bugs won't attack them. For trees, the paint is white. My grandfather adds a little something to make it blue for the house. Every other year my grandparents paint the house and each time, it is a different blue. The paint doesn't last long and it starts crumbling. The small kids like to eat the paint, and we believe it is good for them because it is pure calcium. The kids eat the paint on the wall because their bodies know they need the calcium!

I miss my grandparents 'cause they always treated me with uncon-

Marius' grandparents, Floarea and Silvestru, photographed in 2001.

ditional love. My grandfather is a tall man, about six feet, but rather skinny. He is almost into his eighties, and I think I never saw him shaved. Every time he kissed me I could feel his beard. He was the tough guy who works a lot. Not tough in his soul, though. He is 80; he has two horses, three or four cows, and land to work. He still uses the old plow; the one that the horses pull. You have to press on it to get into the ground. Grandpa had one or two hernias, and he still won't quit working.

I miss sitting there with him and he doesn't say a word. He has that look that only a parent or grandparent has and it showed anytime I went there. He is proud of me.

I miss Grandma, who has a problem with her hip. She's not supposed to walk that much, but every time we get there, she won't stop walking around and she wants to do everything for us. She has really white hair, so does Grandpa.

I miss the mornings with Adrian, my friend, drinking coffee and smoking cigarettes. I remember the times we didn't have any food. I miss working with him on our projects and deciding to skip another class.

I miss my endless quarrels with a friend, Viorel. We would have a six hour dispute on a strange subject like whether motorcycling is a sport or not. On days we had money, we would eat three pounds of meat at once, and then get sick for the rest of the week.

I don't miss my neighbors because they always complained that I was too noisy or I was listening to the Twin Pix Music, a series in the '90s, strange music, and then they'd tell my parents!

I miss my dog, Donna, who died last year and who was my child. I guess that is how I learned responsibility.

I miss having a fight with my Mom; the usual subject was my girlfriend, Andrada. If her mother ever reads this, she would kill me. She was my first girl-

Florica Mateş in her kitchen.

friend. My Mom would say that she was not for me. She is the daughter of a doctor, and we're not on the same level. 'Why can't you find someone in Cluj? You would have to come back here to Baia Mare to see her,' she would say. It could have been any girl. They were either too good or not good enough.

I miss stealing the money from Dad's pocket with his knowledge; if that qualifies as stealing. After 1989, he was a taxi driver and every night when he came home, he asked me to count the money. I would always take one or two bills out and put them aside for me. I bet he always knew how much he had before he came into the house! I would take the money out to buy a shirt or a book. I never really spent money on other things.

I miss having a glass of wine with my Dad. We would sit down and have a glass of wine and talk. We talked about anything. What I want to do in my life, how his life was, about my girlfriend. It was really neat to talk about my girlfriend with my Dad.

I don't miss being poor. I don't miss crying myself to sleep because I didn't have money to buy food when I was in college. It's not being poor; it's being hopeless. There is no end in sight that you'll get over struggling to get your next meal. I felt at that time I would never get over it. It is the fear I thought wouldn't end and that I'd never have time to live; only to survive. I can still see it in me. I am afraid of being happy; because I expect every moment I will wake up and be back. Even though some of those moments were intense it was those times when you get really close friends. I remember when Vio, my friend, and I, we ate dog food. The rule was kind of, if I have food, he has food, but this time there was no food in either house. These are the moments when you really get close cause if you don't have friends you really go crazy. You can get mad together, and cry together.

I don't miss being pushed around by the system, by the people who have money and power. It took me four hours, six threats that I was going to throw someone through the window, to get my transcripts for the university. Three times I had to stand in line, for five hours, talking to the same people in order to get my transcript and I had to threaten them. That is not my nature, I am soft inside, but I had to do it. Now I realize it would take two minutes for the same job in the U.S.

I don't miss being a local. When I worked in a multinational company in Romania, you were either an expatriate [foreigner working in another country] or a local. I was a local, and Will was an American, and therefore, an expatriate. We were both level Eight. I was doing my job and half of his; I was paid $500 a month, he was paid over $6,000 a month. It wasn't just the money; it was that his word was always taken ahead of mine, even though I did more work. If you are a local, the company treats you as if you don't know what you are talking about.

The company did not take me seriously and refused me when I offered to train people in conflict management and negotiation. I offered several times, and was told no each time. About a month before I left (I had given them my resignation), they agreed to give me $80 to teach negotiation skills. The company used to send staff to Vienna for such training and the bill for this was at least $50,000. They had to send all the people to Vienna, put them up in hotels, pay the trainers, etc. I did two-day training for them, on Saturday and Sunday, and when my managers got the evaluation forms, they said I never told them I knew how to offer this training! That was a lie! In that one weekend I saved them $40,000 with no workdays lost.

But most of all I miss the Sunday lunch. It was always the same thing, chicken noodle soup; second course was mashed potatoes and steak. For dessert my Mom would always make some kind of pie. Apple was the one I loved the most. We ate in the dining room, which is rather small, but it's my dining room. We would sit down, me, Mom and Dad, usually a fourth, one of my girlfriends. This was after we would come from church. At the end, the big moment. We would have coffee. The whole meal was the anticipation for the coffee moment.

Even though it sounds selfish that I left my country, and came to the United States to have a better life, it is because I want my children to live in a free society. I don't think I have time to wait until Romania is going to accomplish that. Yes, I will always be a son to my parents, but one day I hope to be a father. I would never want to be forced to have to make the same decision that my parents had to make. To let their only son go.

– 3 –

Magyarország (Hungary)

Hungary is located in Central Europe bordering Austria to the northwest, Croatia to the southwest, Romania to the east, Yugoslavia to the south, Slovakia to the north, and Ukraine to the northeast. It is slightly smaller than the state of Indiana. The population is about 10 million: 90 percent Hungarians, 4 percent Roma (Gypsy), 3 percent German and about 3 percent Slovaks and Romanians. Budapest is its capital, while other key cities include Pécs, Debrecen, Szeged, Kecskemét, and Eger. The Magyar language, spoken in Hungary today, had its origins in the Finno-Ugrian people, the Magyars, who swept eastward from the Russian steppes and eventually settled in the Danube region in the 5th century A.D. The word "Magyar" is used not only to refer to the language, but also to the Hungarian people.

History

Hungary became closely allied with Germany and Italy and entered World War II in December 1941 as part of the Axis countries. However, in 1944, when anti–Axis sentiment arose, German troops occupied Hungary. As the war was ending Hungary was ravaged twice, first by the Germans as they retreated, and then by the Soviet troops as they advanced. At the conclusion of World War II a coalition democratic government was formed, but real power rested in the hands of the Hungarian Communist Party.

In 1948 Stalin demanded strict adherence to the Soviet line and the Hungarian Communist Party assumed complete control of the government, appointing Mátyás Rákosi as first secretary. All opposition to the

Communist Party was eliminated and Soviet troops were stationed throughout Hungary. Nine years later, under then Prime Minister Imre Nagy, the Hungarian Revolution of 1956 began with student uprisings against the Soviets. However, the Soviets suppressed the revolt and set up an administration headed by Janos Kádár, who immediately had Imre Nagy jailed and executed. Kádár resigned his post as prime minister in 1958 but assumed it again from 1961 to 1965 (although he maintained power as Communist Party chairman until 1989). He introduced a formal new economic policy, named the "Goulash Economy," a mixture of Soviet economics and reforms to fit the Hungarian culture.

When economic problems emerged from the oil crisis of 1973, Kádár was forced to make further changes in his policies. By the late '70s large state enterprises were broken up into smaller firms, and small, privately owned firms were legalized. Throughout the early and mid–1980s political and economic liberalization continued.

By 1989, on the heels of Gorbachev's policy of *perestroika* (reform), the Communist Party had lost its monopoly on political power. Finally, a free multiparty election was held in March 1990, and the Hungarian Democratic Forum won. A new constitution was written declaring Hungary a republic — an independent democratic state — with power in the hands of the people and their freely elected representatives.

Éva Monspart and Rudi Ungváry
Budapest, Magyarország

Budapest, Hungary's cosmopolitan capital, is situated on the banks of the fabled Danube River. Since the fall of Communism it has become a center of fashion and nightlife in Eastern Europe. It is also a city of extremes. Women take delight in the variety of styles, but beneath the veneer of rediscovered elegance, many feel insecure and vulnerable. An emerging feminist movement is popular, but many women aren't really sure what it means. Stores display Levi jeans, Chanel perfume, and Italian eye makeup, but most people don't have the money to buy these products. And as the breadth of products and services expands, so does the world of ideas. Inside the coffeehouses and bookstores, students and bohemians discuss politics, philosophy and technology while kiosks, well-stocked with porno magazines, line the streets outside.

Democracy in Hungary has provided young couples with many new opportunities, but most still can't afford to move from their parents' flats. There are now thousands of books to read but little time to read them. Most Hungarians are now working harder than ever. Under Communism, the goal was that everyone should have the same things, not more, not less. Now there is competition, even among friends. "I am your friend, but I must compete with you. Will there be a job for both of us?" A common thought. With a freer economy, new anxieties fill the minds of people accompanied by the frustration of slow economic improvement. Democracy has definitely changed the lives of most, but not all, Hungarians.

My friends Éva Monspart (pronounced Ee'va Monsh'part) and her husband Rudi Ungváry (pronounced Ru'dee Ung'va-ree) opposed the Communist system. They never believed its philosophy and didn't live by its rules. They created their own world within the confines of their family. They raised three children: Krisztián (pronounced Christian), Zsófi (pronounced Jzho'fee), and Fanni (pronounced Faw'nee) to be free thinking individuals. The government threatened them, but it could not and did not control their minds. Unlike other Hungarians, they openly discussed with their children the lack of freedoms under Communism. As I listened to the story of Éva and Rudi's lives, I was struck by a theme that has persisted: they are fighters. They possess a purpose to achieve a sense of individualism. They fought the Communist system, and even after the fall of Communism they continue to be proponents of social and political change.

Éva and I first met at a Soros Foundation workshop held in 1987 in my hometown, Harrisburg, Pennsylvania. She is in her mid-fifties and works as a journalist and an environmentalist. She introduces herself as Monspart, Éva, last name first. All Hungarians present themselves in this way, but Éva is unconventional; she has kept her maiden name. She is a solid and strong woman with short-cropped blonde hair and deep blue eyes. Not only strong in appearance, she is forceful with her words and determined in her spirit. Her voice sings with the high and low inflections of the Magyar language even when she speaks English. She walks with confidence. "Motherhood," she says, "is the only traditional thing about me."

Rudi, an author and historian, is part Hungarian, part Swiss-German, and most assuredly a maverick. At 64, he appears younger than his years. He is of average height, slim build, with a narrow face (not com-

Susan Shapiro and Éva Monspart

mon to most Hungarians), a straight nose, and large, brilliant, blue eyes. A well rounded athlete, he runs twice a week, canoes on the Danube and skis the Carpathian Mountains. Speaking in a soft but commanding tone, he introduces himself as Ungváry, Rudi, in either German or Hungarian.

Not much about Rudi and Éva's lifestyle is conventional. They share the household chores and Éva confides, "Rudi cleans the house, which is not typical for a Hungarian man, and I do the cooking." As a guest in their home, I feel comfortable going to the refrigerator and helping myself. I also assist in preparing meals, this in a country where the guest should expect to be served.

The Ungváry-Monsparts live in a beige stucco house consisting of five large rooms. The living area has oversized windows looking out on the garden and the peaceful residential street. Rudi's father purchased it in 1948 when the country was a "democratic republic." Three years later when they were ready to move into the house, the country was under the Stalinist regime of Mátyás Rákosi and a new Communist law made it impossible for them to live in their own home. There were tenants liv-

Rudi Ungváry in his study.

ing in the house, and they could not be asked to leave unless offered a place of equal value by the landlord. This was not financially possible for Rudi's family, so it was not until 1977 when one of the two tenants died and the other one wanted to move that the Ungvárys were able to move into their own house. They were fortunate that there were only five rooms in the entire house because there was another law that forbade a family with three children to live in a house with more than five rooms.

The house was in disrepair, and it took hard work to bring it to the point Rudi's father had envisioned. Today it is furnished with informal wooden and wicker furniture and simple lighting, not the old European style of ornate chandeliers and velvet sofas. There is no microwave, dishwasher or color TV, but each room is packed with books in many languages. The living room is a quiet area, conducive to study and philosophical conversation. The walls are lined with Rudi's books, magazines, and typewritten manuscripts. His academic presence is a large part of his personality and he proudly displays his favorite books: Mark Twain's *Huckleberry Finn*; *Green Henrik*, by Swiss author Gottfried Keller; J.D. Salinger's *Catcher in the Rye*; and Thomas Mann's *Buddenbrooks* and *Doc-*

tor Faustus. He groups his beloved classics together: Dostoyevsky's *Idiot*, Tolstoy's *War and Peace*, Proust's *Remembrance of Things Past* and Musil's *Man Without Qualities*. Books by contemporary American author Katherine Anne Porter, *Noon Wine* and *Pale Horse, Pale Rider*, are translated into German and are also part of this library. His own works, which have made him well known in his own country, lie together against a wall: *In the Gunscope* (A Gépfegyver Szálkeresztje, published in 1996), and *And Deadly Silence After It* (Utána néma csönd, published in 1994).

The Literary Pages is spread on the coffee table in the far end of the living room. The sofa, covered with a colorful Hungarian shawl, has unfolded newspapers scattered across its pillows. Rudi's lifelong appetite for Hungarian politics feeds on the pages of the newspapers he reads daily; *Magyar Hirlap, ÉS, Beszélö, HVG* and *Élet es Tudomány*, and the German newspaper *die Zeit*. He underlines the political issues he intends to address. "Now that freedom has been achieved, I believe it is not only the politicians' obligation, but the citizens' as well, to be as informed as possible," he says.

It is in the kitchen that the action takes place. Larger than necessary for cooking, it is filled with the aroma of fresh bread and cheese. A large wooden counter, with potted flowers, copper pans, and wooden bowls, occupies one wall. Another wall is decorated with posters and artworks by Hungarian painters. A sturdy oak table seats eight. Across from the table someone is usually standing at the sink, either starting a meal or finishing the dishes. The family, and guests who seem to appear regularly, sit at the table and discuss business, weather, philosophy and their various projects. Most importantly there is a prevailing mood of intellectual curiosity. It is in this room and in this atmosphere that I hear their stories.

LIFE DURING COMMUNISM

In 1956 when Rudi was a student at the University of Miskolc, located four hours away from his home in Budapest. A second-year engineering major, with his future ahead of him, Rudi was the typical student. "My friends and I went to parties some of the time, and I studied a lot. Life was interesting and normal. But then everything changed. It was late October 1956. The bloody Hungarian Revolution!

"There had been countless incidents across Poland and Hungary leading up to the Revolution of '56. However, it was opposition in Hungary, mostly by students like me, to the repressive Soviet regime headed by Janos Kádár that triggered action. University students were leaving the Communist youth organization in droves. Not satisfied with the Soviets' intent, we revived the university association called MEFESZ — Association of Hungarian University and College Students. We asked for new laws for our country. We believed that the people should decide the kind of society they wanted. So we demanded a new government. We did not want violence or force, but we wanted a man named Imre Nagy to be in power because we believed in his ability to make change. But that isn't what the Communists believed. At first we just demonstrated in the streets, but soon the demonstrations got out of hand. The fighting began in Budapest on October 23, 1956."

Rudi and some of his classmates were part of the network of students who led the fight for social democracy. His job was to sit in a dark room in the basement of one of the buildings at Miskolc University and keep track of the daily events. "When I heard that a confrontation broke out between the people, mainly students, and the Soviet army, I had just finished developing a rudimentary radio system that could track the

Revolution meeting at the Miskolc University in 1956.

movements of the Russian troops," Rudi recalls. "Along with several friends, I established the Free Northeastern Radio System (Szabad Borsodi Radio). We heard that thousands had been killed in the streets in Budapest. On October 23, 1956, it seemed the Stalinist government collapsed, but we did not trust the Russians. Our instinct was correct because on October 24, just the next day, Soviet tanks reentered Budapest. The students in Budapest fought back and demanded that Imre Nagy lead the country.

"We then wrote a manifesto, stating that Nagy was the man we trusted. I, like the others, believed that his ethics and dignity could save the country. He was a man of principle, unlike Kádár. For a short time, a revolutionary democracy prevailed. But just days later, the Soviets decided to oust Nagy.

"I was in charge of funneling news to every possible outlet, including the universities. I channeled information to freedom fighters and gave them important contacts, news and travel information and then reported the events to them as the Soviets came back into Budapest with 3,000 tanks and many more army divisions. It was on November 1 that I became aware that Nagy had appealed to the U.N. but received no help. Nagy then sought U.S. support, but was refused. We all felt abandoned. Janos Kádár became the man in charge — approved by the Soviets. I remember sitting in that dark room, afraid of the consequences, yet determined to continue fighting."

As Russian censorship tightened, Rudi's role as a news gatherer became more important. "I worked day and night to keep the station in full operation. But eventually, the Russians discovered the communication system and arrested my classmates and me. I will never forget the night they came and took me away to a concentration camp. Behind bars I swore to myself that I would never give up. I swore to myself that I would never forget. I would fight in any possible way I could. It was in my bones, in my soul, it had become my identity.

"I wanted to live in freedom, yet my entire life had been overshadowed by political regimes that denied me that right. It seemed like a nightmare; once again, forces completely out of my control were determining my life. I was born in 1936 and was only eight years old when the National Socialist terror regime moved into Hungary. I was a child during World War II; Hungary was on the losing side and had to pay a heavy price for its position. In 1945, there were hopes that Hungary might have a 'progressive democracy,' but in 1948, the Stalinist regime solidified its control. Much of my childhood was dominated by political events. As a young adult, I felt the frustration of the Communist aggression. Now I was in prison, fighting against this dissatisfaction. I wasn't going to give up my rights, no matter what it cost me. The atrocities of the Soviets were obvious and in prison I had the chance to reflect on my past. When the guards harassed me, I thought of the injustices of the system, and I wouldn't tell them what they wanted to know."

At this point Éva spoke, describing her circumstances during the Revolution. "The day before the Revolution, I was having a tonsillectomy in Budapest. I had missed a lot of school because I had tonsillitis all the time. The doctor said I should have my tonsils removed immediately. I was admitted to MÁV Hospital because my uncle was a doctor in that hospital, and my mother knew that I would receive the best care possible. There were many hospitals in Budapest, some for the Communist officials, others for the proletariat. Some were well-equipped; others barely met minimal standards. This was one of the better ones. I was just twelve years old, but I experienced firsthand the trauma of the Revolution."

"It was November 4, 1956," Éva recalls. "The hospital was near the railway station, and from my hospital window, I watched as the Russians entered Budapest. It was surreal. I can still remember the feelings of fear and loneliness. My mother wasn't allowed to stay in the hospital with me. I was in a large room with many strangers when I heard the gunshots, saw the Soviet tanks move into the center of the city and viewed the war from my bed. The staff moved the patients to the basement; they were afraid that flying bullets could smash windows. So I recuperated underground, in a cold, damp basement.

"When my uncle would make his rounds, naturally he would always stop by to visit and comfort me. He would tell me what was happening. He listened to Radio Free Europe, which was the news organization funded primarily by the U.S. Congress that broadcast the truth to people behind the 'Iron Curtain.' At first he told me that the Communists were losing. Even though I was only twelve, I knew what that meant and I celebrated along with my hospital roommates.

"But the celebration was short lived. My uncle came to my room the next day and explained that the situation had changed and the Soviets were in control. But he assured me that the Americans would come to the rescue. But it didn't happen. He came back to my room and tried to tell me that the Americans were distracted by the Suez Canal incident, and it just might take a little more time for the situation to turn around. But the Western nations ignored us. The Soviets suppressed the revolt and came into power. I remember my uncle's expression. He didn't want me to be afraid, but I could see the look in his eyes. I didn't understand everything he said. I just knew that he was angry. So were the other patients. So was I.

"Those times were like a roller coaster. I cried so hard when I heard my fellow Hungarians screaming their hatred for the Communists in the streets. But in the end, it was hopeless. Even though the Communist Party soon split into progressive and nonprogressive groups, they were still in command. I watched all this in fear from the hospital. I have never forgotten that time. I wanted to go out into the streets and fight, yet I was only twelve so I also wanted to go home.

"I had been in the ward for about a week when the nurses whispered stories about Russian soldiers. The injured men had been taken to our hospital and were placed in the upstairs rooms. We all gossiped that the Russian soldiers ate better in the Hungarian hospital than they had ever eaten before. Many of us, I must admit, stereotyped the Russians as 'poor' and deprived of basic foods. The joke in the hospital was that the Russian soldiers never even tasted butter and didn't know what to do with it when they saw it next to the bread on their tray. The nurses had to show them how to spread it on their bread! We talked among ourselves and felt that Hungary was definitely a better place to live than Russia. We all agreed that we would never want to be controlled by a system that deprived its own people of basic goods like butter.

"Though many nurses and doctors opposed the Russians, they treated the Russian soldiers with care and respect. They did not blame the wounded for the mistreatment by their society. They took care of the injured. I look back and feel proud of my Hungarian heritage."

The Revolution lasted the entire time Éva was in the hospital. She managed to keep her spirits up by looking at all the positive things that her fellow countrymen did. "I coped as best I could. My uncle told me that there had been no looting in the downtown area even during the heaviest fighting, and he explained how unusual that was. I matured during that time. I recovered but never forgot my hospital experience."

When Éva was fully recovered from surgery, she returned home and went back to school. The political situation grew dark; the Stalinist government took control and executed thousands of non–Communists and imprisoned or deported tens of thousands of others. As Éva studied, Rudi, whom she hadn't yet met, was suffering in a concentration camp near Budapest. He was tortured and beaten for months. The authorities tried to force him to explain how he developed The Free Northeastern Radio System, but he refused and took the beatings in silence. Several months later, he was released, miraculously and without explanation.

The experience deeply affected Rudi. "I changed my lifestyle and outwardly appeared to follow the Communist rules, but inside, my pent-up anger and hatred toward the Communists molded how I would live my life. I would never stop fighting for freedom. The pain inflicted by the Soviets instilled enough fear in me that, at first, I became a 'simple' metal worker and disappeared from the radar screen of the Secret Police, who did not check or care about the average, ordinary person. But I still kept up with politics. I knew that someday I would regain the energy to fight. It was in my blood.

"Because of my prison record, I wasn't allowed to finish at the university. But in 1959, I managed to go to continuing education courses. I was a second-rate worker attending a few classes, and the Communists left me alone. My frustration festered but the timing was not right for me to do anything but remain anonymous. My time would come."

In 1963, Rudy and Éva met at a cousin's wedding. Éva said, "I was infatuated with Rudi's flair, self-confidence, and particularly his courage. I listened to his stories about his role during the Revolution and the work that he still desperately wanted to do. I was impressed by how he had survived the concentration camp, by his pride in having opposed the Communist system, even in prison."

Éva and Rudi had the same beliefs and values. She had a quiet inner strength but was not afraid to express her skepticism toward the government. He had an ability to articulate the injustices and a fire in his eyes to do something about it. They were attracted to each other and began to date. They were drawn to each other because of their commonality of philosophy and determination to fight a system that attempted to control them. Beyond politics, however, they discovered a kindred spirit in each other. She was eager for a stimulating life and he was passionate and expressive about life's pathos. Their relationship grew strong, and they married on June 25, 1966.

By that time, Rudi had finished his continuing education courses and had begun to write poetry, short stories and novels. "I had been quiet since I was released from prison. Quiet means that I stayed out of trouble. But when I wrote, I wrote from my heart. My works were avant-garde and not accepted as appropriate by the Communists. The Communists expected all writing to show a positive and optimistic portrayal of the Communist government, but I did not feel optimistic or positive, so I couldn't write that way. My works reflected my anti–Communist views.

"Convinced that I would never be able to publish my works, but with a growing sense of courage, I went underground with my writings and organized illegal meetings to exchange information. I became involved with people whose values were similar to mine. I spent hours in secret meetings discussing philosophy and ways to fight the system. Éva encouraged me and at times participated in the meetings. But this was only one part of our lives.

"During the day, Éva worked as a window dresser designing windows, something rather mundane. The stores were full of pants, all in brown or black, and lacking in many sizes. People bought what was available. Designing windows was something of a farce. How to make it appealing? And why bother? Still, Éva worked hard because we needed the income. Then she became pregnant with our son Krisztián, who was born in 1969, followed by our daughter Zsófi, in 1972 and a second daughter, Fanni, in 1974. She stayed home with the children until Fanni was three years old. The Communist government had excellent child care policies that provided maternity leave with full benefits, so once Fanni could enter day care, Éva went back to work, this time as a journalist for a women's weekly magazine, *Nok Lapja*."

Rudi worked as a German translator. "I did not get social security benefits or health insurance because I chose to work as a freelance consultant rather than a government employee. It was a difficult choice because of its effect on my family. Our children grew up in a political environment, and learned at an early age that we had strong convictions in opposition to the government."

In the 1980s, Rudi was absorbed in covert operations and information gathering against the regime. During the day, he worked as a translator, but at night he met friends and discussed politics or worked on his anti–Communist writing. Éva was responsible for most of the children's care, and she and Rudi created a routine that provided the children with a sense of security.

Rudi described a typical day in their lives. "Éva would leave for work early in the morning, around 7 A.M. I was in charge of making breakfast for the children; I would put cereal, milk and cheese on the table. But usually I was distracted. The children had to be perfectly quiet while I tried to locate Radio Free Europe on our old, broken radio. I had to place the radio in different directions to get the sound; sometimes I heard the news when the radio was near the window, sometimes I had to put it near the door, and sometimes Radio Free Europe was jammed and I couldn't hear anything.

"The morning often went like this: I would say, 'Be quiet, Fanni. We must listen to Radio Free Europe.' Fanni would reply, 'I want more milk. Zsófi, go and get it for me.' 'No. Krisztián, you're closer to the refrigerator. You go get it.' I would then shout, 'STOP IT. It's important to hear the news. There may be innocent people who are fighting for our freedom. You must know what goes on in the world. This is the sound of freedom. It is our link to the free world.' But then Fanni would cry, 'I want more cereal.' I was determined to hear the report from Radio Free Europe; Fanni, only a child, was determined to have her cereal." Rudi remembers how he frantically turned the dials and moved the radio around while classic sibling rivalry raged around him. "The fighting inside me persisted. I wanted the children to understand that we needed to hear what was said on the radio. We needed to know the sound of freedom.

"After a typically hectic breakfast, the children would hurry off to school and I would wash the dishes and go to work. Éva would come home around 6:00 P.M. and make dinner. Sometimes we had chicken and vegetables; other times cheese. Always soup. We would sit down together as a family and talk about the day's events, what homework the children had to do, and the plans for the rest of the evening. We would have a normal family conversation, amid the children's chatter, while I told Eva the latest news from Radio Free Europe. Then we would wash the dishes, trying to get Krisztián and Zsófi to participate.

"Éva would make certain that the children were busy with their homework and then we would decide who would go to the underground meeting. Often I went alone because Éva wasn't interested in the agenda, or more importantly, the children needed her attention. If it were a special event she would join me. She especially liked the concerts."

"When I did attend," Éva said, "I would always make sure the children were settled before we left. We often had to check the location of the meeting; the members of the underground had developed a complex communications system, placing notices in different parts of the city. The meetings were never held on a regular schedule and for security reasons they switched apartments each time. Just before the meeting, the members would scatter about the city and write the location of the meeting, always trying to confuse the police. We had secret places where we posted the information — sometimes in a phone booth, other times by the train station, occasionally in a café, taped under a table.

"We would have to take at least one bus and two trains because most of the meetings were on the Pest side of the city, across the Danube. We usually entered a large old Communist apartment building and, more often than not, the elevator wouldn't work. So we climbed the stairs and quietly hurried into the flat without knocking, took off our shoes and nodded to the few people gathered in the living room. We went directly toward the bedroom. Entering the back room, my sense of excitement would increase. There would usually be about 20 people standing around; not a sound would be heard. We would acknowledge the familiar faces and the event would begin sharply at 7:00 P.M."

Éva recalls one such meeting. "It was a concert night and we listened to Bach's piano concerto playing on an old record player hidden in the closet. The sound was muted by a pile of dirty clothes stashed on top of it. Most of the guests were huddled together, practically arm in arm, listening to the Klavier Piano Concerto. Even though there was static and the sound was unclear, no one seemed to mind. I loved that music.

"Three elderly ladies sat on the tiny bed, placing their healthy ear toward the music. This time we were in the home of Pal Petrigalla in District 5, Vecsey Utca, one of the more interesting participants in the Hungarian underground. I had come because I wanted to hear the music; specifically Bach's B-Minor Mass, my favorite work. I love Bach's Fugue, Mendelssohn's Violin Concerto, and Mahler's Second Symphony, all works that were not exactly forbidden by the Communists but certainly not approved. You see, these composers believed in God. Many countries forbade music by composers who were known for their religious beliefs and it was forbidden in the Soviet Bloc to play Bach, Mahler and Mendelssohn. Many nationalistic composers, such as Webern, Berg, and Stravinsky, were banned as well. But it was the B-Minor Mass that touched me the most. Rudi came for the interaction and for the political discussions that followed. Sometimes during these gatherings there were concerts, other times art exhibits or lectures; but always there were discussions focused on political events."

Éva continued, "Rudi was an important member of this strong underground network that flourished during the 80s. It was a small network so everyone knew everyone else. As an underground writer, Rudi researched new concepts on art, culture, and social issues in a different way than the Communists would permit. They demanded that the society be uniform. Any artist or writer who thought differently from the traditional propaganda was at risk and, if caught, would be labeled a political activist. While we didn't understand exactly what the consequences were, we did not fear imprisonment or the severe consequences that we have since learned dissidents in other countries endured. For example, neighboring Romania, ruled by Ceauşescu, had no underground network because people would be put to death on the spot. We also heard that Czechoslovakia had few people protesting that regime. Rudi and his fellow members liked the freedom they felt during these meetings. On the streets we had to talk in slang and hidden codes so our words would confuse the authorities, but in these private meetings, we felt free.

"The political discussions began immediately after the special event and focused mostly on the violation of human rights. Special topics were discussed; a priest spoke on religion and the role of the Catholic Church under a Communist system; a former prison guard talked about life in the prisons. And an undercover spy gave us information about the Party.

"I was interested in politics and the underground but my major responsibility was my family," Éva said. "As the concert at Petrigalla's ended I left for home to make sure that the children were settled. I suspected that they might turn on the TV, something that neither Rudi nor I allowed. Or they might be playing chess instead of doing their homework. I entered our flat quietly. Krisztián and Zsófi were busy doing their homework while Fanni was fiddling with the TV. Rudi and I had made a rule that the children were only allowed to watch TV once a day for only 20 minutes and that was to see a fairy tale. They were never permitted to turn the channel to Communist programs, which other children watched. We were determined that our children would not be filled with Communist propaganda, even if it meant getting rid of the TV."

The TV programs were limited and manipulated by the government to spread the ideology of the Communist Party. Speeches by leading Hungarian politicians were aired and there were vivid stories portraying the positive effects of the Communist system. There was never any mention of the atrocities against humanity that were occurring daily. Though Éva and Rudi could function on two levels, in the public arena and in their own private space, allowing their children to take in Communist propaganda from the media would threaten their long-term goal of raising independent thinkers.

"Once," Éva recalled, "when we had left the children for the day,

Zsófi, Krisztián and Fanni Ungváry

Rudi and I had detached the TV wiring in our apartment and hidden it in my closet. But Krisztián, on to our game, searched the apartment, found, and re-installed the wiring. When we got home, we knew that the TV had been on for hours. So imagine, we took the wiring with us when we left the children for any length of time. This evening I hadn't bothered to take it with me. But I didn't like seeing Fanni at the TV.

"This time Zsófi and Krisztián had stopped their homework as I took off my sweater. They started to play their nightly game of chess. Fanni turned away from the TV as she saw me enter, and quickly asked her brother if she could join in the game. They bantered back and forth. Who should play the first game? I sat down with a cup of tea, and started to relax when the phone rang. It was my dear friend. 'Hello, Éva. Can you hear me?' The phone system in Hungary was one of the worst in Eastern Europe and often connections were either cut off or there was much static so people often had to shout, 'Can you hear me?' 'Yes, I can hear you, Edith.' We had our own hidden language, and there were key words we made up as a code. There were always these codes, hidden messages. Nothing was said directly, especially over the telephone. The government no longer interfered in our everyday lives, but no one knew what the Communists really would do to maintain control. So we played it safe, and didn't take the chance of talking about serious matters over the phone. The kids went to bed around 9 P.M. Rudi came home often after midnight. I was usually asleep by that time. This is pretty much how we functioned under Communism."

THE FALL OF COMMUNISM

In the late 80s, life began to change. Hungary became open to Western ideas. The country was less repressive than most other Eastern European republics as Janos Kádár's politics became relatively more conciliatory. In addition, Kádár revised his economic policies; he introduced reforms that loosened government control on medium-sized businesses. This led to moderate affluence in Hungary. The Ungváry-Monsparts benefited from both the social transformation and institutional changes that finally led to the downfall of Communism.

Rudi continued to go to political meetings, but they were different from the underground ones. Now there were Monday night talks held in midtown Budapest apartments with as many as 400 people in attendance. And there were amateur theater groups and "local heritage" clubs. They no longer spoke in hidden code over the phone, and there was hope in the air.

In 1988, Kádár was deposed and the political structure changed to a multi party system. On June 16, 1989, the prime minister, the president of the National Assembly, and 200,000 citizens of Hungary attended the state funeral to rebury the remains of Imre Nagy. It was a clear statement that the Kádár regime was a puppet state of the Soviet Union. This was the beginning of Hungary's declaration of independence and the last of the public demonstrations against Communism. The Ungváry-Monspart family celebrated.

AFTER THE FALL OF COMMUNISM

Many of the dreams for which Rudi and Éva struggled have come true. Now their country is a democracy and they have unimagined opportunities. Private businesses have been established, new laws have created a popular form of government, and spirituality is acceptable and even valued. However, Rudi and Éva are not yet satisfied. Éva works to make changes in environmental policy, an area of major concern to her. Now, she can lobby for environmental issues without worrying about personal ramifications. She writes magazine articles for nonprofit organizations and lobbies for more stringent environmental laws. The streets of Budapest are dirty and she is unhappy with the contamination that clouds the city and endangers its monuments.

"I will not own a car because of my commitment to the environment," she said. "I have been an active advocate of environmental issues since the late '70s, when I opposed the Hungarian-Czechoslovakian dam project, and demonstrated against it. The project began in 1977 as an agreement between Czechoslovakia and Hungary to construct a huge system of dams, reservoirs and canals along the Danube River, which flows through both countries. I opposed the dam because I believed that it would disrupt the ecology of the region. I fought the Communists on this issue. It only made sense to try to save the Danube River. Today I write about environment issues but I can have my views publicly acknowledged."

As for Rudi, he continues to work with politicians to address the issues of the old regime. He is beginning to write a book that exposes the horrors of the past. But now, he will be able to publish it without consideration to what might happen if someone disapproves of its content.

Rudi says, "Now I can finally publish my books without consideration of what happens, but I have to search out publishers who themselves are operating in a completely new environment. Today I have to make money in a capitalist economy. That is a new phenomenon for me. There is much to think about and change so that the old system will never return. Even though we never followed the rules of the Communist regime, I never imagined that I would be able to speak openly and espouse our views publicly. I feel so lucky to live in these times."

I made several trips to Hungary between 1990 and 1993, staying with the Monspart-Ungváry family while working for the Soros Foundation implementing the Health Education Program in the schools. Éva had started to work as a freelance journalist. This required frequent trips to other European nations. Every time she left the country, the old anxieties would surface. "Was a democratic Hungary real? Will it be there when I get back? Could the Communists work their way back into the system?" There were so many psychological adjustments to make. "I can't get used to walking outside my home without looking over my shoulder. And discerning the truth takes on new meaning; finding reliable information is now not only possible, but more important than ever," she said.

Beyond environmental issues, Éva is an activist in the emerging feminist movement. "I speak out for women's rights, particularly on the issues of job placement and political positions. I oppose discrimination toward any group, including the Gypsies, who are so often mistreated. There are very few government programs that help them. Most Gypsy women live in terrible conditions. Their culture is quite different from Hungarian culture so it is hard for many people to understand them. It is not only among my friends that I am outspoken. I write editorial articles and have directed TV programs that support my views."

With unrelenting energy, Éva also wanted the Hungarian population to increase their awareness of their poor eating habits. She wanted them to change a diet that is typically high in sugar and fat. Hungarian desserts are made with butter or lard, eggs and sugar. Grease, whipped cream, whole milk, and cheese are all common ingredients. Since I was teaching a nutrition curriculum in the Hungarian schools through my work with the Soros Foundation, Éva contacted the national TV station and had a newscaster tape my nutrition class. We brought a can of lard and a bag of sugar to the school and each child calculated the teaspoons of fat and sugar they eat in one day. Students stood in front of the camera as they measured the amounts. Fellow classmates and the TV viewers watched as some students counted over 100 teaspoons of sugar (none is needed for good health) and 80 teaspoons of fat (30 is acceptable). The visual impact of this was effective. People began to see that the foods that were part of their culture were not part of a healthy, long life.

Éva and I worked together for many months. It was helpful that several of her colleagues came to the class to support us with our "revolutionary" teachings. "I was persistent and change occurred," Éva said. "I wrote articles explaining the need for good nutrition. All across the country, I promoted the idea that these changes would affect the health of the children in a positive way. I cited statistics that overwhelmingly showed that we Hungarians had major heart problems, cardiovascular disease and high blood pressure. With a healthier diet, the number of nutritionally related diseases can be reduced and we can have a healthier nation. The public began to accept this information and schools initiated nutrition programs."

Éva practices what she preaches. "I make Hungarian göulash with

tofu, soybeans and cheese instead of a beef base. My granola is homemade and differs from any cereals available. I use only Hungarian ingredients but I often must travel to stores across town, on two subways, to
get the products. I believe eventually they will be more accessible to all
Hungarians."

Rudi and Éva's political commitment has had varying effects on each
of their three adult children. I talked with them as we sat around the
kitchen table. Krisztián, thirty-one years old, follows in his father's foot-
steps as an author and historian. His works concentrate on the politics
and history of Hungary with a special emphasis on war crimes. It has
been his passion since he was six years old.

"My dad is the living history, and I ask him to edit all my works,"
he said. Krisztián has spent years working on books that show the harm
done by the Communists. His special interest is in the siege of Budapest
in 1945. "I am publishing the third edition of my book, *Siege of Budapest
1945 (Budapest Ostroma, 1945),* which, I must say with modesty, has received rave reviews from the press. My English translation is now ready
too. There are many theories, and I don't claim that I know the truth,
but I do know that the Communists were not fair to us. I was brought
up in a home that allowed me to think on my own. Today I can say what
I want anywhere. What a great feeling that is."

I asked him what he likes to do when he isn't writing. He enthusi-
astically replied, "My hobby is wine. I am developing a winemaking business, in the famous wine region of Tokaj."

Zsófi, twenty-eight years old and the middle child, is a free spirited
young woman who has traveled in the United States, Italy, India, and
Asia. She lived in New York City for three years, first working as a nanny
for an American-Hungarian family, and then studying art at the Fashion Institute of Technology. Zsófi said, "I feel insecure and unprepared
because I grew up under Communism in a poor country, but nothing
stops me from venturing out into the world. I am an artist and graphic
designer and I have something to offer the world."

Fanni, twenty-six years old and the youngest, is married to a Hungarian, István, thirteen years her senior. They have a six-year-old daughter, Hanna, a four-year-old son Fabian, and an infant son Simon. She is
a devoted mother and works with organizations to promote the inclusion of private schools in the educational system. Fanni said, "I am comfortable living in Hungary now that the society is more open, but there
is much confusion here. People are more individualistic today. During

Communism there were not many personal choices to make; everyone was made to be the same. There wasn't color in clothes; there wasn't color in homes. There weren't differences in style, speech, or status. But there was a common bond of suffering, so we united in that bond.

"Today I feel frustrated. Friendships and relationships have changed because we lack this common bond. People are spread out — going in many directions. Now there is less time because people want to make money. There is so much more to buy in the stores. The simplicity of life is gone, and the sense of community no longer exists. And that brings about confusion. People aren't used to the pressures and the decisions they have to make. On the one hand they want the goods that a free market economy brings, but on the other hand they don't know how to go about getting what they want. That makes for much confusion.

"Let me give you an example. My husband, István, is 38. His best friend in high school has a construction business. It is a big company and he is very rich. He has enough dollars to be safe, but he is so stressed. His link is to the Christian Church and he gives charity, but he really doesn't understand the religion. He wasn't brought up with it, but for some reason he believes that is what he should do. He doesn't have many friends anymore; we have grown apart. He is confused. It seems there is less time for friendship now. During Communism there was that bond of suffering. Today people are more individualistic and that is good, but everyone is missing the common bond. No one is sure what will happen in our society.

"Remember, Zsófi, how we used to talk with our friends? How we hated the system! We had passion for what we believed. We had a cause and were joined by that cause. I think there was a lot about those times that were great, and that we didn't appreciate."

Zsófi nodded. It was an era that they not only survived, but they actually relished parts of it. Even though their parents despised the government, there was the play of melodrama in their youth.

"Remember how Dad fought the system, hated it and wouldn't let us talk during breakfast because we had to listen to Radio Free Europe," Fanni continued. "Our task was to fight the system, but even those who were Communists, they, too, had a cause. There was a strange excitement to life. When I used to go out, everybody went out together. Zsófi, remember how we went to the phone booth across from Moszkva Square and turned to page 67 in the directory and learned where that night's party would take place!"

In the '80s the Communists no longer forbade parties and gatherings, but they did not organize much for young people. Because no alternatives were offered, private parties, with a somewhat limited number of people, were the "in thing."

Zsófi smiled. "Yes, page 67, then we'd go to the party. The parents would be away, and there'd be 100 people in a tiny flat. We could barely move! Yet we danced. Danced into the night. What you didn't know, Mom!"

Fanni continued, "Now, people are too busy. Too, too busy to be friends anymore. Everybody goes in separate directions. I imagined free life without uncertainty. During Communism, I was young so my perspective was immature, but today I see chaos. The young are focused on making money, something we could never do when we were their age. And at night they are tired. So people don't go out like they used to. They keep to themselves. I miss the old times. Still, I would never go back to Communism. I do wish for more self-confidence for all of us."

On that note, we turned our attention to the little ones crying for attention. We all decided that it was time to make dinner. "I want göulash soup," said little Hanna. "I don't," replied Zsófi. "I'd rather eat something vegetarian."

In 1994 I was working in Budapest, and once more I stayed at their home. Rudi was at his computer developing a Hungarian thesaurus and an information retrieval system so that people could learn to speak more clearly. He explained, "I want to assist my countrymen in the transition to 'direct language.' After so many years of speaking in code, burdened by fear, basic communications skills need to be rebuilt. I have completed a 248-page book, *And Deadly Silence After It (Utána néma csönd)*, which describes the Revolution of 1956, specifically the happenings at Miskolc University when my friends and I developed the Free Northeastern Radio System. I am proud to say that it is now given to every graduate of Miskolc University. I felt an urgent need to interview the people involved in the revolution, record their individual testimonies and document their statements. I felt compelled to chronicle my activities on the Revolution committee, and explain the complex, if spontaneous, communications system that had provided important news for the entire country. I am also writing my new book and have developed several documentaries on Hungary's role in the Nazi era and on Communism in Hungary. I have produced a TV documentary on Hungary's role in World War II that has been broadcast nationwide. And I have published an existential and psychological novel, *A Gépfegyver Szálkeresztje* (*In the Gunscope*), a work that, without a doubt, would have been forbidden under the old regime."

Éva feels that the transition is complicated. "It is still an emotional experience for me to go to a western country. I take any opportunity to travel. But every time I return home, as the plane lands, I still wonder whether anything will have changed while I was away.

"I have a passion to save our environment and I have attended conferences in Germany, Austria and Switzerland. I recently co-founded the NGO Eco-counseling Association (KOT), an environmental nonprofit organization. I know that it will take generations to change the environmental hazards caused by the Communists. But I will continue to work hard to do so.

"I still have it in my blood. I will never forget how I fought to save the Danube River."

In 1996 Éva had an experience that would not have occurred under the Communist system. She became the editor-in-chief of a women's magazine owned by a Dutch company. They assured her that they would teach her sales and marketing skills because she was responsible not only for content, but for sales. Sales and marketing techniques, a capitalist concept, were never a part of the Communist system, so Éva struggled to understand how to increase sales. She had the ability to design the magazine so that it taught new concepts to the Hungarian population; how to refurnish their apartments with little expense, how to make do with the items they had, how to be creative. "During Communism there was no style," she said, "and furniture and household supplies were colorless and limited. Now an abundance of materials was introduced into our country, but most people couldn't afford to buy new things. However, they could make small changes with what they had. I gave explicit directions how to make curtains, how to redo a room to bring color and light into it, how to make an ordinary flat appear larger. I even told them exactly where to buy inexpensive products."

But the new marketing manager, also a Hungarian woman, fired her, claiming she inadequately promoted the magazine. It was a painful experience for Éva. She enjoyed the challenges in sales and marketing and felt that she was learning these skills. It was also quite interesting for her to work with a Dutch company because during Communism a foreign organization would never have been permitted to own a company in Hungary. Éva was shocked when she was fired because no one was ever terminated during the old regime. Then, people maintained their positions whether their work was high-quality or deplorable. She said sadly, "The Hungarian community has missed an opportunity to learn how to do all of this."

Éva added that she learned a lot from that experience. "I was forced because of that situation to think about how I express myself. I could have fought harder for my job. I am more vocal nowadays and certainly more outspoken and assertive. But I do feel that people must adjust to all different situations in life: their government and their jobs. There are always issues that can cause some people problems. During Communism I did not allow the system to control me even though there were limits on what I could do. During my work with the Dutch company, I wasn't as strong. But it was only temporary; I am strong again today. During Communism, I used to think that once we were free, everything would be fine. Now, I realize that even after the fall of Communism, there remain so many things to change.... What do you think, Susan?"

I replied, "I see major changes in Hungary since my first trip here. People walk the streets and don't look scared and sad. I remember when I first stayed with you and we had to go to the police station for me to register as a foreigner. Now your lives are much the same as mine. Sure, underneath the bustle of the crowd, there is frustration, but with an open society, I see positive changes. What amazes me most is that no matter whether one lives under a Communist government or in a democratic society, our lives and what we cherish are very much the same. You, Éva, worry about your kids, just as I do mine. I remember how you worried about Zsófi when she lived in New York City, so grateful that I was only three hours away in case she needed help. And you have described your marriage and the responsibility that Rudi carries and how comparable it is to my husband's. I used to think that people in Eastern Europe were so different from me. But here we sit in your kitchen and talk about the same things I talk about at home: family, jobs, health, politics, athletics, weather and so on. We even tell the same 'mother-in-law' jokes and Ron asks 'what's for dinner tonight' in the same tone that Rudi uses! So very much is similar. I wonder whether this is true for everyone."

Éva agreed, "I am convinced that there are universal internalized hopes and fears that exist — those things we can control; only our external circumstances vary — those things that are out of our control. I am not sure that any of us will ever totally recover from the Communist world when we felt constrained and deprived of our human rights. We had our own individual struggles. Do you know how much needs to be done here? I believe it is most important to work here. The Communists lied to us about everything. For 40 years, the Hungarian Communist system brainwashed the people. They falsified information and said that we produced more than the U.S. and Germany. Most people didn't know any better. Now they do. And it is up to us to better our world."

In the summer of 2000 I again worked in Hungary and stayed with the Ungváry-Monspart family. As we gathered around the kitchen table I thought about their lives. In some ways, political and economic freedom has been different than they had expected. Though enjoying many freedoms, they have had many adjustments to overcome.

Under Communism they had a common enemy; the Soviet political and economic control was a unifying factor. Now there are many political parties with various platforms creating uncertainty and confusion in the electorate. Then, the standard of living was fairly consistent for everyone. They all had jobs, food and housing. Now, the family sees homeless people in the streets, unemployment and crime. Compromises and adjustments have taken place on a national, local, and individual level which often make the transition overpowering. The Ungváry-Monspart family may at times feel overwhelmed, but they do not stop moving forward in their work. They fought under Communism, and they are still determined to make a difference in their society.

As in all families, there is change. This family claims that life inside their home has remained very much the same. But outside their home, all of them, in their own ways, have become examples of the new democracy, a new state of mind.

It will be a long time before Rudi and Éva will forget all that occurred prior to and during the 1956 Revolution. I wonder if they would have been different if the students rather than the Soviets had won. Would Rudi and Éva have fought for freedom if Nagy had been in power? Would Rudi have been content? Would anyone believe that a family could live in the midst of a Communist society, relentlessly fight the system, and yet remain free? Even with all these questions, one thing remains certain: no matter what political or economic system surrounds them, they will always have their freedom, sitting in the kitchen of a house — on a small street in the Buda Hills.

– 4 –

Česká Republika
(Czech Republic)

The Czech Republic, located in Central Europe, borders Austria to the south, Germany to the west, Poland to the northeast, Hungary to the south and Slovakia to the southeast. It is slightly smaller than South Carolina. The population is approximately 15.6 million, of whom 81 percent are Czech, 13 percent are Moravian, 3 percent Slovak, and 4 percent other nationalities. The key cities are Prague (the capital), Brno, Ostrava, and Olomouc. The official language is Czech. Czech culture had its origins in the Czech tribes who, in the 5th century A.D., settled in the Moravian and Bohemian regions.

History

Czechoslovakia gained independence at the end of World War I and remained an independent nation until Hitler invaded and occupied the country from 1939 until May 9, 1945, when the Red Army entered Prague. During the next three years, Eduard Beneš, the president of Czechoslovakia, tried to maintain power by making constant concessions to the Communist Party, but on February 25, 1948, the Czechoslovakian Communist Party (KSC) took sole and absolute control. Two decades of strict Communist Party rule followed. Dissidents were arrested and killed, religion was banned, farms were collectivized, and the arts and media were censored. Then in 1968, Alexander Dubček, a reformist party secretary, advocated an "Action Program" to democratize socialism in Czechoslovakia, politically and economically. This period of hope was named the

"Prague Spring" of 1968. However, on August 20, 1968, the members of the Warsaw Pact, led by the Soviet Union, invaded Czechoslovakia. Dubček was arrested and Gustáv Husák replaced him as first secretary of the party. For the next twenty years the Communist Party preserved the status quo.

As was the case in other Soviet satellite countries, when Gorbachev advocated *perestroika* in the mid-eighties, party control was challenged. A group calling itself "Charter 77" had formed in Czechoslovakia demanding openness in communication and artistic expression. Václav Havel, a well-known Czech writer, was one of the central figures in this group. In January 1989, he was arrested and put on trial in 1989 for his dissident views. After his release in October 1989, he became spokesman for an organization known as the "Civic Forum." In November 1989, a peaceful student demonstration in Prague grew into mass demonstrations throughout the country. These peaceful demonstrations, which heralded the end of Communist rule, became known as the "Velvet Revolution." The Czechoslovaks immediately reconstructed their legislature and elected Václav Havel as president. Havel worked with the new parliament to modify the constitution, to eliminate all mention of the Communist Party and to create a social democratic approach to government. This changeover led to clear differences in the politics of the country, specifically those of the Czechs and the Slovaks. A vote was taken in 1992 and, as a result, on January 1, 1993, Czechoslovakia was separated into two countries; the Czech Republic and the Slovak Republic.

Věra and Ivan Janík
Nový Jičín, Česká Republika

My Journal, November 20, 1989, Czechoslovakia—
I haven't written during the past several days so here is my update. First of all, I am now in Czechoslovakia. I finished teaching my umpteenth class in Budapest on Thursday at 3:00 P.M. and took the subway and train back to Éva Monspart's house where I was staying. Shortly after I arrived there my friend Gábor (the Hungarian psychologist Ron and I met on our first trip to Hungary) called and asked if I would like to accompany him, his son Andy (who lived with us in the United States for a year) and his daughter Viki on a trip to Czechoslovakia. Even though exhausted from having spent last weekend

in Romania, I never seem to be able to turn down an invitation for adventure. He said he would pick me up at 5:00 A.M. the next morning at Éva's house. Éva and I rushed to the American Embassy (arriving moments before closing) so I could get my visa. For some reason I was not as overwhelmed by the formalities of filling out the necessary forms. Well, maybe I am just getting more used to government bureaucracy!

Government bureaucracy is one thing but cultural time differences are another. I have learned that Hungarian time is quite different from U.S. time, running at least one-half hour late so I didn't expect Gábor to come before 5:30 A.M. I must say I was a bit frustrated when he arrived at 6:00 A.M. We drank espresso with Éva, and finally left around 6:30 A.M.

Gábor drives an old Russian Lada. I think it is gray, but it is so dirty that I really can't be certain. I haven't seen one car wash throughout Hungary, and I haven't seen any hoses lying around, so I can't blame him for the dirt covering my face and clothes from the opened windows.

For nine hours, the four of us were squeezed into his Lada between the luggage and food. Viki, his twelve-year-old daughter, blasted Hungarian music so loudly that we could hardly talk. We stopped only to go to the bathroom, usually "au naturale" since there were few rest areas en route. The two-lane highway was pretty smooth but the car itself shook so much that my body was in constant motion the entire trip. It's amazing that I didn't get sick. Gábor told me that I should be glad that he didn't drive the Trabant, which is an East German car, made out of pressed cardboard and plastic. I guess everything in life is relative!

As we arrived on the outskirts of Prague, Gábor said that he had reserved two rooms for us in the three-star Hotel Prague, in Wenceslas Square, the center of the city. He had picked up the necessary documents at a Hungarian hotel to verify our reservation.

However, just as we started toward the downtown, we saw a barricade manned by guards. A policeman stopped our car and said that we weren't allowed to go on. Gábor asked why, but the policeman remained silent. In broken Czech Gábor then tried to reason with him; we were just sightseers and we had reservations at the Hotel Prague. But that didn't seem to matter. A few passers-by came over to hear what was going on. Guards were crawling under the windows and looking in our car on one side and the barricades blocked us on the other side. Finally, Gábor took one of the policemen aside, and, I think he may have slipped him some money. In any case, we were given permission to walk to the Hotel Prague. We left our Lada parked on a side street somewhere near the barricade. With our luggage in hand, we walked slowly (I felt like a refugee) towards the hotel.

Strangely, there were no cars on the road. We actually walked down the middle of the street. Gábor stopped an elderly man and asked what was happening, but the man just shrugged his shoulders and walked away. We joked about how eerie it was, but underneath our laughter, we were nervous. Czech flags hung from the windows of every building. Never before in my travels had I experienced such an outpouring of patriotism. Something unusual, perhaps beyond our wildest imagination, was in the air.

We registered at the hotel where we were the only guests, I think. Wenceslas Square was virtually empty; a woman with orange dyed hair walked her dog, two young boys talked softly. Otherwise it was too quiet. Where were the people? The receptionist shrugged her shoulders, and said something in Czech that I didn't understand. Well, maybe it was a holiday that we didn't know about so everyone was at home.

I had my own room. It was decent, at least compared to the ones in Romania, and I took advantage of it. I had two studio beds, not very comfortable, but sufficient. Electric chandeliers hung from the ceiling, but most of the bulbs were burnt out. There was a balcony that overlooked the Square, but the door wouldn't open. The sheets were clean and crisp and the room had been dusted. I showered in the lukewarm water and dressed. Gábor said we should meet in his room at six before going out for dinner and I had a few minutes so I decided to call home to make sure everyone was all right. I hadn't told Ron that I was going to Czechoslovakia—calls from Hungary were very expensive, and calls they sometimes took hours to place. In this first-class hotel, it might be easier.

I went to the lobby and asked for assistance. One receptionist tried to help me, but her lips puckered as she spoke in broken English. She asked her colleague, who called an operator and arranged for my call. I gave her my home number, which I wrote down very carefully so that my numbers were written in European style.

The young lady stumbled over her words, but I understood that the operator would call my room. It seemed to take forever, but finally, through much static, I heard Ron's voice. He asked me where I was and I told him I was in Prague. "Why?" he quickly asked. I explained that Gábor unexpectedly arranged for me to accompany him and his children there.

But Ron cut me short. "You know that there is a revolution going on in Prague right now?" I said, "No there isn't, Ronnie, don't worry. It's so quiet here." I decided not to tell him about the barricades and our adventure because he might get more nervous. "There are hardly any people in the streets." He responded, "Susan, I'm watching CNN right now, and there is a revolution on the streets of Prague."

From the quiet of the hotel, it was hard to believe, but obviously true. Ron described the location of the demonstration but I had no idea where the action was taking place. I told him that I would be extra careful. We spoke a few more minutes, said goodbye, and then I ran to Gábor and Andy's room, where I screamed the news of the revolution.

We dashed down three flights of stairs to the lobby. The receptionist shouted at me that I could not leave the hotel unless I paid the $120 in cash for the five-minute phone call. Needless to say, I just stood there in disbelief. We argued that such an expense was impossible, but to no avail, and I grudgingly paid the full amount. The four of us left the hotel to try to find out what was happening. We checked the newspaper stands for information, but there were no papers left. We asked a woman at a vegetable kiosk and she said something was happening but would tell us nothing more.

We surmised that the Communists were suppressing the news. One man finally told us there were a lot of people two blocks away holding a political demonstration. It wasn't on the Czech news he said, or on the TV or radio. We felt an urgent desire to locate the demonstration, so we walked quickly through the streets of Prague. Still no crowds and no demonstrations. Finally, the sun was setting, and we were tired. We could find no indication of the revolution seen around the world on that day, and wondered what had actually happened.

By this time we were getting quite hungry so Gábor went from one building to the next asking people where we might eat. We couldn't find a restaurant and we were growing impatient. Finally a man directed us to the entrance of a restaurant in the basement of an old building. There were no signs outside to suggest that it was a restaurant. He had said that if there are heavy red curtains that often means it is a State restaurant. The curtains were red and made out of that typically Soviet-style heavy fleece material. The menu was limited to a few beef dishes. We each ordered one of them and a round of the renowned Czech Pilsner beer. The portions were just enough but the food was quite good. Unfortunately, the waiter stood over our table, listening to our conversation much of the time. He told me that he was trying to learn English. I guess it is unusual to meet an American. I was uncomfortable as he stood there, but we really weren't discussing anything personal or politically incorrect. Oh, before we left I did sneak a few pieces of Russian rye bread into my pocket!

We spent Saturday walking the city, seeking signs of the revolution, but with no luck. The stores and restaurants close at noon on Saturday and open on Monday, so we made do with leftovers from the night before. The Russian rye bread came in handy! On Sunday we asked the people on the streets about a revolution. Still, no answers.

So we returned to the hotel, packed our belongings and checked out. Before we left Gábor remembered that our car was low on gas. Our hotel receptionist had, among other things, told us that we had to have certain coupons to buy gas, especially since we were foreigners. Gábor tried to buy the coupons but he was turned down at three different stores. He was disgusted by this time because he knew I had told Éva Monspart that I would return to her house in Budapest by dinnertime. Gábor prowled the streets and observed the people. He finally chose a young couple walking their child. He asked them to go into the hotel and buy coupons for us. He secretly handed the man a twenty-dollar bill. It was scary; if we were caught, it might have caused an international incident. Gábor was forced to trade on the black market. Every day in this part of the world, it seems that we are involved in a situation where we must do something illegal. We were fortunate once again. The couple smiled because American dollars, though illegal, were in high demand. They made a few dollars and we got our coupons.

We filled our tank with the cheapest gas, but the adventure didn't end there. We drove to the border, ecstatic to be leaving the country. And they wouldn't let us out! I WAS THE PROBLEM. The guards said that this border was not for Americans; it was the Czech-Hungarian border, near the Slovak part of Czechoslovakia, so we needed

to go to another one, hours away and travel from Czechoslovakia
through Austria into Hungary. Gábor argued with them, but this time
he didn't win. We turned around and drove an additional three hours
and we are now trying to enter Austria. We have been waiting for one
hour at this border so I am sitting in the car, knees up to my chin,
writing this. They have checked our car, our passports, everything,
twice. Still we wait. More later.

NOVEMBER 21, 1989

We finally got out of Czechoslovakia and found a McDonald's in
a small Austrian town. What a treat that was! We didn't get back to
Éva's till the middle of the night. The whole family was waiting up
for us — nervous — I think, maybe even a little bit annoyed. They, too,
had heard about the revolution in Prague. I had tried to call them earlier in the day, but didn't have the phone card you needed in Austria,
and I couldn't call from Czechoslovakia because the lines were all occupied, probably a result of the revolution that we couldn't find.

THE FAMILY'S STORY

Unbeknownst to me, as I was struggling with Gábor and his children to get out of Czechoslovakia, a family living in a small town four
hours from Prague were in the midst of a crisis. On Friday, November
18, 1989, Ivan Janík (pronounced Ee'vawn Yawn'ik), his wife, Věra
Janíková (pronounced Yawn'eekova), and their three children were in
their apartment in Nový Jičín, Czechoslovakia. They were trying to
remain calm as they discussed their future, but a very serious situation
confronted them — the possible imprisonment of Ivan. On Monday morning, November 21, 1989, the Communist Committee would
give their final decision on whether Ivan would be permitted to remain
as a teacher, or would be fired and possibly arrested.

Nový Jičín is a picturesque town of 30,000 located in the hills of
Moravia, where the Janiks live with their three children, Anna, Filip and
Martin, and Věra's mother, "Babichka." Daily life is usually simple for
the people of Nový Jičín, with much commercial activity and most social
interaction taking place in the town's resplendent Romanesque square.
Just one-half block off the square, above the *Květinářstvi* (Wednesday's
Love) flower shop, is the second-floor flat of the Janíks. It consists of a
spacious living room, master bedroom and office, children's room, kitchen
and bath. Věra and Ivan were alone in the kitchen, keeping the fear in

Ivan Janík, Babichka and Věra Janíková

their voices from Babichka, who was knitting a sweater in the living room.

Years later, Věra described to me what happened to her family on these tense days in November 1989. The year had been filled with frustration and anxiety for the Janíks. Ivan was a teacher at the school for children with special needs, *Čechy pod Kosířem*, just off the square, and it was the teachers in this particular school who realized that there were problems within the local school trade union, one of the major organizations that supported the Communists. The chairman of this school's trade union organization, and a member of the Communist Party, was siphoning money from the union funds for himself. Almost everyone in the country was a member of the trade union, but those like Ivan and Věra, who had not joined the Communist Party, were looked on with suspicion. Ivan and Věra had attended the union meetings regularly. After it was found that the chairman had been stealing money, Ivan and many other teachers came to the next meeting well prepared.

It would be a risk for anyone to show their anger and question the chairman in an open meeting, but on this day in March of 1989, Ivan took it upon himself at a full membership meeting to question the local party leaders, thereby forcing the trade union committee (made up of Communists), to investigate the situation.

During this time, Gorbachev was the Russian leader, and changes were occurring throughout the Soviet bloc, including Czechoslovakia. Because things seemed to be "opening up," Ivan at first was not concerned that he had asked that the chairman's records be examined. The party checked on the funds and found the chairman had definitely diverted the funds for his own use. He was just an aide in the school, without teacher status, but his role of chairman gave him power in the community.

When the committee found the chairman guilty, the school principal, also a member of the Communist Party, had to take some action. On one side was the chairman, a politically powerful person in his community; on the other side was Ivan, a non–Communist teacher. The principal blamed Ivan for raising the question at the meeting. Ivan had a degree in advanced psychology, but he was not a Communist and therefore not eligible for advancement. He was now in jeopardy of losing his career, or more. He was the ideal target.

Although everyone knew the chairman had stolen the money, the principal asked the regional party secretary to have Ivan dismissed. The regional secretary agreed and told Ivan to leave. When Ivan refused, he was summoned to appear in front of a committee comprised of local and regional Communist Party members. They asked hundreds of questions, often repeating them. He answered them all, over and over again. The officials distorted the answers he gave them, trying to prove misconduct by Ivan.

Next, they tried to bribe him with the promise of a better paying job (referred to in political terms as "the carrot"). When he rejected their offer, they threatened him by saying that Věra would be fired from her teaching position (referred to in political terms as "the stick"). This would have been a terrible blow to her, as she had worked so hard to overcome the political roadblocks created by the Communists. Věra described these difficulties: "When I was eighteen years old, I wasn't admitted to the university in my hometown of Ostrava because of a situation that occurred with my father, who had been a member of the Communist Party. When the Russians occupied Czechoslovakia in '68, he was ordered to go in front of the Communist Committee and state his allegiance to the Russians and the countries in the Warsaw Pact. The Czech government demanded that everyone announce to the committee that this was 'Friend's

Help' and not an occupation. He instead claimed that the Russians came into our country and occupied it. He was thrown out of the party, and this became a black mark on my record. I was rejected from the university because of my father's political position. Yet my parents had divorced when I was three years old. Even though I hadn't seen him since I was three, I still had to pay the price for his actions. I became a simple worker for one year, but repeatedly attempted to enter the university. I was finally approved and received my degree from the pedagogical institute."

The fact that the committee was going to try to make trouble for Věra would have hurt Ivan more than if they fired him, but Věra wouldn't let him give in to their demands. So Ivan again refused to leave his position in spite of their threats and pleading. He spent his days at school and his nights discussing the risk he was imposing on his family. But Věra and Ivan would not stoop to the Communist demands. To do so would have been a denial of the values they were instilling in their three children.

Early in November 1989 Ivan went from one commission to another trying to clear up the situation. He was tired but persistent. The committee said they would come to his school on November 21 and give their ultimate decision. He expected that he would be told to leave. The Communists would not back down.

On Saturday, November 19, Věra and Ivan sat in their kitchen discussing their situation. Babichka's apple strudel sat untouched on their plates. Věra had lost weight and looked gaunt. Ivan was unshaven and pale. "How are you really feeling?" Věra asked, probably for the hundredth time. Not only was she panicked about Ivan's job; he had been under such stress that she worried about his health. Ivan felt pain and tingling in his left arm and Věra was afraid he might be having a heart attack. "Ivan, what should we do? I know that three of your teachers feel badly, but they are afraid. I am touched that one person stood up and spoke so openly at the last meeting."

At that moment their twelve-year-old son, Martin, stormed into the apartment, telling them that they must turn on Radio Free Europe. "Something is happening in Prague," he told them. Ivan tried to tune in to Radio Free Europe, but it was blocked. He moved the portable radio from one place to another in the apartment until he finally heard bits of news, but with much static.

Petr Uhl, a news reporter for Radio Free Europe, announced that a number of students had been brutally beaten and one student killed in Wenceslas Square. (They later learned that there were no deaths.) Uhl said that the crowds came onto Narodny Street, near the Magic Lantern Theater, and the police blocked their way. More and more people were protesting the regime, and the numbers of people in the streets were growing every minute. Věra and Ivan looked at each other. They knew the exact location of the demonstration in Prague, and they were both nervous and excited.

The Janíks talked about the demonstration and the events that led up to it. It didn't surprise them that people were frustrated. In the prior week, thousands had gathered in the streets of Brno, the largest city in Moravia, just two hours west by train from Nový Jičín. The students at the University of Brno were attempting to get the government to make changes. Certainly Czechoslovakia had to be affected by the fall of the wall in Berlin, but Věra, thinking aloud, said she was too scared to feel optimistic that Communism could really just collapse, but maybe, just maybe...

Martin went to talk with his grandmother while Věra and Ivan thought about some of the hard times that they had survived. Ivan said, "I don't want a recurrence of the past. Things have improved lately. I don't want life to go back to the way it was in the '50s and '60s, when I was a young adult. The fear I had just walking out my front door."

Věra answered, "Everyone had fear. I was always so scared."

Ivan said, "I walked the streets with my head down so no one would notice me."

"Me, too," Věra said.

She continued, "I don't want a repeat of 1968. Ivan, don't you remember how excited everyone was at first? We had such hope that life would change when Dubček was elected." Věra was referring to the "Prague Spring" of 1968 when the Central Committee of the KSC (Communist Party) had elected Alexander Dubček, a moderate reformer, to be first secretary. He advocated an "Action Program" to democratize socialism in Czechoslovakia. It included new freedoms: freedom of the press, freedom of assembly, and freedom of expression. New economic policy was also set in place. Some democratic principles were established within the legal structure, but most of the reforms caused major disagreements with members of the Warsaw Pact.

Ivan and Věra loved Dubček. "Yes," Ivan said, "to think that I even joined the Communist Party for a brief time because I wanted to support Dubček." But on August 20, 1968, the countries within the Warsaw Pact, led by Soviet troops, invaded Czechoslovakia. Věra and Ivan's lives changed drastically from that day on.

"I will never forget that time," Věra said. Ivan looked at her intently. "Yes it was on the night of August 20, 1968, that Dubček was arrested. The good times were short-lived, and I remember exactly where I was when I heard that the armies of the Warsaw Pact invaded Czechoslovakia and put in a new leader, Gustáv Husák. I heard it over the radio, sitting with my parents."

The Soviets forced Dubček to comply with orders to tighten party controls. He remained in office until April 1969, when Gustáv Husák was named first secretary of the Communist Party. The party leadership was once again purged of reformists. Husák's regime demanded conformity and obedience. Limits were placed on literature, art, and music. Ivan said, "That's when the Communists brought me before a committee and banned my poetry. What terrible times we had."

During that period Ivan left the party and actually went in front of the committee, and just like Věra's father, said that the invasion was an occupation, not "Friend's Help." Because he was an ordinary teacher, and many people were disagreeing at that time, nothing happened to him. Ivan was fortunate because soon after he appeared before the committee the situation changed, and people who expressed their disagreement with the regime lost their jobs. Many of them were imprisoned.

"The demonstration going on in Prague," Věra said, "really brings back the old fears of 1968. Will there be change for the positive or will the old regime win out?" Martin then stormed into the room and disrupted their conversation. He showed them a message he had just finished typing.

> PEOPLE, IT CONCERNS YOU AND YOUR CHILDREN. SUPPORT THE STUDENTS. SUPPORT THE GENERAL STRIKE ON MONDAY, NOVEMBER 21 FROM 12–14 O'CLOCK. WE DO NOT WANT VIOLENCE! WE WANT REAL DEMOCRACY! WE DISSOCIATE FROM PROVOCATIONS! TO DIALOGUE PEACEFULLY

He ran from his flat, gathered his friends and went around the neighborhood taping the statement on the doors of houses throughout Nový Jičín.

Věra and Ivan waited and listened from their apartment. Radio Free Europe came on loud and clear in the evening, and they learned more about the events leading up to the demonstrations. Again Petr Uhl of Radio Free Europe described the situation. "An incident occurred today

in Prague that may change the course of history for the people of Czechoslovakia. The Official Socialist Youth Union gathered together and organized a ceremony to commemorate the murder of a Czech student, by
the Nazis, fifty years ago." Uhl noted that it was very clever of them: the
government couldn't cancel such a ceremony since it was anti–Nazi. "The
ceremony grew into a massive demonstration. It started in the Vyšehrad
cemetery, and has continued with more and more people joining hands
and demonstrating. Right now," he said, "it is moving into Wenceslas
Square. The information we are receiving seems to show that the numbers are growing larger and larger." Uhl had given Věra and Ivan the
information that they hoped would change their lives, but they still had
to plan Ivan's course of action. He would go to school no matter what.

As Věra and Ivan talked, Martin returned from the square shouting
that peace and justice had come. "I believe it is for real this time. Students in Prague are demonstrating and hundreds of thousands of people
have jammed Wenceslas Square. My friends here in our square heard of
the police beatings going on. We aren't going to sit still. We are going
out into the streets." Soon, every city and town across Czechoslovakia,
including Nový Jičín, joined in the protests. They were demonstrations,
later called "The Velvet Revolution," because there was no violence. The
Communist leaders of Czechoslovakia, along with the rest of the world,
heard the angry protests that Ivan had expressed so often before.

It was a suspenseful weekend, with little sleep for the Janíks. On
Monday the country was in chaos and the Communists did not have
time for a decision relating to Ivan. The Communist leaders were consumed with their own survival. Ivan was saved.

After the Velvet Revolution

During the revolution Věra and Ivan experienced a new world. People wore ribbons with red, white and blue stripes, the colors of the Czech
flag, to show their allegiance to their country. Věra had only worn this
ribbon once before, in 1968 during the Soviet occupation. Shortly after
"The Velvet Revolution," Věra and Ivan witnessed all sorts of changes.
People wore clothes with color as a symbol of support. They smiled on
the streets; TV stations reported both national and international news;
shelves in the stores were soon filled with Western products and the newspapers now included an editorial page with letters and columns.

With the fall of Communism, the Czechs immediately reconstructed their legislature and elected Václav Havel as president, replacing Gustáv Husák, the man the Soviets had placed in power. Havel's writings defined the political and artistic conscience of the people. As president, he worked with the new parliament to modify the constitution, to eliminate all mention of the Communist Party and to create a social democratic approach to government. He also brought back Alexander Dubček as chairman of the assembly.

The political scene continued to change over the next few years, but it was when Ivan read about the Soros "Open Society" Foundation in the national Czech paper that Věra's world shifted. The foundation, established in ten countries, provided educational programs and exchanges with Western nations. Health education was in great demand in many of the countries, so the Soros "Open Society" Foundation (its main office in New York City) planned a seminar to be held in Budapest, Hungary, in April 1992. They advertised in the Czech paper for educators who spoke English. Ivan cut out the advertisement and insisted that Věra should apply. On April 3 she boarded a plane from Prague to Budapest.

The next day, April 4, at seven o'clock, there was a reception honoring the participants in the Health Education Program. About 60 people milled around, drinking wine, eating cheese and nibbling on Hungarian pastries. Everyone wore name tags that had small country flags drawn on the right hand corner: Lithuania, Estonia, Hungary, Romania, Czechoslovakia, Yugoslavia, Russia, Bulgaria, Poland and Ukraine.

The atmosphere was tense as these educators, many of whom had never left their country before, or even met anyone from another Eastern European country, were meeting for the first time. For some it was their first plane ride. All knew Russian, as required by the Communist regimes, but now English would be their common language. The Lithuanians spoke English even when they were introduced to the Russians. (Speaking Russian was distasteful to them.) People tried the food, smiled awkwardly at one another, and made small talk in English. I was the hostess, along with my colleague, Carol Flaherty-Zonis.

And there was Věra. She radiated. Tall, slender, like a ballerina. Her long, blonde hair flew across her forehead. Her blue eyes revealed a curious mixture of sharpness, sensitivity and bashfulness. There was something very sophisticated in her manner. She spoke optimistically as she told me about her life in Nový Jičín.

Věra and I met for breakfast in the morning before the workshop; took our lunch breaks together, and often we just sat in the lobby, talking well into the night. I observed her as she interacted with other participants during the workshop and saw that she was a natural, a born teacher, never strapped for words. A woman of principle, Věra knew that she wanted to lead her country into new teaching methodology and information about health education. She said that she especially wanted to introduce sexuality education into the school curriculum in Czechoslovakia. She helped create an open atmosphere in our workshop as she led her colleagues into discussions about homosexuality and gay rights. She plopped herself down on the floor and drew detailed sketches of the male and female human body, and then brought her new Russian friends down on their knees with her. There was a camaraderie, and even laughter, that was unfamiliar to the participants. They were learning a kind of education not permitted in the former Soviet Bloc.

In one week a new world opened up for Věra. She learned a great deal about the program and herself. She took a personality inventory and discovered that she was a nurturer, an idealist, and one who believed that she could make change. What Věra didn't know was how these discoveries would affect her life. The new teaching methods fascinated her, and she particularly liked the exercise called "lifeline," which involved groups of four. Each participant had to describe the highs and lows in their lives, how they dealt with these periods, and what their feelings were. Everything was confidential so they felt safe in sharing their intimate thoughts. It was a new experience for all of them.

Věra left the workshop with a whirlwind of plans. She became the Czech coordinator of the Health Education Program but she immediately encountered problems. Many administrators resisted the changes and opposed the new "democratic ideas." The Ministry of Education had to approve her workshops (and their allegiance had been to the Communist Party). She had to convince teachers that it really was possible to modify their teaching methods.

Soon teachers began to sign up for her workshops. Věra, with Ivan's help, decided to offer a special weekend workshop on sexuality education and blend old methods with new ones, so as not to offend many of the old-line professionals. These workshops proved so successful that the number of applications overwhelmed them. Věra and Ivan worked with teachers so they could clarify their understanding of their "own" sexuality before they decided what was appropriate to teach. Under Communism, sexuality education was not taught in the schools. Now the teachers had to introduce new concepts and they had to be familiar with the information. Věra and Ivan did not tell the teachers what to teach; they offered information and gave teachers questions for thought.

Many teachers made significant transformations in their professional and personal lives. The new ways of communicating were, in themselves, inspirational. Teachers realized that they could have a voice in creating a society that is more open and tolerant. They saw that they could become positive role models in their school and in their community. They learned how to make decisions and solve problems. The program spread across the country; teachers, health professionals, and finally school administrators wanted to participate, and Věra and Ivan became well-known throughout the educational community in Czechoslovakia.

But in December 1992, another change occurred in the country that affected Věra's career. The government voted to split Czechoslovakia into two separate nations; the Czech Republic and Slovakia. Věra would no longer be the health education coordinator of Czechoslovakia. Instead she would direct the program only in her new country, the Czech Republic.

Věra and many people in Czechoslovakia were saddened when the split-up was announced. To understand their sorrow it is important to recognize the history of the region because there had been political and economic differences between the two states for centuries. As far back as the fifth century A.D., Czech tribes settled in Bohemia and Moravia, two regions of the country. Four centuries later these Czech tribes united with neighboring Slovak tribes to become the Great Moravian Empire. But five hundred years later they divided. The Slovaks became part of the Hungarian Kingdom and the Czechs, part of the Holy Roman Empire and then the Hapsburg Empire. This division led to the development of distinct Czech and Slovak nationalities. In the middle of the 19th century, during the Austro-Hungarian Empire, the Slovaks were under the control of the Hungarian Empire while the Czechs were ruled from Austria. In the late 1800s the leaders of the Czechs and Slovaks had significant contact and the idea of a Czechoslovak nation emerged. However, it wasn't until the end of World War I that Czechoslovakia was proclaimed an independent country.

Although the Czechs and Slovaks were not totally integrated, Czechoslovakia survived as a nation for the next twenty years. In 1939 Hitler negotiated a breakup of Czechoslovakia by arranging for the Slovaks to proclaim their independence. Shortly thereafter he marched into Czechoslovakia.

In 1945, at the end of World War II, the Red Army entered and occupied the region. Czechoslovakia (Czech and Slovakia) was once again declared a sovereign state, although it was heavily influenced by the Communist Party. Then, in 1948, the Communist Party assumed full control and Czechoslovakia became a Soviet satellite republic for the next forty years. When the Velvet Revolution heralded the end of Communism in 1989, clear differences between Czech's and Slovak's aspirations, political and economic, surfaced.

Acording to Věra, these issues surfaced within the government, not among the people. She called me at midnight, December 31, 1992, on New Year's Eve (Czech time). The country changed from Czechoslovakia to the Czech Republic on January 1, 1993. "I am so sad. So very sad," she said. "There is a great deal of depression among all the people now that our country is splitting into two. But at least it is without violence. Many people that I know say that if there had been a popular vote, the country would still be united. I agree. This is not what I want. Even though we have our differences, we still could be one country."

It was not to be. On January 1, 1993, Czechoslovakia was separated into two countries; the Czech Republic and the Slovak Republic.

Věra was named coordinator of health education for the Czech Republic. "At least this separation did not bring on fear. At least," she said, "we live in freedom." In March 1993 I assisted her in a workshop. This time my passport was stamped "The Czech Republic."

During the next several years my family also became involved in the Janíks' lives. Dan (my son) had developed a peer-counseling program in several countries in Eastern and Central Europe that taught communication skills to teenagers. The Soros Foundation, with Věra's help, sponsored the program in the Czech Republic. Her son Martin became a participant. By the end of the workshop, Martin and Dan had become close friends. Also, my husband Ron spent a week with me in Nový Jičín in 1994 and helped Ivan understand the changes the U.S. has made concerning the rights of the disabled. This topic is of special interest to Ron because his sister is crippled. Ivan's work is especially noteworthy because in many Eastern European nations, the disabled have been "written off." There were few people like Ivan who took an interest in anyone who was born with physical or mental handicaps. Special students were placed in separate schools, many times out of contact with the outside world. Mental problems were ignored. Wheelchairs, crutches and physical equipment were antiquated. The handicapped were basically forgotten.

Věra and I continued working on projects via Email and phone. I also made several trips to the Czech Republic. In September of 1999 I sat with Věra at her kitchen table nibbling on Babichka's apple strudel. We had just completed a workshop in Prague. I asked her about the changes in their lives. "There are now hundreds of seminars on the virtues of democracy, the role of nationalism, human rights in new democracies, and changes in the arts," Věra said. But those were not the topics that we discussed. Instead, our conversation focused on their daily life and the remnants of the Soviet system.

"How have you changed since 1989?" I asked.

"You see, I am still just a teacher, and I don't want or need fancy things. Remember how I told you when we first met that I was just a teacher? Now I have traveled to many countries and I have seen a lot. But I am still an ordinary person. That doesn't mean that I haven't changed. I have experienced new things, and I feel better about myself, but I am still just a teacher and an ordinary person with a wonderful husband, who is so good to me, and whom I love dearly, and three beautiful children. I worry about them, of course, every mother worries about her children, but I am blessed."

"Yet, you have developed the leading health education program in the Czech Republic and you are known throughout the country. Does that fit in with being just a teacher and ordinary?" I asked, recognizing that Věra has maintained her modesty.

"I think so. Professionally, my career is very different. Yes, I am still a teacher, but not in the school down the road. Since I went to your workshop, I became inspired to teach communication skills, sexuality education and conflict management to our teachers. The Communists controlled our school system and I decided that I wanted to help change the minds of our people. When I taught in the elementary school, I was forced to teach the students in the way of the Marxist ideology. What I mean is that the system forced us to ignore the existence of any other spirituality than Communism, which was not really spirituality. We were not allowed to be original, but always equal. Now I feel free to express myself, and to teach people in my country how to reach peace and have good self-esteem. That is what our country needs, for each of us to feel our own self-worth. I never could have imagined it would happen to me."

"That's a major task, to have people change how they feel about themselves."

She answered thoughtfully, "Most people are craving new rights, freedom of speech, and yet they don't know how to express themselves. I didn't either, although Ivan and I always have had an unusual relationship and we have been open in our communication. That was in private. In public, I had to learn new skills. I am still learning and practicing how to be more open with people. All my life, there was a totalitarian government, and I learned not to trust anyone outside of my own family and close friends. Now, I am teaching others trust. And I am teaching them the meaning of democracy. This topic is very important. Ivan and I offer workshops together to teachers across the whole Czech Republic and if I may say so, we are very successful and very popular. Teachers from every region call us and want programs in their schools. We even have a long waiting list. So interesting, how our lives take paths that we never expected."

I asked, "Now that Ivan is the principal of the school for special education (a full time position), how can you offer workshops across the country together? When does he have the time?"

"It does sound impossible but we go every Thursday to another school region to give a workshop. It is hard on Ivan, because he drives on Thursday (sometimes it is a six-hour drive). The workshop starts that night; Ivan and I do the first activity together. Then we stay in a small hotel. He gets up at 4:00 A.M. to drive back to his own school in Nový Jičín. It's the same school that he worked in as a teacher under the old regime. He even works with some of the same teachers who opposed him during that terrible time. But it was the times, and he forgives them. He works Friday at the school and then returns to work with me. He drives back to my workshop on Friday night and we work all day Saturday, and finally we return home sometimes on Saturday, usually Sunday."

"I know you worry about your kids. You have written that to me several times. Where are they when you are on the road?"

"Babichka, my mother, stays with them. It is hard for me to be away, but I believe in our work so much. Although I worry that I leave the kids too much. Babichka does a great job, but she is getting older and it is hard on her. But the twins are also getting older, and are quite responsible now. Martin is out of the house, living in Prague. You see, the children believe in our work, otherwise I couldn't do it."

"You are away three days; I can imagine that the rest of your week is rather busy!" I exclaimed, knowing Věra does not often sit still.

"I spend time with my children and prepare for the next workshop, answer the calls and correspondence. We get far more requests than we can handle. I would love it if we had money to develop more programs and hire an assistant. I hire to answer the phone, do all the typing, all the copying of the material. Everything is on me. I do it alone and our equipment is old and run down so it is hard to get things exactly right, but somehow I manage. We don't have the money for anything but the bare essentials and even that's a struggle. Ivan helps me at night, when he has the time. Looking for funding to develop future programs is not my strength, so often we go ahead with the workshops and are paid very little. We never learned how to raise funds under Communism, and I don't seem to know how to teach myself. And what's more, we do workshops for teachers, not for business. In the school system there is little money. But I am not complaining; I am thankful for the opportunities I have."

I asked, "Tell me about Ann, Filip, and Martin. They really have grown up."

"Ann and Filip are fifteen now. Ann is outgoing. She is a ballet dancer, and about three years ago was even asked to study in Prague. Ivan and I knew that this could be a fantastic opportunity for her, but we didn't want to give her up. At twelve years old, she would have had to live in

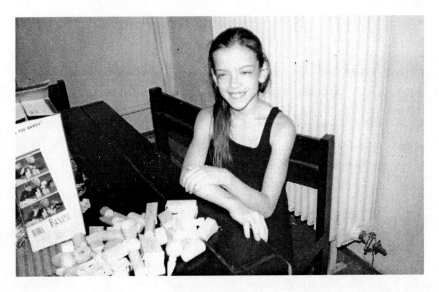

Ann Janíková

Filip and Ivan Janík with grandmother "Babichka."

Prague, in a dormitory. We are four hours away, and a twelve-year-old shouldn't be left alone in the city. Those were our thoughts. She is fine with the decision. I hope she doesn't regret it later. She is an excellent athlete. Filip isn't outgoing like Ann, and I worry about him, but he is a blessing to us. He is more of a homebody. As twins, they are very different. They go to school by 7:30. I eat breakfast with them before they go. Babichka is usually up making pancakes or hot cereal for them. They walk to school and do their sports after school. They don't get home till 6:30. Then we eat together and they do their homework till bedtime. Schoolwork keeps them very busy. Ann likes to talk on the phone, but she only talks on weekends. During the week, she is too busy with school and her studies. They were only five years old when the old government fell. They had little first hand experience of life under Communism."

"And Martin?"

"Martin is twenty-two and is working in Prague, doing computer work, translating English into Czech. His English is excellent, better than mine. He loves the big city, but he comes home some weekends. He says he comes home for Babichka's food. And she sure does feed him well.

Martin Janík

She makes him apple strudel, chicken soup, all sorts of cakes. He always takes food back on the train with him. She spoils him. Oh, Martin still plays basketball all the time even though he has problems with his spine."

"Does Martin remember the revolution?" I asked.

"Yes, but in such a different way than we do. He was so young then, just twelve. He remembers typing on that old typewriter and running through the streets. He talks about the excitement of those times. I remember fear, fear for Ivan. But I am glad that Martin's generation is spared the fear that we grew up with."

"I know there were problems in Ivan's school during the Communist era. And I remember the old dilapidated building and how depressing it was inside. Has it changed?"

"Ivan has done the most amazing work at his school. We will take you and Ron there to see those changes. During the old regime, you are right; it was dark and dreary, and very depressing and he couldn't do anything about it. He was only a teacher and didn't have any power. Now, he has transformed it into a new environment. Children hang bright pictures on the wall; teachers are trained to be kind to their students, and to show students the respect they deserve. The walls throughout Ivan's school are repainted, and the dorms, where some of the students have to live because of the distance from their homes, are colorful, with pictures of American and Czech movie stars and lots of MTV posters. It looks like a totally different place. The chairman of the trade union is gone, and doesn't work as an aide any longer.

"Actually, it is different emotionally for the teachers and the students too. Ivan is in control now, and his demands are reasonable. Ethics, respect, and even affection are part of the curricula. Ivan is often seen with his arm around a student, helping him through a difficult situation." During Communism, the children with special needs were really disregarded. Many things improved but some still exist. A problem that will take time to correct. We still don't have provisions for the handicapped that are available in the U.S., but at least we are making sure in Ivan's school that the children are treated fairly and with respect. Ivan is working to try to get legislation passed. Ron helped Ivan understand the laws concerning the disabled in the U.S. It is a major issue in our country. I have heard that all the former Soviet Bloc countries neglected the handicapped. I remember that they were seldom seen in our streets. Often parents were ashamed of them. Now there are programs that support the children and their families with special needs."

"It seems that so many aspects of life have changed. During Communism, you were not always informed about the politics. You said that you didn't know what was going on. What surprises you now, and what have you learned that you didn't know then?"

"*I didn't know what was going on.* The Communists were hiding so much from everyone. But the dissatisfaction grew and as events in Poland and the German Democratic Republic unfolded, and then Gorbachev appeared, people started to express their disagreement. But so much happened before the revolution that we did not know. We could get information only from our friends or from Radio Free Europe, not from the official news. Now I know.

"I didn't know the extent of Václav Havel's activism. I had heard of him, and knew that he was in jail. At the time no one believed that his imprisonment had any significance. We heard about the demonstrations in Brno and knew that there was tension and anxiety there. We didn't know about the demonstration in Prague until we heard it on Radio Free Europe when Martin came storming into our house, telling us the news.

"We didn't know that on Sunday, November 19, a group of artists and writers, the avant-garde, was meeting in an art gallery in Bratislava to form the Public Against Violence (*Verejnost'proti nasiliu*, VPN). At the same time, Havel was organizing a meeting of the oppositionists in Prague and *Občanské Fórum* was founded."

"You have a special feeling for Václav Havel. Your smile shows all."

"I now hear about all the work that Havel had done with Charter 77, which was the first activist group. Under his leadership, the members of Charter 77 moved from human rights advocacy into political activism. He is a remarkable man. He helped to bring freedom into our home. We had never known what was going on because the Communists had controlled the media. I still can't get used to hearing unbiased reporting on Czech radio and TV."

"How has the new freedom changed you?"

"Life today is so different. I have no idea what would have happened if 'The Velvet Revolution' had not occurred. We suffered so much during those eight months that the Communists persecuted Ivan. We felt so alone, except for the one man who stood up for him and said they were all crazy. Well, this brave man who fought publicly for Ivan went to Yugoslavia over that summer, then from Yugoslavia to Austria, and now lives in Australia. He had problems living here.

"My work has changed dramatically. I would never have thought I would be responsible for changing the teaching methodology in over 3,000 schools, and that Ivan and I would do workshops on health education, communication, environment and human sexuality and that people would express themselves openly. I will never take freedom for granted. I breathe it. Nevertheless, I see sometimes that people do not understand what 'freedom' means. They do not know that freedom and responsibility are two sides of the same coin. It will take generations for us to change."

"Are there things that haunt you, or that you just can't forget?"

"I often think how many times Ivan spoke up, afraid, but not able to surrender his principles. I think about them daily. They are engrained in my mind. Ivan and I talk about them too. How he would have lost his job or gone to prison rather than give up his principles? That stays with me every day. Now we are glad that we have had this personal experience. You know, that nothing ever happened to Ivan because the people were all too busy trying to adjust to all the changes. It just disappeared. So amazing to me. So unbelievable."

"And your dear Ivan, as you call him, what has changed for him?"

"Just yesterday he said that maybe he should write poetry again.

You see, before 1968, Ivan's hobbies were acting and writing. He loved to write poetry and his works were often published. He wrote plays for the acting troop, but the Communists read them and got hold of his poetry and claimed it was subversive. They called him in front of the committee and told him he was forbidden to write. So he began writing children's fairy tales. In 1973 these were adapted for television, and children across Czechoslovakia watched them. Morals and values were hidden in these stories so that children could get something of substance while watching TV. Ivan always fought the injustices of the Communist system. Yes, maybe he will start writing poetry or children's stories again."

"Are your dreams fulfilled?"

"Sometimes I feel disappointed now, for life is not changing quickly enough, but I know ten years is not a long time. It will take many years, probably generations, to detach from the horrors of the past. My family and, in fact, all the people in our entire country continue to adjust to the changes that have occurred in our past from Nazi control to Communism, from Czechoslovakia to Czech Republic and Slovakia. Sometimes I feel the transition to the new democracy and capitalist economic system is moving too slowly, but other times I see that life is improving and we are enjoying our freedom from the repressions of Communism. There are now more goods in the stores, although most people don't have enough money to buy the newer things, but life is better. What is important for us is that we can speak openly, and without fear. But the changes are too slow. The system has changed but the manners of many people have stayed the same."

"Věra, I recall that Ivan once eloquently described your life under Communism."

"Oh, yes, imagine that you are standing in quicksand and the mud is rushing to the space between your upper lip and under your nose and you are drowning. You can't move. Yes, you are still breathing, but barely. You believe you will soon drown unless you are rescued. Our freedom under Communism was the space between your mouth that is covered with mud, and your nose where you breathe. That is what we felt. Fear of drowning. So much was lost."

E-mail from Věra, February 4, 2002:

Dear Susan:
    I write and apologize; I know you do not believe that I am writing to you … I know. You are maybe disappointed by my silence. But my

thoughts are with you every day especially since September 11. Now you as Americans are experiencing pain as we have and that makes me sad. Please forgive me. I swear that a million times I (or we all) thought about you all. But I felt so exhausted as never before. I do not know how we — Ivan and I — "survived" to Christmas. I really prayed that Christmas would come at last for I needed to be alone for some time. Now we counted how it was, so: we had 22 three-day workshops from the 28th of August to the 18th of December. If you count how many weeks this time has you will know that we had workshops twice a week and no free weekends. I felt like a "rumpled sponge." I had no strength, but people didn't know that as they demanded more and more time, and I could not disappoint them. All of the time en route, from one end of the Republic to another, many times without water, sleeping in different beds, sometimes cold, sometimes hot, and throngs of people — no intimacy. I felt exhausted not only physically but mentally and emotionally. When all this work was done, we had to send about 500 people Christmas letters. I know that the card was the same but we wrote a special note to each one every year. Then we had to write 500 envelopes — not by computer, but by hand. And then, I wanted to be alone with my family, I could not communicate with anybody else; nevertheless I love you and miss you. I did not lose my relation to you or my love but I was exhausted and I did not have what to give. I hate computers so I did not sit to it.

Susan maybe you can think I am crazy, but do not worry, I am O.K. And imagine, Ivan! He also had his school!!! I worried about him very much, I tried to simplify it for him, so when we were close to Nový Jičín, that's when we were alone. Ivan took me to the workshop on Thursday afternoon, we began the workshop and the next day in the morning he left for school and came back to our workshop in the afternoon. I worked that day alone. Nevertheless I worried about him as this winter was really unusually full of snow and snowstorms and it was sometimes very difficult and dangerous to drive. But enough. It is behind us.

It would be so great to sit with you again and talk, not through the computer. Maybe you would ask me why we do it all, why we do not work less, it is so difficult. First we like this work as we are convinced that it is so necessary. Second, there are quite strong institutions which do very similar things and if we refuse to do workshops maybe we would lose the interest of the people who had wanted us. They would ask the "competitors." Third, it is my job, it means money. Enough about work.

Now, about our family. My mum, Babichka, broke her wrist in the beginning of December and until now she has it in plaster. I hope she will be okay and as if that were not enough Ivan had his left shoulder out of joint. Ann, my beautiful daughter, decided not to do sports in autumn as she really was "muscles and muscles" and she did not feel good as a girl but just last week she felt that she misses it, so today she went back to the training. So we shall see. Filip, he is still my good boy who fights with himself and both Ivan and I see that he is more successful, mainly in finding himself. The teachers love him and he has good friends in his class and it is very important. Martin is still in Prague and no changes. Only that all three children had birthdays in January; Martin was 25, and Ann and Filip 18. I can't believe that our children are so old when we are still "young." And as they are 18 so Ann and Filip are looking now for some summer job abroad as they want to earn money and improve their "languages" and see other countries. So they seek in internet and as they do it now — in winter — I think that they will find something.

So enough for today. Please, I beg you once more if you could forgive me. I really love you. And Susan I miss you.

Big hugs to Ronnie.

— 5 —

Lietuva (Lithuania)

Lithuania, located in northeastern Europe, borders Latvia to the north, Belarus to the east and southeast, Poland to the south, the Russian region of Kaliningrad to the southwest and the Baltic Sea to the west. It is about the size of West Virginia. Vilnius is the capital and its largest city, while other key cities include Klaipėda (a seaport), Kaunas, and Panevėžys. The estimated population is 3,500,000. The official language is Lithuanian.

History

Lithuania was an independent state from the end of the First World War until the Molotov-Ribbentrop Non-Aggression Pact between Germany and the Soviet Union was concluded in 1939. As a consequence of this pact, in 1940, free from any Nazi interference, the Soviets entered Lithuania and established the Soviet Socialist Republic of Lithuania. However, just one year later, in 1941, the Germans did an about-face and declared war against the Soviets. The Germans then marched into Lithuania and in a few days occupied the whole country. It wasn't until the summer of 1944 that the Red Army began driving the Germans out of Lithuania and by January 1945, near the end of World War II, the Soviets achieved total reoccupation of Lithuania.

Lithuania remained under the strict control of the Soviet Union for the next four decades. Although there were pockets of active and peaceful resistance, there was no major threat to the Communist Party rule during this period. It was not until 1988, a few years after Gorbachev initiated his policy of *perestroika* (reform) that the Lithuanian Reform

Union became a driving force for change. At a demonstration in Vilnius in the summer of 1988, 100,000 Lithuanians turned out. By the end of 1989 the Lithuanian Communist Party had split from the Communist Party of the Soviet Union and it was only a short time later, on March 11, 1990, that independence was declared. However, the Soviet Union did not accept this declaration and invaded the country. After a few bloody skirmishes in Vilnius, the Red Army retreated. In February, 90 percent of Lithuanians voted in favor of a referendum to declare independence and on September 6, 1991, the USSR conceded. For a short time after independence the popularity of the Lithuania's anti–Soviet parties dropped, but in 1992 the Democratic Labor Party gained control and in 1996 the Conservative Homeland Union Party was voted into power.

Zina and Alfredas Baltrenai
Kaunas, Lietuva, 1995

Laura Baltrenaite (pronounced Bultray´naita) was unlacing her Adidas running shoes. Zina, her mother, was frying some fresh eggs. I was sipping a cup of pitch-black espresso. I asked Laura, "How many kilometers did you jog?"

"About 10K," she replied, breathing heavily. It was an October morning and a numbing Baltic mist enshrouded Kaunas, Lithuania. It felt like early winter, not early fall.

"Are you heading to class now, Laura?" Zina asked.

"In a bit. Right now, I have to shower, if there is any hot water, and get dressed."

"At the moment, there is." Zina heaved a sigh of relief.

Laura continued, "I hope it stays that way for the next twenty minutes. I'll be really mad if I have to go to school with shampoo in my hair again. And why can't we have heat yet, it's cold!"

Zina took a deep breath. "There is nothing I can do about the water or the heat. Don't blame me!"

And indeed, Laura was right, it was cold. Regulation of the heat from central power plants was a remnant of Communist days. The government would not turn it on until the temperature reached six degrees Celsius (43 degrees Fahrenheit) for three consecutive days. Energy was still a precious commodity, and if the temperature stayed below six degrees for two days and twenty-three hours, but then rose in the last hour, there was no heat.

Zina tried to placate Laura. "If the hot water goes off, I will boil some water for you. It won't take a minute." Then she ran to the door of the bathroom and shouted, "And you can take a cab to school if you're running late."

It was October 12, 1995, and I was staying in the house of Zina Baltreniene (pronounced Bul tre'nee an a), her husband Alfredas Baltrenas (pronounced Bul tre' nus), and their fifteen-year-old daughter, Laura Baltrenaite. (In Lithuania, each family member has a slightly different surname.) The Baltrenŭs lived comfortably in a typical "flat" on the second floor of a Communist style apartment building on B. Sruogos, a street in the Žaliakalnis district near the Kaunas University of Technology. The front door of their flat opened into a foyer and the doors to six other rooms. The closet-sized toilet, aptly called the "wash closet," or "WC," was on the left. A door led to a long, narrow kitchen, with a wooden table and two stools that slid under the table to save space. Alfredas (or Fred as he said I should call him) had recently remodeled

Fred Baltrenas and Zina Baltreniene.

the sink and countertop, so they looked fairly modern. A microwave sat next to the new, black, electric stove. Although the kitchen was quite long, it was so narrow that two people could not stand side by side. While Zina stood over the stove, I sat across from her on one of the hard stools. It was not the custom in Lithuania to help the hostess, and Zina told me to relax. She did the cooking and serving. I was the guest.

Zina and Fred's small bedroom was next to the kitchen. Their bed and a small wooden dresser filled the entire room. It was cluttered, not because Zina is messy, but rather there was no other space to put anything. It seemed that Zina used the dresser and Alfredas had to make do. His sweaters were on top of the dresser, and his ties hung from the doorknob.

Straight ahead in the foyer was the bath and shower, from where Laura now shouted, "Mother, the water is sooty and black which means it is going off again, and I have suds in my hair." Zina ran to boil water. Once the pot of water was hot and filtered she handed it to Laura. While still ranting, Laura washed the suds out of her hair.

Zina pointed me to the living room–dining room and told me to wait there until she finished dealing with Laura. I sat patiently on the worn plaid sofa. A dark oak dining room table where we had dinner with several of Zina and Alfredas' friends the night before was on the far end of the room. A huge armoire filled with Lithuanian china and glassware rested against the wall near the window. Shelves filled with books lined the entire room. All of it was Eastern European — old books, dark heavy furniture, and dim lighting. I turned on the 1970s style television set, which faced the sofa. The picture was clear but I couldn't understand what was being said on the "tele" or in the next room where Laura and Zina were speaking to each other in Lithuanian. They had moved into Laura's room. A few minutes later, Zina rejoined me and explained, "I told Laura that life is changing for us. It will take time, but things will be different."

Laura walked into the living room, dressed to perfection, and kissed me goodbye. While hurrying off to school, she said, "Maybe I will meet you later for hot chocolate on Laisvės Aleja," the pedestrian mall in the *centrum* (downtown). When she talked, her almond-shaped gray eyes looked serious. Laura was thin, almost too thin, but quite attractive. Wearing black, tight pants, a white and black striped turtleneck, and platform shoes, she looked like a model waiting to be photographed, not a student going to high school. Laura dashed out the door. Zina gave a motherly sigh.

Zina is five feet tall and carries her head high and chin up, appearing taller than she actually is. Her short brown hair, cut at the local Moderna Salon, was pulled back off her face with every strand in place. I thought her weight was just right, although Laura and her friends were always telling Zina to exercise more.

Zina and I went back to the kitchen to finish our breakfast. We talked about the challenges of raising a teenager. I was intrigued by the similarities. Zina was raising a teenager in Kaunas, Lithuania; I, two teenagers in Harrisburg, Pennsylvania. She was raised in a Communist society. I had lived in a democracy. Our backgrounds were so different, but the tones, the actions and the reactions toward our children were quite similar.

Laura Baltrenaite and Susan Shapiro

We looked at the clock and realized that we must head to her office to begin our work. Zina's office is in the central section of Kaunas, in the main downtown area, which is centered on an outdoor pedestrian mall, Laisvės Aleja. It is the shopping district and the center for many businesses and organizations. She worked in the middle of the mall, in an old, dark, stone building where Vytautas Magnus University, one of the two colleges in Kaunas, is located. Her office had a balcony that overlooked the major department store, Merkurijus. Next to her building were kiosks, small shops, and one well-known restaurant, the Astra, that served the best kugel, a Lithuanian specialty made with grated potatoes and pieces of ham, browned in an old oven. The bricks were heated with burning logs and the kugel was cooked on the hot bricks. We decided to have lunch there later.

We spent several hours at her office. We wrote the agenda for a workshop that she and her colleagues, Jurate and Vida, would give to teachers and social workers in Klaipėda the following week, organized a smoking prevention and drug and alcohol education workshop for two school districts, and answered several phone requests for health education trainings. At 4:00 P.M., we walked onto the mall and headed for the restaurant.

The rain was mixing with snow flurries. Zina spotted a copy of Laura's favorite magazine, *Cosmopolitan*, at a nearby kiosk. The availability of goods was made irrelevant by the fact that most Lithuanians could not afford to buy them (a special problem for parents whose children seem to want everything). Then we stopped at a local bakery. The bakeries of Eastern Europe — what a special treat! Bread and cheese were the foundation of the Communist diet. The shelves in this bakery were lined with loaves of pumpernickel, rye, and other varieties. I felt one of the loaves. "It has such a hard crust and solid center; this is real bread — no air," I smiled and said to Zina. "Taste a piece now and we'll take the rest home." Carrying two loaves for 10 minutes made my arms ache. Ofttimes, Zina and I would eat a whole loaf just while walking in the mall. This particular day, we bought three loaves of fresh, dark, black rye bread that we carried in our Lithuanian plastic bag, but we refrained from eating too much because we were headed to the Astra Restaurant.

Laisvės Aleja was bustling with people waving to one another and stopping to chat. Teenagers walked the streets, and boys and girls laughed and held hands. I noticed the Lithuanian girls, with their long legs and blonde hair, wearing their platform shoes and tight dresses and pants, just like Laura. Many sat in small groups at the cafés drinking hot chocolate or espresso, gossiping, and as Zina put it, "talking girl talk." Juxtaposed to this picture of youth were the old women who walked the mall, holding tightly onto their plastic bags containing grocery items. It was not possible to discern their ages; their faces were more wrinkled and weathered than those to which I was accustomed. Many wore brown leather, old-fashioned tie shoes, and often their ankles looked swollen as they hobbled along the cobblestone streets. Their print or plaid housedresses did not match their woolen sweaters. Most had their heads covered by colorful babushkas; some with plastic rain hats. They were vestiges of the old culture.

Zina said, "Most people who walk Laisvės Aleja were born in Kaunas, go to school in the city's elementary and high school, marry in the Catholic Church, Soboras, raise their children here and die in Kaunas."

In fact, there was an eerie lack of diversity in the population. There were few, if any, Blacks, Asians, or Hispanics. No boom boxes, no high fives, maybe a few Chinese restaurants. Zina continued, "Under Communism, the only black people we ever saw were students from African nations aligned with the Soviet Union, attending one of the universities in Kaunas. A few weeks ago I saw black members of a visiting United States basketball team walking Laisvės Aleja—you can imagine the stares of curiosity. All heads turned to look at them. Not that there is discrimination or resentment, but it is more a case of fascination."

Statistically, the population is Caucasian with 80 percent pure Lithuanian, 16 percent Russian or Polish, and the balance a mixture of other Eastern European nationalities. There was such sensitivity to nationality that in Lithuania, as in most of the former Soviet Union, an individual's passport was stamped not only with citizenship (Lithuanian) but also nationality, for example Jew, Hungarian, Chinese. Multiculturalism now enters even the smallest of nations through art, film, music, and the Internet. In time, even Laisvės Aleja will have the energy of diversity.

Students strolled the mall, many smoking cigarettes. Zina sighed, "Oh, the need for a smoking prevention program! Maybe in years to come, there won't be as many students lighting up. We are pressuring the government to put warning labels on the cigarette packages and to make ads showing the long-term effects of smoking. But we can see that we have stiff competition. Right now the tobacco companies entice the government with the jobs they create, and we need employment. The problem is down the road when health care costs due to cancer, high blood pressure, and other diseases attributable to smoking begin to skyrocket." The mall was also busy with businessmen and women hurrying to the post office and bank, and young mothers walking their babies, most with old-fashioned carriages, but a few with new strollers.

As we entered the Astra, Laura ran up to us with five beautiful young girls trailing her, all svelte, with long, thin legs and blonde hair. "Can we eat lunch with you, Mom? I want my friends to meet Susan." Zina was delighted, and we changed our reservation and ordered a table for eight. Most of the conversation was in Lithuanian, so I didn't know much of what was said.

The next day, Thursday, we took a bus to the town of Panevėžys, two hours from Kaunas, where Zina's mother lives. Her home is a five-story, weathered-cement building—Communist style—right in the center of the town. A small food shop was next door and a kiosk practically blocked the main entrance. Old rusty bicycles were parked on the small balconies and clothes hung from the rails to dry. Young tenants were sitting on the balconies smoking cigarettes and enjoying the sunny but cold day. A shirtless old man was shaking out his dusty carpet, and a middle-aged woman, babushka covering her head, was hanging her underwear to dry. We walked up a flight of stairs and rang the bell.

Sofija, Zina's mother, welcomed us, and we sat down to an assortment of goodies. She is a strong looking woman, tall with a broad build and thick brown hair streaked with gray. Her eyes are blue, the same as Zina's, but they are almond-shaped like Laura's. She has chiseled features, with a constant expression of seriousness and stoicism, I presumed, learned in Soviet times.

Zina translated as Sofija filled my plate and listened as Zina talked about Laura, her school and friends. Sofija kept shaking her head, unable to understand her granddaughter. "Why does she need so many clothes? Do they have to be so tight?"

It seemed as though Laura and her grandmother lived in two different countries. Grandmother's quiet disposition and usually complacent attitude were very different from Laura and Zina's. Her body had begun to age, but her mind was sharp. The oldest generation has been the most adversely affected by the latest changes. Not only were the elders more resistant to societal transformation, they were the generation most negatively affected by it. Sofija used to be the one in charge of everything but now it was hard for her to manage her family. Much more of her time was spent apart from the nuclear family, unlike when she grew up, because her children were no longer within walking distance.

Zina talked about her mother as Sofija prepared more snacks. "Now she no longer has any savings left; all the rubles she had put away for her retirement years are worthless. The ruble had devalued to a pittance at first, then there was another form of money and now there are Litas. She no longer has totally free health care — those days, in reality, are over. Today, it is pay [under the table] if you want good care when you need it. One thing she does still have is her flat."

Sofija's apartment was large enough to comfortably sleep one person, but actually had once been the home shared with her husband and their three children. We sat in the living room–bedroom and Zina told Sofija about Laura and the hot water incident of the day before. Grandma shook her head, said nothing and grimaced. She was becoming too familiar with that kind of story. Zina's mood improved dramatically as she released her pain onto her mother. She had been translating for me but then became too absorbed in the conversation to bother. Often, throughout my travels, it seems the translations of everyday conversations for my behalf would alter what they wanted to say. When Zina and Laura were at home, they usually spoke English in my presence (unless Laura was really upset).

The subject changed quickly. Sofija's hands trembled as she began talking about her hip problem. She couldn't walk well, and her hands were arthritic, but she would not dwell on her condition. She still had her sharp mind and the respect of her children. The extended family was very close under Communism. Often, three different generations lived in the same apartment. There were no nursing homes, no special geriatric care, and no senior citizen adult programs. The elderly had their small pension and their family. Sometimes, because many apartments had no elevators (or if there were, they usually did not work) some of the elderly were shut-ins because they did not have the physical strength or ability to walk up and down the steps. Zina's mother, though, was still mobile enough to get out. In fact, she was taking the bus the following week to meet us in Kaunas. It was getting late now. We kissed and said our good-byes.

ZINA BALTRENIENE'S STORY

Zina began her story on the bus ride home.

"My grandfather died when my mother was very young. It wasn't long after that my grandmother died too, so my mother took care of her brother. Then he became sick and died. My mother was only 16 years old, too old to go into an orphanage, but she had nowhere to go. Her teacher let her live in the cloakroom of the school. She put a bed there and that's where my mother lived. She finished school and then met my father, who was 13 years older. I guess she needed someone to take care of her. He was a forester.

"My father's parents escaped Lithuania during World War II. They were forced to flee because my grandmother was a teacher and my grandparents knew that the Soviets would deport them to Siberia because of her education. It was known that officers of the resistance were deported, but it is also important to understand that many of the intelligentsia — university lecturers, high school teachers, artists, writers — were also taken away. My grandparents spent several years in a Displaced Persons (DP) camp in Germany before they finally moved to Australia.

"My father ended up staying in Lithuania because, as a forester, he was working in the forest and when he was about to go to the bus to meet his parents to leave the country, there was a shooting in the forest and he couldn't get to the bus. He missed the bus but his parents were on it. He didn't have contact with them for years. Hard to believe, isn't it? But that is just the way life was.

"My father was imprisoned in Russia for three years. I don't know why or where the prison was located. I really think that my parents didn't talk with one another about the circumstances. I believe that my father had knowledge of the terrain, being a forester, and this may have been a factor in his incarceration. He could possibly tell people how to escape. I just have to accept that I will never know the whole story.

"My parents married in the late 1940s. Once they married, their life was normal; as normal as it could be considering the times — two hundred fifty thousand Lithuanians were forced into labor camps and fifty thousand members of the resistance were dead. They lived in a village, Tytuvenai, in the western part of the country.

"I was born in 1952. When I was quite young, we moved to Pandelys, a town in the northern region of my country. My parents focused their lives on us three children, Vitalija, my older sister, me and my brother Gintaras. They never talked politics or their dislike of the Soviet system and neither parent was a member of the Communist Party. At the dinner table, we discussed the day's events, our homework, and the weather.

"While living in the small town of Pandelys my father became something like the mayor. He was an important and prestigious person in the community and life was smooth until he received a letter from his parents through the Red Cross. He hadn't heard from them since they left Lithuania in the '40s.

"A letter arrived postmarked for him but it did not go directly to him. It went to the chief of the Communist Party in our town. He approached my father and told him that he had a choice. If he took the letter, he would be fired, but if he wanted to maintain his position, the chief would destroy the contents. No one would know anything more. We took the letter, and were forced to leave town. My father lost his important status and never regained it. In 1962 we moved to a remote Lithuanian forest village called Kupreliskis, where he worked again as a forester and where I walked two kilometers to the village school. Vitalija, my sister, had to sadly move away from our family and attend school in Panevėžys. There wasn't a high school in our village.

"My father then began writing letters to his parents, and they renewed a long lost relationship. We were always so excited when the mail came. We'd sit down at the kitchen table and read each word over and over. They sent us clothes and gifts, new kinds of candy, and colorful pajamas.

"However, my mother grew despondent. She could never adjust to living in the forest. She sewed for a living. She could no longer be a bookkeeper, the job she had previously held and loved so much. She suffered a lot in those years. She worked quietly and didn't say much. Eventually we all moved to Panevėžys and into the flat where we sat all day today. I lived a normal life, going to school, playing with friends, doing my homework.

"I married Alfredas in 1976. We lived a simple, Soviet lifestyle. We worked, went out with friends, and visited family. We didn't have many decisions to make; the Soviet system made most of life's important decisions for the people. After high school you either went to work or to the university. There is a value of freedom and independence inborn in all of us, but we just didn't talk about it. Why should we? We couldn't do anything about it. People were frightened and didn't ask a lot of questions. Anyhow, publicly there was little or no difference of opinion. Of course the Communist system now seems dysfunctional. But it isn't so easy to say that it was all bad, because it wasn't. I cannot speak negatively about the entire system. Parts of it, yes. We were part of a big machine. We all turned the wheels the same way. I didn't fight the system. How could I?

"I taught school. We had very little choice in the subjects we taught and, of course, we had to teach the Russian language and Marxist doctrine classes. There was no choice of schools for students as you have in the U.S. such as private schools, parochial schools, or schools with special teaching techniques. We didn't decide what size flat we wanted to rent because if there were two people, then you had two rooms. If there were three, then you could have three rooms. So when Laura was born, we were allowed three rooms (two bedrooms and a living-dining room). We were lucky to even get our own flat — most of our friends, when they got married, ended up moving in with their parents.

"Our flat was built after the mid '70s, the last of four types of apartments built from the 1920s to the late 1980s. The "Stalinist" type built from the late 1920s to the mid–1950s had three to five stories and an exceptionally large living space: high ceilings, mainly parquet floors, wide corridors. Although one family initially lived in this type of flat, eventually the state required two, maybe even three families to live in them [depending on the calculation of the number of people per square meter]. Each family would occupy one or maybe two bedrooms and share the rest of the space, i.e., kitchen, bath, living-dining room, as common area with the other families in the flat.

"The second type of housing, 'Khrushchev,' built in the 1960s under then Party Chairman Nikita Khrushchev, had five to eight stories with low ceilings, very small kitchens and corridors, little separation of rooms, and bath and toilet in one room. Living conditions were cramped even for one family. The third type was built after the 'Khrushchev' period but was similar to the 'Khrushchev' model. These were four to six stories with most rooms now separated again, especially bath and toilet. The last type built by the Soviets since the mid–1970s were seven to sixteen stories with a little more space. Rooms were usually separated, kitchens a bit larger, and they had separate bath and shower. We lived in this last type of building.

"Our life was not complicated. You might say we could decide what to do on weekends. Would we go to Fred's parents' or mine? But we did have good food, health and education systems, elder care programs and cultural activities.

"I worked hard as a teacher. When classes were over, at 2:00 P.M., I went home and taught private lessons until 9:00 P.M. I taught English, which turned out to be a real advantage for me after independence. I had a true passion for languages. Our schools required serious studying by all students. Teachers demanded respect and students obeyed. There was little, if no, interaction, between student and teacher. I can already see how the West has influenced our school systems and I do not like it when some of our teachers now accept poor behavior.

"I never joined the Communist Party, but I had to comply with all the teaching methods set by the Communist Party members. The textbooks always mentioned how the Russian Army was the best, the greatest. Lots of propaganda. But I had to comply or else I could only be an aide, not a teacher. You see, the Party pretty much controlled what would be taught and how it would be taught. But teaching was very important to me so I followed the Party rules. Socially, we had a few close friends, but we were very selective — you had to be careful who your friends were.

"The Party just about controlled everything — what we saw on television and heard on the radio, what we read in the newspapers, where and when we could travel, even the mail we could read. But as I hinted before, that doesn't mean all was bad. My education had been high quality. So was Alfredas'. But let me explain other things the system did that was right and what worked. We had fantastic cultural events (of course, censored by the Party) at reasonable prices, affordable to everyone. The ballet was Russian caliber, tops. As was our opera, classical music, and theater. And we all took advantage of it. Students went to the ballet in the past like they go to the discos today. When I think about the books that we read during Soviet times, I realize how uncultured our society is becoming. We read only the classics; those books that are worth reading. Nothing else was available. There are some lessons to be learned from those times.

"We, in Lithuania, never struggled over the basic necessities. We know that many countries were often without food. But we never were. Actually people would come by busloads from other countries like Belarus and Poland to buy meat, milk and butter from us. Lithuania, as an agricultural country, always provided us with the basics. But this caused problems for us. It took a lot of our time to stand in queues because the people came from the other countries to shop in our country.

"Life changed for all of us in the late '80s. The Soviet government was not so strong and the control was not so tight. In 1988, two things happened that gave Alfredas and me insight that life was changing. First, we bought a car, a Russian Lada, and second, I went to England for three weeks for an educational program. In Lithuania, during Soviet times, most people would never dream of owning a car. It was impossible to go to a car dealer and just buy a car. One needed a special license; usually you had to pay off an official to get one, and that was difficult. It was far more money than most citizens had. But Fred and I managed to get the license and a car. We each had worked thirteen-hour days at two jobs for several years. Fred had worked at the Kaunas Cardiology Hospital in its computer center. After his regular work, he secretly cleaned trains at the Central Station. This second income, combined with my private teaching, gave us the money for the car.

"My trip to England was of even greater significance to our lives. I was selected to go to England to attend an educational program for English teachers. The Komjaunimas (the Young Communist League in Lithuania) made the arrangements. Actually only one-third of the people selected spoke English; two-thirds of those taking part were Soviet controlled government officials. While I was there I met an Englishman named Petras Bulaitis whose parents had emigrated from Lithuania. He was so happy to meet 'real Lithuanians' that he talked with me for several hours, amazed that I spoke so openly. But this was 1988 and life was changing.

"One year later, in 1989, this same Englishman rang our doorbell. He visited with us and asked if Fred and I could do him a favor. A friend of his, an Englishwoman named Tish, was of Lithuanian descent and she wanted to search for her relatives who still could be living in Lithuania. If she came with a friend could we help her locate her family? We agreed, and Tish came to Lithuania with her friend Maureen a few months later. We actually located Tish's grandparents. Tish and I became friends and wrote to each other. There had been restrictions on foreign correspondence but that had been lifted by 1989. In 1991, Maureen and her husband Barry called and said that they wanted to come to Lithuania to visit us. Barry and Alfredas became friends, and Barry encouraged and even assisted Alfredas to import products from England to Lithuania — water heating devices which were installed directly into the pipes. We had nothing like that, no hot water heaters. Our hot water came from a plant directly to the flats just like cold water. We had no computers and very basic kitchen appliances. And so Fred became a businessman! Something I would never have imagined! Then you know the rest of the story. We met at the Soros Foundation seminar and because of your workshop I am now the coordinator of the Health Education Program. And Alfredas must tell you about his life because I think it, too, is interesting."

Zina and I had arrived back in Kaunas on Thursday night. We spent Friday at her office working on her different projects. On Saturday, Fred and I went for a walk on the same central pedestrian mall, Laisvės Aleja. In the new section is a famous Catholic church — "the Wedding Church" — where Lithuanian men and women marry every Saturday beginning at noon. The church has regained its strength since 1991. Ninety percent of the population is Roman Catholic with about 700 Roman Catholic churches. Religion is growing in the country, but for many, it is also unfamiliar. It was about 12:10 P.M. when we arrived, and Fred wanted me to see the "action." There were several young girls, in their early twenties, milling around the church, wearing long, white, handmade wedding gowns, veils of elegant fabric, and fancy jewelry.

Fred explained, "There will be several wedding ceremonies, one after the other. People in town gather to watch the parade of glowing Lithuanian beauties marry their handsome beaus!" There was a glimmer in Fred's eyes. Perhaps someday Laura would be among them.

After watching several ceremonies, amidst the cheering of relatives and the snapping of cameras, we walked through the center of town to the other end of the mall, the "Old Town" built in the European tradition. Its architecture was similar to the capitals of other Eastern European countries and, from 1919 to 1940, it actually was the provisional capital of the Republic of Lithuania. There are cobblestone streets and tiny antiquated stores that display Lithuanian amber, wooden sculptures, decorative costumes and fancy European shoes. Small restaurants seat up to thirty people, but many of these eateries are so well hidden that they are only known to the natives. We stopped to eat lunch in Eliza, an expensive restaurant with white tablecloths, fresh flowers, and a warm atmosphere. An elderly man in a tuxedo sat at a piano playing soft classical music. The waiter was polite and courteous; the atmosphere sophisticated, European, and intimate — a contrast to the cold, cavernous Soviet style restaurants with their heavy red drapes and oft-times rude waitresses dressed in the standard leopard print uniforms. We dined on tender chicken, mashed potatoes and delicious dark bread. Fred shared his story.

ALFREDAS BALTRENAS' STORY

"I was born in Panevėžys, an identical twin. We were like two cups of water, so very much the same," Alfredas said of himself and his brother Raimondas. "We lived in a small house. There was enough space for me and my brother to share one room, my parents to have their own separate bedroom, and my grandmother, who lived with us, to have her own tiny room. My mother, Liucija, was the youngest of four children. The other three of her siblings had left the country to escape possible deportation to Siberia. My mother stayed to take care of my grandmother, who refused to emigrate because she was old and wanted to die in Lithuania. This produced a dilemma for my mother because the only means of communication with her brothers and sisters abroad was by mail, which made her suspect in the eyes of the local authorities. The police constantly questioned her because of the mail she received. She still managed to send letters at her own risk; she never lost touch with them.

"I attended the most famous high school in the country — Balĉikonis — where I excelled academically. I never had problems with the officials other than my mother's monthly call to police headquarters. We did not have a lot of possessions but we did not live in want. I just had what I considered to be a happy childhood: family, school, sports, and friends. I worked, met Zina and we married. As Zina says over and over again, life was not complicated.

"Late in the 1980s I began to attend meetings for citizens who wanted Lithuania to become economically independent from the Soviet Union. We were not against socialism or Communism — it was still very dangerous to speak against the system, but we wanted to create an independent Lithuanian Communist Party. The meetings were held during the Gorbachev administration in Russia at a time when the head of the Supreme Council, Vytautas Landsbergis, was extremely popular. He invited Gorbachev to Lithuania and told him what steps the Lithuanians would like Gorbachev to take for Lithuania to gain economic independence. The Lithuanian Soviet TV publicized this discussion across the country. It was unheard of for an official of a Baltic Republic to tell the president of Russia what to do. Everyone was shocked at how brave our prime minister was. The prime minister told Gorbachev to go home and get answers and send the results back to the Lithuanian people. It was an amazing time in Lithuanian history. Gorbachev knew it was impossible to live under the same conditions as years ago because the Soviet style economy was getting worse and so he was open for change. At the same time the Lithuanian intelligentsia worked for a more open society. Together, these events led to Lithuanian independence on March 11, 1991.

"After Independence," Fred continued, "I became interested in business, and I saw that the time was right to change our lifestyle. I wanted more for Zina and Laura. A lot of small companies appeared. There were small shops and a new law was issued that said we could start our own companies. I realized that I had business sense. Big companies had problems; small ones were more flexible and had an easier time. State businesses were failing because of the inefficiency inherent in what had been a centrally planned economy based neither on supply and demand nor on profit motive.

"The transition to democracy brought many problems. I had to be careful not to move too fast yet not let opportunity slip by. It was a balancing act. I heard a lot of different stories at the time, and I had to sort them out and see how they fit for me. For example, I have a friend who negotiated with an Italian company to make tomato paste, but he couldn't open the factory here because the laws kept changing and prices continually got higher. So big business was hard and I decided against it for me. I knew that I wanted to go into a small business. When Barry, our friend from England, asked me to start a small importing business with him, I said yes. Of course, the major problem with going into business in any of the former Soviet republics was getting startup capital. Banks, even when they had the slightest interest in your business plan, were initially loaning money at very high interest rates, sometimes 50 percent to 75 percent, and then you 'had to know somebody.' This made borrowing almost impossible except for the very short term. There were no other sources of funds — except of course, family and friends, here and abroad — and no grant programs. I was lucky to have Barry and some other friends to help me with an initial investment."

Fred then explained, "Most people were afraid to actually start a business because self-motivation and self-initiative were really not tolerated and, in fact, could be dangerous under our old Communist system. If you had an idea for improving production, manufacturing or agriculture, it was difficult to have it implemented; many times a superior would steal it as his own idea. The planned economy did not create much invention or innovation."

This could have contributed to its own demise, I thought. Employment for all (or inversely, zero unemployment) was a primary tenet of the Communist economic system. Therefore, any ideas or inventions which would have dramatically increased the productivity of the worker were not a priority. Individual ownership was also nonexistent; there was zero tolerance for such a radical idea. The state owned everything, property, all means of production, buildings, farms, and restaurants.

Fred continued, "Now things are slowly stabilizing. There are positive signs — little things. We can own our own land, own our own company, and we are free to travel abroad. We are learning to form our own opinions and debate political issues — things that seem so basic to you. The social climate has changed. Can you believe Zina and I are now even thinking of buying property and building our own home! Now, let's get going. We must pick Laura up at her friend's house."

The next day I went to the airport in Vilnius. As I sat on the airplane I thought about Zina and Fred's life. Communism had ended four years earlier and many things had improved, yet their family still had no heat until the temperature reached 6 degrees for three consecutive days, and the hot water was often turned off. For them, these were minor inconveniences. But now they could listen to the BBC; they could read Keynes, de Tocqueville, Darwin, Williams; they could scour the *London Times* or the *Washington Post*; they could attend Broadway shows or rock concerts; they could view abstract and impressionist art; they could choose to work where they desired; they could go to a school of their own choice; they could, they could ... the new freedoms and possibilities were endless. Even two phone books, one a Yellow Pages, had opened up a new world for them, because phone books were difficult to obtain during Soviet times, an attempt to make communication between people difficult. Zina was beginning to get email at the office and Fred had a successful import-export business. Times were changing rapidly for the Baltrenų family. I was satisfied that their lives were improving.

THE TRANSITION TO DEMOCRACY

It was in September 1999 that my husband Ron and I returned to Kaunas. It was a month after Laura had arrived in the United States to study for one year at Duquesne University in Pittsburgh, Pennsylvania. She had been selected for a scholarship from students all over Lithuania. Zina and Fred had their new house completed. Laura lived there for only one year but would return after she completed her studies in the United States. Zina and Fred gave their flat in the city to Zina's mother. The four of us sat at their kitchen table in their new house talking.

The first thing Zina discussed was how much she missed Laura. "Laura often popped into my office, just to say hello. I always knew or, at least, had an idea where she was. In fact, Fred had even bought her a cell phone before she left for the States, just to keep her in constant touch."

Under Communism, education was different than it is today. Tests were given at certain levels of education and only the top students were chosen to enter the tuition-free state universities. It was almost unheard of for a child to study out of the country unless there was some diplomatic connection. In fact, very few colleges here had dormitories and most students went to institutions of higher learning while living at home. Now, Fred and Zina were coming to terms with a new world, which included their daughter's absence. At the same time, they were happy that she had the opportunity to study abroad.

For Zina, the past four years of her life had been a kaleidoscope of events. "My job takes a lot of time, more of my time than I would like, but the Health Education Program has been a huge success; so successful that I have decided to expand my work and start a nonprofit organization." She identified a number of important issues that had to be addressed in Lithuania, such as career counseling, environmental education, and curriculum development. "I spend more time at the office than I think is fair to Fred, but I do have peace of mind knowing he is also busy with his own projects."

Now Ron, who has been a businessman all his adult life, inquired about changes in land ownership: "Give us some insight into the initial privatization process."

Fred replied, "The right to own property was quite novel to us since under Communism individuals could not own property. The resident to whom the flat was registered was able to purchase that flat. Most often it was a grandparent or parent because most apartments had two to three generations of the extended family living in them. Usually the sale from the state to the individual was at a very nominal price but supply and demand soon made these initial purchases quite valuable."

Fred went on, "Of course new responsibilities were now thrust upon the apartment owners as the state no longer was responsible for maintenance of common areas; hallways, landscaping, and roofs. It took the new apartment owners like me quite a while to gain the mentality that we would now have to pay and care for such things ourselves, even common areas, or that the buildings would have to be bought by companies (investors) who would now be our landlord," Fred continued. "Also, land itself was initially viewed as having little, if any, value of its own. Most of us could not separate the value of land from the value of the actual living unit, and it took quite a while until we realized that land had its own value. Another major issue for the government, on the local level, was plotting and recording the owners of land and buildings. Initially this led to much scandal, the typical situation of insiders in collusion with some government officials, but proper recording of ownership of land has finally been established."

Zina joined the conversation. "Now with proper legal recording of our purchase, we felt comfortable in searching in the city or the suburbs for property. And here we are sitting with you at our kitchen table." Zina and Fred live in a wonderful old village, Kalautuva, nestled in the woods, approximately 20 km from Kaunas. Back in the 1940s it used to be the vacation spot for many Lithuanians, especially Jews. Zina went on, "Fred and I bought a piece of land here, but it was adjacent to a strange looking, old, dilapidated cottage. The government had an ordinance in Kalautuva stating no new homes were to be built, so the only way we could bypass this ordinance was by attaching our new house to a cottage that already existed. So, we bought land next to an elderly farm couple and attached our house to one wall of their cottage. Eventually we bought the house from the neighbors and tore it down. Yes, it looked a little unusual when we first built it, but we now have our, as you say in the U.S., dream house."

Zina had a glimmer in her eyes. A few short years ago, she could not have imagined a lifestyle like this for her family. Now, she had a three bedroom, two story home with a garage, living room, and dining room. It was well equipped with all of the newest technology and conveniences; microwave, bread machine, dishwasher, sub-floor heating system, and hot tub.

"Fred's new business has prospered, so he invested the profits into our home. He drew up the plans and directed all facets of the construction himself," Zina said. General contractors are not part of the culture; the future owner has to be his own general contractor.

Fred presented the situation in this way. "Because bank interest rates were so high, borrowing a large sum, even as a mortgage, was financially prohibitive. Therefore, for most would-be new homeowners, it took a long period of time to complete the job, usually two to five years, while they earned the money themselves. The house across the street from us is still only half finished and the construction began two years ago. Sometimes people just run out of money and try to sell their partially completed homes; or they just halt construction until they have the money to continue. It is certainly not like in the West where there is a very competitive mortgage market and homes are built in months, not years." Fred continued, "It took over two years to have this house built. Before going to my business in the morning, I would pick up the workers in the city and take them to the construction site in Kalautuva; then after work I would pick them up, check on their work, and take them back to Kaunas. I did most of the design work, engineering, and purchasing. I had to; who else would have done it the way I wanted it done?" he asked.

Zina repeated her excitement, "Who could have believed! Who could have believed!" She sat at the kitchen table and just looked around. Three cell phones, two separate telephone numbers for their home and two cars in a garage with an automatic door. She recently passed her driver's test, and Alfredas bought her a German Volkswagen. She contemplated how she felt about her new lifestyle and where she was right now.

"My work is my means of giving back. I spend hours writing grants to the European Union, and other private and public foundations requesting funding to expand my programs to include violence and child abuse prevention and communication skill building. I am also doing work in the area of alcohol abuse, school debate, environmental protection, and smoking prevention. I so desperately want to make life better for the people of Lithuania." Her organization, called Youth Career Center, is unique in the country.

We talked about changes in the lives of the people as we drank espresso and munched on nuts and apples. I was sensitive to the position of Jews in Lithuania and had wondered about anti–Semitism. I had been raised in a culture where I was told that many Lithuanians were anti–Semitic. Now, an adult, I am working in that country. Yes, there had been anti–Semitism, a great amount of prejudice toward the Jews. But after doing workshops for hundreds of teachers, psychologists, and social workers from across the country on the topics of cultural diversity, tolerance, and issues of stereotyping, I would like to believe that attitudes are changing. The manifestation of prejudice, war, violence, and occupation have worn the older generation out, and with the spirit of its rebirth, Lithuania is looking for peace and hope.

"The Lithuanians have not forgotten the genocide of the Jews or the anti–Semitism that permeated our country during the '40s," Zina said, when I asked her about anti–Semitism. "I want you and Ron to visit a Lithuanian museum to learn the present and past history of Lithuania, and to go to the IX Fort, outside Kaunas, to learn about the Jews of Kaunas during the German occupation. It is important for me to have you go there, not only because you are Jewish but because my parents lived a short distance from the fort. But it is not a subject you can ever get my mother to discuss."

Only 5,000 Jews remain in Lithuania, after a very large population known as the "Jerusalem of Eastern Europe" was wiped out by the Nazis before and during World War II. Museums display artwork that shows the atrocities of the Nazis. Several synagogues remain throughout the country; one in Kaunas, the other in Vilnius. The elderly are the main congregants. The Kaunas synagogue still does not have prayer books or any of the religious items worn during the services (yarmulkes, talles). Under the Communist regime, children were not permitted to learn Hebrew and no Jewish education was permitted. What the elders remember and what was taught in the privacy of the home is what remains. A small amount of anti–Semitism exists that seems closely connected to anti-democratic feelings or resistance to change.

We spent several hours in the Lithuanian Museum where the exhibits depicted mass deportations of *kulaks* (formerly wealthy peasants who resisted collectivization), writers, and teachers under the Soviet regime. Then we entered the IX Fort. It was 1999, six years after the 50th anniversary of the legendary escape from the Kaunas prison camp, IX Fort. We saw pictures and memorabilia and read how the events unfolded. It was the amazing escape of sixteen men hopelessly imprisoned and condemned to die by the Nazis.

After the visit to the IX Fort, we went back to Zina and Fred's and had a glass of wine, toasting the miraculous action of the prisoners. Zina's mother was staying with us.

I asked her to share her story with me. She answered only, "I remember the time."

Zina and I washed the dishes and forced ourselves to lighten the mood. We turned on Lithuanian folk music, and Zina taught me some Lithuanian dances. Her mother laughed when I continually tripped over my own feet. Ron and Fred sat by the fireplace discussing business. After meeting several times in 1995 (both in Lithuania and the U.S.), they planned and established Lekrona, a Lithuanian-American joint venture to export vinyl siding from the U.S. to Lithuania. They had chosen this product because Alfredas, on one of his early business trips to England, had seen siding on some of the homes. He knew that many of the homes and buildings in his country were dilapidated and in need of repair. Their intention was to import the siding from the U.S. until production would start somewhere in Europe. They heard that a company in Poland was considering building a plant.

Starting and conducting this joint venture had not been a simple task. There were licenses, stamps, and taxes. There were questions to be answered: How do we market this new product? Will it be seasonal? How do we train crews to install it? Fred, having set up his own company, Albana, in 1991 had gained firsthand knowledge of the problems associated with customs and the protection of shipments arriving at the dock. Fred explained, "Understanding how to pick up merchandise was vital to me because many companies' shipments were being totally or entirely stolen from the time they arrived until they were picked up. I knew how many men I would need to protect the shipment and that I had to be at the dock from the time of the container's arrival until I had it on my truck for transport from the Port of Klaipėda to our warehouse in Kaunas. Security of the goods was of utmost importance. We rented that warehouse space which you saw, Ron, but we had to pay a lot of money to have it protected by armed guards. You saw them, behind our showroom."

The conduct of business in Lithuania was novel to Ron back in 1995. He had to learn the business culture in order to work with Fred. As Ron explained it, "Because buying on credit is still unheard of due to the high unemployment rate and the job insecurity, all sales are in hard currency only. A checking system is still suspect due to employment insecurity and problems within the banking system itself. Many banks that opened do not have proper reserves; they are undercapitalized, or have fallen victim to loan scandals. In the early years after independence, bank failures were frequent and consequently many people were afraid to put their money in the banks. Fred and I keep most of our money in a 'safe' bank in a dollar account and the monies we need to conduct daily business we keep on hand in the local currency, Litas." He went on, "We keep our money in this dollar account in case of any future devaluation of the Lita. Fortunately, the Lita has maintained its value *vis-à-vis* the dollar. Business invoices are also paid through the banking system instead of by check. When Lekrona owes the *Kaunas News*, as an example, for advertising, Alfredas takes the amount due in cash and deposits this amount, along with the proper paperwork, in Lekrona's bank. Lekrona's bank then forwards the money to the bank which the *Kaunas News* uses. As the business and employment situations stabilize, I think a checking system will prove quite valuable for future growth."

Fred added, "Many new companies are having problems adjusting to the new system. Employees here in Lithuania have to be stimulated, a new concept for our society. Employees must be told everything, and then you have to check what they do. Basic rules, like being prompt and finishing tasks on time, must be stressed, along with an understanding that the company has to make a profit or the employee won't get paid. Every day it seems there are unforeseen infrastructure problems. One day there may not be water, the next day the phone may not work. Faxing a letter to the United States can be a major headache." Ron and Fred ended their conversation well past midnight.

The next several days were busy. Zina and I consulted on her projects and the men worked on their business. The morning before Ron and I were to leave, the four of us ate breakfast at the kitchen table: black bread, homemade jam and a white cheese similar to cottage cheese, but traditional to Lithuania. We discussed our plans for the day as we drank coffee from their new coffee maker. Zina had arranged for us to drive two hours to Sovietland, a unique park owned by a friend of theirs. "You'll get clarity from this venture, how mad our society once was, how we survived as citizens of a country made up of exploiters. Today will be a day of reflection," Zina said as she dried the last dish. Alfredas nodded in agreement.

We packed into Fred's ten-year-old Audi and drove past the familiar houses of Kalautuva, noting the beauty of the surrounding forest. Hiking paths led down to the Neris River, only a quarter of a kilometer away, where mothers were unpacking box lunches while their children played and waded in the water. The sun shown brightly through the car windows, bringing some warmth to this chilly morn. It was June, but I sat in the back seat with Zina, with a sweater wrapped around my waist and two pairs of heavy socks on my feet. Zina wore a sleeveless top, and Fred wore a tee shirt. We looked like we were living in different seasons.

We drove past the tiny village church in Kalautuva. It could seat up to forty people on wooden pews, but it was filled to capacity only on Christmas. We then stopped at the village bakery, housed in an old stone cottage. It was our fifth and last visit in one week. We had befriended the owners and loved their *rugalach*, bite-size pastries filled with nuts or raisins. Zina explained, "Two brothers own the bakery and their families take turns running the business. Each week one family is responsible, and the other family has the entire week off. The one week is really tough on the family, with long hours, and they say that it takes them the entire second week to recover." I watched the mother managing everyone in the back room, where the bread and cookies were baking while the teenage son, Adomas, waited on customers. He weighed the cookies on an old aluminum scale and counted the money on an abacus. The father was the overall administrator and he took the orders for wholesale distribution to bakeries and restaurants in Kaunas. I told him, "In all my life I have never tasted cookies like yours! You must use some spices and sugars that are unavailable to us in the U.S. Let's start an export business and export them to the U.S." The father glanced shyly at me, proud of his product, and thankful for the compliment.

Zina, looking at her watch, urged us to get moving. "It is getting late and Mr. Malinauskas is waiting for us at Sovietland." We drove away with our bakery friends standing on the street, waving goodbye.

Lithuania has one main four-lane expressway, the Autostrada, which runs from Vilnius, the capital, to Klaipėda, the only seaport. We were on this road for a short time when Ron noticed there were a number of Russian trucks passing us. He questioned Fred on his observation.

"There is a geography lesson involved in answering this question,"

Fred explained. "After our independence, it was very important to the Russians to maintain control of their seaport city of Kaliningrad and surrounding territory. As you know, Russia's port of St. Petersburg (formerly Leningrad) is far to the north and is not as accessible in mid-winter as Kaliningrad. So, if you look at a map you will see that Russia is really to our east and our west. We have given permission to the Russians to transport goods going to and from the Kaliningrad region across our country. The Russian trucks you see use this Vilnius-Klaipėda Expressway to get to and from that Kaliningrad region."

While we were speaking of Russia, I had a question for Fred: "I notice at night, especially during dinner, you watch the news shows on the Russian television stations. This just seems strange to me since you are now independent of Russia. What is your attraction to Russian television?"

Fred looked at me and smiled, "This might be hard for you to understand since you come from such a big country with really no present or former history of being dominated by a foreign power since your independence. We are a small country, located next to many countries who have ruled us over the centuries. Not only small, but Lithuania is, for the most part, quite flat with few natural barriers. Therefore it is possible for a foreign aggressor to march across our country in a very short period of time. This is why I watch the Russian television newscasts. You know there are still many in Russia who would like to see their country once again expand into surrounding, recently independent countries like ours. All it could take is one 'crazy' to get the Russian 'nationalistic soul' stirred to action. I do hope you understand my concern. Russia could be a real threat to us. We have come so far in the past ten years — my country and my family — just too far."

This conversation on the way to Druskininkai certainly set the stage for what we were about to experience. It made Fred's concerns seem real to Ron and me. Just two hours later we entered a whole new world — Sovietland, a land where Stalin and Lenin still stand tall and Lithuania's recent past comes alive.

SOVIETLAND

They once stood in the central squares of Lithuanian cities, but now the statues of former Communist leaders stand in a park, Sovietland or Grutas Park, as it is called in Lithuanian. There are sculptures of lead-

Susan Shapiro in Sovietland in front of a statue of Lenin.

ers — Stalin, Lenin, Dzerzhinsky, Soviet soldiers, and the People — the common worker with arms outstretched, a mother with child in her arm, and a farmer with shovel in hand — that fill the Grutas forest, near the town of Druskininkai. The four of us walked amidst this surreal setting guided by a Lithuanian businessman, Viliumas Malinauskas (pronounced Mal′ lin owskas), who is the owner of the park. He won an open competition organized by the Lithuanian government for the right to create this park of Soviet sculptures. We walked up to Lenin, and stood next to him, read the inscription about his role in Lithuanian and Soviet politics, and then meandered several yards farther into the woods where we came upon a group of Soviet soldiers, so large, actually awesome. The trees surrounding the men gave me the feeling that I was entering a hidden territory. It felt eerie.

Fred said, "Most governments destroyed their statues when Communism collapsed, but Lithuania decided to preserve them. In Latvia, they were smashed. No one wanted to look at them." Zina continued, "Hungary has a similar park, although not as highly defined with all the extras that Malinauskas is planning."

Mr. Malinauskas started speaking quite rapidly in Lithuanian, and

Zina translated for us. He told us each detail that surrounded his mission to preserve the statues. Zina began, "He is hoping to expand the park, and construct a copy of a Soviet *gulag* [forced labor camp], an underground Lithuanian partisan hideout, and a railway. People then would be able to go onto train carriages which are replicas of those that transported hundreds of thousands of Lithuanians deported to Siberia by the Soviets. The trains would cut through the forest, just as when they carried the prisoners to the Siberian cities of Novosibirsk and Ekaterinburg. He already has erected a watchtower, similar to the ones that were placed at the borders."

Zina continued, "But there are right-wing members of parliament and an organization called *Labora*, comprised of people who are mostly anti–Communist, that want to halt his project. They claim the park glorifies the Soviet leaders and that it is located in an area where anti–Soviets hid and fought for freedom after World War II. *Labora* wants to destroy the sculptures. *Labora* insists that 'genocide makers' should not stand on land 'soaked with the blood of the partisans.' They label it a political Disneyland, and claim all efforts in Lithuania, public and private, should be on the restoration of the country, not on such a 'commercial pop show.'"

Mr. Malinauskas said, "My father died in the Siberian camps, and my relatives were murdered in post World War II times. I want to document these Soviet crimes, and tell the tale of the Lithuanian resistance, because the Lithuanian people tried so hard to fight back."

Fred and Zina nodded in agreement. Many Lithuanians have similar histories, but Mr. Malinauskas has the money to do something of historical importance. He is the owner of the Hesona Company, the largest exporter of Lithuanian mushrooms. He has put two million Litas (about a half million dollars) into Sovietland. He said it would probably never return profit to him. "I will never financially get back what I have put into it. That is not what matters to me."

Also on this property, just a short walk from his house, he has built one of the most successful enterprises in all of Lithuania, Hesona, a mushroom processing plant. He described his factory to Zina and she translated, "The main factory has over 500 employees who are responsible for picking, cleaning and preparing the mushrooms for distribution." He walked with us to the factory. "Lithuania is known for its wide assortment of mushrooms, but there are over thirty that are poisonous. I must be certain that my employees know the difference in the mushrooms, because many mushrooms look very much alike, yet one can be deadly, and the other wonderful and meaty tasting. After they are picked, some of them are then dried; others just cleaned, and canned. My business also exports tomatoes, garlic, carrots, peas, and an ever-increasing number of different types of produce. I am expanding and exporting meat and fish products and all sorts of fruits to countries across Europe, Scandinavia, and Israel. Lithuania is an agricultural state, and always has had plenty of food, and I know what to do with the excess."

Mr. Malinauskas' business head is in the mushroom business, but his heart is in Sovietland. He spoke freely to us about the reasons that he wants to design this park. "I am not at all overwhelmed with developing two businesses simultaneously, even though they are so different. I have so much energy and I don't get tired. I intend to succeed in a capitalist world but, most importantly, I very much believe that families who have had experiences similar to mine need to know that they have not been forgotten, and the public must forever remember the atrocities wrought upon the Lithuanians by the Soviets."

While he talked with us, his cell phone rang, and his staff came to ask questions. It is his deepest conviction, he repeated several times, to expose this park to the world. "These were wicked people who did wicked things. Now that we are free, we must speak the truth. And never allow this country to be occupied again."

We spent five hours with the Malinauskas family. Mrs. Malinauskas, in her early sixties, spends her days quietly in the house and garden. She is an unpretentious woman, simple, and very pleasant. Her face tells stories of her past, and her simple dress was in contrast to the elegant surroundings of their home. Her husband is the breadwinner, and she, the homemaker. Zina explained, "Their three adult children assist with the mushroom and export business, but Mr. Malinauskas controls Sovietland. The eldest son lives on the property, about one mile away, and he brings his young boys to their grandparents' so they can run around the yard and be supervised by grandma." They all seemed comfortable in their expanding home and enterprise.

We dined with them, a meal prepared by their private chef. It was actually an assortment of all of the products we had seen in the factory, laid out very elegantly on their enormous dining room table — cabbage and potato salad, herring, smoked salmon, pasta salad, and pickles. We drank Lithuanian champagne, fruity and sweet. We sat on carved wooden chairs in their palatial dining room that matched the gorgeous oak table. I could have imagined it in the White House dining room, except here there were trophies and stuffed deer and bears hanging on the walls. The chandelier that hung above the table had hundreds of crystal, spiral drops. The ceramic tile floor covered an enormous area, from the dining room through the halls, with a geometric design that looked handmade. While we feasted in luxury, I looked out the window and saw an enormous statue of Stalin staring at me.

After the meal I paused to look around. It is quite unusual to have two major businesses and a family estate all on one property, with the "Disney-like" park on one side, a factory with over 500 employees on the other, and a huge mansion in the middle, but it seemed to work for them. We left this exceptional family late in the afternoon. Mr. Malinauskas handed me a special gift, a picture of a Lithuanian village made out of small pieces of amber. We hugged goodbye, and the four of us got into Fred's car for our return trip to Kaunas.

Late that night, upon returning to Kalautuva, we sat once again at the kitchen table, eating our last meal with Fred and Zina. Zina asked Ron and me, "Do you see big changes in our country since your last time here? How do you compare Lithuania to the other countries in Eastern Europe?" Ron answered her briefly, but then she changed the subject. "Oh how I miss Laura. It's so hard for me to have her so very far away. I know that this experience for her in the United States will transform her in ways I will never understand. When I think of my child, I realize that she has been exposed to the West in ways that I could never have imagined. Remember when she spent the summer as a nanny in England?" Zina looked at me and I nodded. "I can't believe that she is now studying in the U.S. To think that our daughter won a $20,000 scholarship to study at Duquesne University," she said to Fred. Zina continued, "She really is a child of the nineties. She goes online, knows how to use the computer like it is a part of her, loves rock music, dances and parties, and demands to be independent. She exercises at least four times a week, spends hours in front of the mirror, and watches every morsel of food that she puts into her mouth. It is all so new to me. I doubt that she will remember the statues that we saw today or even that shampoo residue in her unrinsed hair."

Zina went on. She seemed so comfortable talking with us. "At the other extreme is my mother. The medical care is no longer sufficient, and since Communism fell, the pensions for the elderly are smaller than ever. I worry a lot about her health and her social problems. She is an old-fashioned grandma, not like your mother as you have told me, Susan, or the grandmothers in the States, who take Tae Chi, eat dinner out, and retire at an early age so they can play golf or take college courses. My mother knits sweaters for her grandchildren, doesn't complain or demand anything from any of us, doesn't own or drive a car, can't understand the need for high-tech, watches TV in black and white, and cooks the old traditional dishes. I know she remembers every one of the statues, and what each political figure meant to her and her family. But, as you can see, she won't talk about the past."

I studied Zina as she talked. She shares characteristics of both Laura and her mother, Sofija. Her clothes are not as up to date as Laura's, but not as old fashioned as her mother's. She has basic computer skills, but nothing like Laura's. Sofija just shakes her head when Zina says that Laura emailed her. I can see that she has no idea what Zina is talking about. Zina likes classical music, not the loud rock that Laura loves. She walks in the forest of Kalautuva for daily exercise but she can't imagine joining a gym, let alone exercising four times a week. She drives a car but only for necessity. Laura likes to "drive around" and visit friends. Zina, like her mother, still loves to cook the old traditional Lithuanian dishes. She can't understand how Laura can live on pizza and salads. Zina fits into both her mother's generation and Laura's.

She summed it up, "I am a middle-aged working woman, a motherly woman, and maybe I have put on a few extra pounds. A little confused, but happy. I am fortunate to live in such exciting times and to understand my past, something I fear my dear Laura will forget. And my dear Mother only lives in the past, with every statue in her mind, every detail of those times. I can see it in her eyes. Yes, I am united to both, a woman in the middle, not totally understanding either world, but not separated from either."

– 6 –

Republika Makedonija (The Former Yugoslav Republic of Macedonia)

The Former Yugoslav Republic of Macedonia is located in southeastern Europe in what is commonly known as the Balkan region. Slightly larger than Vermont, it borders Albania to the west, Bulgaria to the east, Greece to the south, and Serbia and Kosovo to the north. The population is estimated to be two million people composed of 67 percent Macedonian, 22 percent Albanian, and 11 percent other nationalities. The official language is Macedonian, which had its origins in the Slavic tribes who first settled in the Macedonian region in the 6th century A.D.

History

Macedonia, from the 11th century to the 15th century, fell under the influence of the Roman Empire, Bulgaria, and Serbia. At the end of the 14th century the Turks invaded and Macedonia became part of the Ottoman Empire for the next five hundred years. In the 19th century, as the Ottoman Empire declined, a new Macedonian consciousness developed. However, this Macedonian nationalism was short-lived. In the early years of the 20th century two Balkan wars were fought, the first in 1912 to rid the Turks from the Balkans, and the second in 1913 to settle the aspirations of the neighboring countries of Greece, Serbia, and Bulgaria, each of which partitioned sections of Macedonia. Macedonia remained partitioned until the end of World War II. It was not until

1948 that Josip Brož Tito, the leader of the Yugoslavian Communist Party, declared an independent Macedonian Republic of Yugoslavia.

Tito moved Yugoslavia ideologically away from the Stalinist "line." He organized the central government to ensure his control but, at the same time, he delegated more authority to the Yugoslav Republics. All Yugoslavians had educational opportunities, jobs, food, and housing regardless of nationality. Tito, seen by most as a benevolent dictator, brought peaceful co-existence to the Balkan region, a region historically synonymous with factionalism. After his death unemployment and inflation beset the country and in 1990 the Communist Party lost power. One after another, each of the republics declared independence, Macedonia on September 8, 1991. As in the other Balkan regions of Bosnia and Kosovo, where ethnic differences have led to wars, Macedonia is now in turmoil. The Albanian population is demanding greater representation in the government, better housing and schools, higher paying jobs and recognition of Albanian as an official language. The people of Macedonia continue to search for a peaceful resolution.

Darko Jordanov and Herbi Elmazi
Skopje, Republika Makedonija

NEWS UPDATE:
SKOPJE, MACEDONIA (AP)
The Associated Press, June 17, 2001 3:48 P.M.

Negotiators in Macedonia ended a third day of talks Sunday with no word on whether a deal to prevent full-scale war between ethnic–Albanian militants and Macedonian government forces was any closer. Politicians are considering a peace proposal drafted by President Boris Trajkovski that calls for a cease-fire, amnesty for most rebels who disarm voluntarily and greater inclusion of minority ethnic–Albanians in state institutions. Trajkovski's plan may also include the removal of references to ethnicity or religion from the constitution and add Albanian as a state language.

No area brings so much confusion to people as the Balkans. Mention the word Bosnia, Macedonia or Serbia and the reaction is often: "I don't understand what is going on there." Or, "The situation seems volatile although I am unclear about their problems." Or, "NATO should send troops to disarm the rebels." Or, "Our boys shouldn't die over there. It's not our business."

What is it that makes religion and nationalism such divisive forces? Children and elderly shot, women raped, towns destroyed — all in the name of God or Country. Conflict — what lasting power it has over people. Conflict — frozen by fifty years of Communist rule in Yugoslavia. Conflict — is it part of an inner consciousness or is it a creation of politics and religion? Macedonia has conflict. I remember the great hopes for Macedonia after independence. It is hard to believe that just ten years later I would fear for the lives of my friends in this small Balkan country and that their conflict would become my conflict. This is the story of two very exceptional men who are from different cultures and are best friends. They have been working together in an organization to promote peace and co-existence in the Former Yugoslav Republic of Macedonia.

Darko Jordanov and Herbi Elmazi, both 34 years old, live in Skopje, the capital of Macedonia. Although both are Macedonian citizens, Darko is of Slavic descent and a member of the Orthodox Macedonian Church while Herbi is of ethnic Albanian descent and practices the Muslim religion. Macedonia has been their home and the home of their parents, grandparents and great-grandparents.

Herbi is quiet and reserved. He stands about 5 feet, 8 inches tall, and is slight of build, with deep blue eyes and curly brown hair. In his youth he was an archery champion and excellent basketball player and still participates in both sports. He speaks Macedonian, Albanian, Turkish and English. Herbi is organized, efficient and very detail oriented.

Darko, on the other hand, is outspoken and emotional. He has a round face with dark hair, dark eyes and a flirtatious smile. Of stocky build, he is a little less than six feet tall. Very sensitive, but quite talkative, he knows how to hold an audience's attention whether speaking in English, Macedonian, Serbo-Croatian or Dutch. Unlike Herbi, however, Darko struggles to be organized and looks at the whole picture rather than the details.

Herbi and Darko have their own ideas concerning the future of their new country. Darko, as Slavic Macedonian, claims that the ethnic Albanians should have a limited voice in policies, as they comprise only 22 percent of the country's population. Macedonians of ethnic Albanian descent, like Herbi, reject those statistics and claim that there are more ethnic Albanians than the Macedonians acknowledge.

The political situation dominates Herbi and Darko's thinking. "The world is looking at our country now because again there is a possibility of war in the Balkans," says Herbi. "Until recently Darko and I were proud that we had been spared the violence that surrounded us during the Bosnian War. During that war thousands of refugees ended up in camps inside Macedonia so we heard firsthand about the horrors. We saw the terror. Bosnia is such a close neighbor to us and we know so many of the Bosnian people."

Darko adds, "They are our friends and relatives. Macedonians and Bosnians don't forget that once we were two regions in the same country. We were proud that there was no fighting on our soil. Now that has changed."

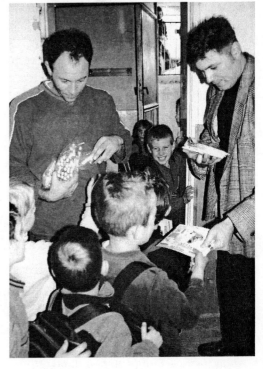

Herbi (left) and Darko working at the International Red Cross.

Herbi and Darko come from very distinct cultures. Herbi speaks Albanian in his home and Darko speaks Macedonian in his home. Herbi, as a Muslim, attends the mosque, and Darko belongs to the Macedonian Orthodox Church. Most of Herbi's father's family have lived in the country and in villages where agriculture is their work; the land has supported them for generations. Darko's family has its roots in the city.

Herbi and Darko disagree on many aspects of life in Macedonia. Herbi says, "I live in poverty compared to Darko, yet our work is similar."

Darko replies, "At one time Herbi had a higher salary. He had five more years' working experience with international organizations which pay two or three times more than Macedonian companies. Sure there are differences. There always are with any two people. I live in an apartment

I inherited from my parents that they got during Communism and it is twice as small as Herbi's parents' flat."

Herbi often reminds Darko, "My people are treated as second class citizens. The constitution states that Macedonians and all minorities have full rights. This statement alone shows the separation of ethnic Albanians. I want the Albanian language to be recognized as an official language just like the Macedonian language."

Darko feels that the constitution gives everyone equal rights. "There should be some extension of the Albanian language but I want the Macedonians to be in authority. It is Macedonia," he says adamantly. "I know that I don't have the same pressure in looking for employment, although it is not easy finding a good job for me either. I worry about the number of Albanians who have moved into Macedonia. It could happen that there will be more ethnic Albanians living in Macedonia than Macedonians. As of today, the number of ethnic Albanians continues to grow. They have more children in their families than we do. Under Communism we felt sorry for the Albanians who lived within the geographical borders of the nation of Albania. Their dictator, Enver Hoxcha, was a tyrant and forced them to live under terrible conditions. So when many of these Albanian people fled that country we accepted them. But now, the situation for us as Macedonians is grave."

Herbi says, "My family didn't migrate from somewhere to Macedonia. We are living here for centuries; then something changes, we remain inside the borders and we are treated as second class citizens in the universities, and in job status. Macedonians have job priority over Albanians."

Cultural and economic differences complicate the relationship but both men say, "It's not impossible for us to still be best friends." They work and socialize together, have barbecues in the countryside, and family holiday get-togethers. They want their children to learn to live together. They are not always in agreement, but they are considerate of each other's points of view. Darko says that the ethnic Albanian rebels' aggression is a violation toward the Macedonian population, but he does not let the emotions created by those acts affect his relationship with Herbi. When Herbi thinks that Macedonians discriminate against ethnic Albanians, he does not hold it against Darko personally.

Darko and Herbi are only two people of two million, but they are two men trying to find answers to the complex issues that surround them. As one pebble affects the flow of the river, perhaps two men can influence their region. They each want the same things for their children — the pursuit of happiness and a life free of violence and fear. Together they work for peace.

HERBI'S STORY

It was April 2001: We sat on the couch in my family room. Herbi and Darko had been in Harrisburg visiting with my husband, Ron, and me for two weeks. It was Saturday morning around 7:30. Darko was still sound asleep. Our family room has one large couch that faces the back yard. Herbi and I sat next to each other and commented that the trees were soon going to show the signs of spring. His body seemed more relaxed, much more than on his arrival. He felt comfortable in our home. He went to the refrigerator when he was hungry, washed the dishes, and even figured out how to use our washing machine. He knew that we really liked him and Ron and I felt that he liked us.

Herbi began, "It's important for you to understand my roots as an ethnic Albanian living in Macedonia. I cannot talk about me or my family without telling you about some of my history as an ethnic Albanian.

Bona, Selesta, Ammar and Herbi Elmazi

Long before I was born my ancestors lived in Macedonia, as Albanians. My origin comes from the Ilirs who resided in the Balkan Peninsula.

"Just like the other people in the Balkans, we were under the Ottoman Empire for five centuries. The Turks tried to assimilate all the Albanians into their culture. They selected very young children, sometimes even babies, and sent them to Turkey to grow up in the Turkish spirit, and even changed their names to Turkish ones. They trained them to fight and sent them back and gave them the territory to manage. One very well known person in the Albanian history was Gjergj Kastriot, who as a child was sent to Turkey and they changed his name to Skenderbeg. After he was trained the Turks sent him back to his land to rule for the Turkish occupation. Instead he organized an army and rose up against them. Skenderbeg fought against the Turks and managed to create an independent state. He signed a peace agreement with the Turks in Skopje in 1463. But he broke the agreement with them and expelled them from all the Albanian territories. After his death in 1468 those territories again fell under Turk occupation. And that lasted for five centuries.

"You might ask why I need to tell you all about Albanian history. I, as an ethnic Albanian, have a different history than Slavic Macedonians even though we live in the same place. We, as Albanians, have fought for our rights and our independence for centuries. The Ottoman Empire claimed Albanians were Turks. The people of Serbia, Montenegro, and Greece launched prejudice against us.

"Around 1878 Albanians wanted to have their own land and they wanted to be recognized as a nation. When the Turks were driven from our land, the borders were redrawn arbitrarily. Many ethnic Albanians were no longer living within the boundaries of the Albanian nation. Unfortunately, this has caused problems for my people.

"If I talk about the history of Macedonia and I don't tell you the Albanian perspective, then you are missing a big part of the story. We are part of that region, just like any of the other people. The Albanian history must be understood or we will never resolve the situation and never live in peace.

"My own story begins with my mother's parents, my grandparents. My grandmother comes from a very famous Turkish family, very high status. She was only fourteen when she married my grandfather, who was a poor Albanian. Her parents, you can imagine, were very much against the relationship so my grandparents eloped. My grandfather worked in a factory but my grandmother's family never accepted him. The two of them had a true love.

"The Muslim religion was very much a part of their lives. They went to the mosque every day. In the early part of the century, they had no problems practicing their religion. There were mosques in cities and villages across Macedonia. My grandmother, or 'Aga,' as I call her, prayed five times a day. She is still alive and it is so much a part of my life to see her stand up, walk to the window and pray. About five or ten minutes each time. Aga never misses her prayers. My grandfather followed the tradition in many ways. He was the head of the household, tough, but very respected. Everyone was afraid of him; he had big power. It had nothing to do with money because he was a very poor brick laborer and worked about 15 hours a day, just to get enough bread for the family.

"My grandmother wanted to raise their six children as Turks, which was okay with my grandfather. But it didn't work out that way. My mother became an Albanian, the only Albanian in her family. The rest of her siblings are Turkish; they speak Turkish and follow Turkish customs, but not my mother," Herbi said in a matter of fact tone.

"How did that happen?" I asked.

Herbi explained. "My mother was the oldest child in the family. When she was seven, she started school. But since my grandma worked endless hours inside the house, she didn't have time to take my mother to school to register her. My mother accidentally walked into the wrong classroom, and sat down. When she finished the first year, she brought home the diploma. My grandma was shocked. She recognized it was not Turkish letters. She asked my mother, 'What is this?' and my mother said, 'I am going to an Albanian class.' By the time my grandmother realized this mistake my mother was settled into a routine and doing very well and the teacher didn't want to let her go. She convinced my grandma to leave her where she started because if she went into the Turkish class she would have all sorts of troubles. So today she is Albanian, and so am I. Just because my mother walked into the wrong classroom."

"Then your mother married an Albanian?" I asked.

"Yes—a poor man. He, my father, was born in a village, Cauzhaney, close to the second largest city, Bitola. He was a teacher in an Albanian high school and my mother was studying at the same school. They fell in love and married. My parents consider themselves ethnic Albanian even though my mother has Turkish blood. They have lived much of their lives in poverty. One loaf of bread and water was often dinner. My father was the first in his family to be educated. My aunts and uncles had no schooling at all.

"We lived in Skopje because that's where my father got a job. When I was very young, my grandma and my aunt took care of me while my mother went to work. I was probably around five. My mom and I would get on the bus early in the morning; I held her hand tight because the buses were crowded. All I could see were people's legs; that's how short I was. When we passed through the area where my grandma lived, my aunt would be waiting for me. When the door opened, my mom passed me to my aunt and I went to my grandma's house.

"I spent a lot of time with my grandmother while I was growing up. I know that she is an ordinary Muslim wife, but to me she is exceptional. She is respected, as all the elderly are, by her children and grandchildren. I often picture her right after Ramadan, the Muslim fast that lasts for one month. This was and still is our tradition. When the fast ends, all the families get together. The first night after, we all go to my grand-mother's. Imagine her sitting in the corner of the room, the head of four generations. She has her sons and daughters, who have their sons and daughters, who have theirs. She is the grand-grandma. But even though there are so many grandchildren, since I am the first, we have a special relationship. I joke with her. I can make her laugh. Everyone else treats her with such serious respect, but I can just make her happy.

"In the early '70s I was in primary school. It was during Josip Brož Tito's regime. Tito had a social consciousness and believed in unifying all the peoples of Yugoslavia not only by honoring the rights of the citizens of each republic but also by creating a national Yugoslavian identity. During my childhood there was interaction and cooperation of ethnic groups in almost every facet of life. At weddings my family combined Turkish dances with Albanian classical music. Intermarriage was common, like in my family, with estimates of two million intermarriages in a population of almost 22 million. I made many friends from all parts of Yugoslavia while serving in the army. My family vacationed in the same resorts as everyone else across the country. We watched the same TV stations and heard the same news. There was one common language in the whole of Yugoslavia — Serbo-Croatian, even though we spoke Albanian at home.

"I always lived in the same neighborhood, in a Macedonian district, which was a humanitarian project, developed with the help of the Russians after the Skopje earthquake in 1963. There were several apartments facing each other. Not fancy, but who needs fancy? They were of a Communist style, with four floors made of concrete block. A big garden right in the middle of the apartments provided us with room to play. No streets, so we could bicycle, play ball, and our parents didn't fear the traffic. I played with Macedonian kids all the time and we all liked each other. I guess that I am different in that respect from many other ethnic Albanians who weren't surrounded by Macedonians.

"For four years my parents sent me to a mixed Albanian and Macedonian school which was one hour away by bus. But it was too hard to get there so they decided to place me in the school 100 meters distance from our flat, even though the teaching language was only in Macedonian. They just wanted me to be educated no matter what the language was. I could walk to school and not have to take public transportation. I had a lot of friends and spoke the Macedonian language quite well. But it was street Macedonian which was different from the terminology I had to use in the school. You know street talk, I am sure you have it, one word used in the streets while the other in the school.

"I put a lot of effort to be a good student but it was difficult because of the language. An example for you; one teacher asked me a question which according to me the information did not exist in the book. But that was not the case, because the textbook only used other terminology. I arrived at home and I complained to my parents about what happened. We found out that the question was in the book but with the other terminology used, and unfortunately I didn't know it. It was frustrating for me because I knew the subject but just because of different terminology I received an F."

"But usually my grades were good. I remember as a young child one particular memory. You know how one thing can stand out. Well, this one does for me. When my grades were good, my parents would take my friends and me out for a special lunch. Usually at the end of the school year, so once a year."

I asked, "To a restaurant?"

"I wouldn't say a restaurant. That didn't happen. It sounds funny because we would go on an outing and eat kebabs. They are made on a stick. We would picnic and my mom would give me as many kebabs as I wanted. It was a treat. It wasn't that kebabs cost so much, but my parents made it seem like this was an extraordinary occasion. They convinced me and I believed it. Once they bought me a new bicycle but usually for good grades, it was kebabs.

"But anyhow, I graduated from primary school and my parents decided I should go to a school that specialized in electronics. That would be a good career for me. They thought that way I could always get work.

Since the only secondary school in Albanian was for general studies, I attended an electro-technical secondary school in the Macedonian language. I had no choice because the only other school in the Albanian language was in Kosovo, and for that we needed a lot of money. I would have had to rent an apartment and get support from my parents and with their salaries as teachers, we couldn't afford that. I was the only Albanian out of 500 students. I had to study twice as hard as the Macedonians to receive the same grades. But I have to mention that the teachers and the students really accepted me very well, I had no problems at all in the secondary school.

"I was happy. My life was representative of most kids, a little unusual for Albanians because my mom did not educate us in the traditional Albanian way. If you have a son and a daughter, then the son is like the king in the house and the women serve the males. This was not permitted with my sister, Lindita, and me. If I got into a fight with her, my mom would defend Lindita, if she was right. My father also maintained our equality. They both said that we were equal. On the other hand, my mom taught Lindita how to cook and take care of the house. So some of what she did was traditional."

"Is it part of Albanian culture that the male is so valued, or is it part of the Muslim religion?" I asked.

"Both," Herbi answered. "Religion plays a part in our lives but it is more cultural than spiritual. It's interesting how important it is to have a male. Just four years ago my wife was due to deliver our first child and she shared a room in the hospital with another lady, an Albanian. The lady said to my wife, 'I hope my child is not a girl because if it is, I can't go home. I have six daughters and if this one is also a girl, my husband is going to kill me.' She was serious," Herbi said.

"I assume that would never occur in your family?" I asked.

Herbi answered, "No, maybe because my family is not religious and we are different from many other ethnic Albanians in that sense; we'd never play favorites on the sex of a child."

"Were you ever afraid of the Communist system?" I asked.

Herbi replied, "As a teenager. I had the fear that I might say something wrong and end up in jail, or get in some kind of trouble. So I didn't say anything. It just wasn't a big deal. If I didn't have a Coke to drink I never made problems. We had parties at houses. Drugs did not exist and life was not complicated. We may not have had what you call freedom of speech but is it always a good thing? Imagine that you go to a 76ers basketball game and you sit down to enjoy the game and you hear people shouting racist remarks, 'You dirty Jew,' and no one stops them. Today we hear people shouting all kinds of derogatory statements against Albanians in public places and Albanians shouting back at Macedonians. It's awful. Freedom of speech today is misunderstood. It results in violence. We were happy under Tito's regime. Then, there were no racist remarks or ethnic tension.

"To us Tito had a certain, what do you call it, *charisma*. To me, unlike some of the Communist dictators in other countries, he put our welfare ahead of the 'line.' Or you might say he combined it to produce the best situation for all of us. It allowed us a decent life and the opportunity to live well. And we were all Yugoslavians. I, as an Albanian, had more rights than I do in Macedonia today. We were not second-class citizens. We had our university, our high schools, everything. As citizens we had the same rights as the people from Slovenia or from Croatia. Co-existence was on a high level. Tito promoted brotherhood and unity. And we were economically powerful. My citizenship gave me status. I had official documents that permitted travel to any of the other republics. My passport was recognized worldwide due to the good relations that Tito had with almost the entire world. Tito asserted Yugoslavia's national interests in opposition to Soviet rule and my family lived in peace and relative prosperity. What could be wrong with that?"

Herbi focused on the positive of his youth, but I asked about the growing nationalistic opposition. "I read that Slobodan Milošević from Serbia made nationalistic remarks in the '70s, that he was a regular on TV, declaring that the Serbs had been unfairly treated, especially in Kosovo. Didn't he speak to large crowds on the streets in Belgrade about human rights for the Serbs and say that the Albanians denied the Serbs the right to live on their own land?"

"Yes," said Herbi. "My father recognized that nationalism was creeping into our lives and was slowly challenging the socialist ideology. He talked about it at the kitchen table.

"In 1975 my parents began to fear for our future. I remember overhearing their conversations as they talked with neighbors and friends about the situation when we sat in cafés. I thought, was it a Pandora's Box — problems that had already existed but were now out in the open? Was it the fault of power driven politicians? Or were ordinary citizens demanding their rights? No one had answers. One thing was certain — the political status quo was changing," Herbi said.

"It was around the time of Tito's death, in 1980, that my parents really began to notice definite changes. The economy began to go down hill and the political climate was tense. The cost of food was rising and tension was mounting among the different ethnic groups. As a minority ethnic group, we stood to suffer the most."

"When Tito died in 1980, what happened to you?" I asked.

"I wasn't hurt by the nationalistic feelings at that time. I only heard my parents talking. In 1981 I joined a group called the 'Working Action.' The 'Working Action' was part of the organized youth life but it was very difficult to get a placement in the organization. Imagine that from my town, Skopje, which had around 600,000 inhabitants, only 15 youth were selected to go on this working action. I felt special."

"Is it like the Communist Pioneers?" I asked.

"No," Herbi answered emphatically. "The Pioneers was a youth organization everyone joined. The 'Working Action' was organized to do important work in the country, like building dams, streets, roads, and railroads. It was very powerful to work in this organization. It lasted 30 days, during the summer. I mingled with 500 youth from all around Yugoslavia. We slept in barracks. After breakfast we did the physical labor, up until early afternoon. We were then brought back for lunch and afterwards we played soccer, chess, watched cinemas, and they even gave us training like driving, painting, and riding horses. A lot of new friendships, relations and even marriages happened during that time. I was once sent to the capital of Croatia, Zagreb, to work in this working action group called "Sava 81" named after the second largest river in Yugoslavia. Imagine, I was only 14 and I was 600 miles away from home, but had nothing to worry about because safety and friendship were on an extraordinary level. Now the youth do not have such opportunities. So for me I wasn't troubled like my parents were.

"You know I was inclined to believe that life would continue the same as always. When you live in good conditions, you don't think it could be otherwise. I was comfortable. Then things changed for me. I was getting older and I realized that nationalism did exist. Especially when it affected me.

"I was at the university by this time and one teacher — I don't want to name her — asked me my name. I told her. Then she asked what nationality I was. I said I am an Albanian and she very simply told me that I would never pass my exam. She was an angry woman. I never did pass and I had to leave the school. I did not lose my motivation though.

Maybe because I had such support from my parents. They accept me totally, just as I am. That was very important to me. So I didn't give up that easily. I waited for one year, and then I went to another school. That teacher frustrated me, but she didn't stop me."

"You just accepted the situation?" I asked.

"Yes. Albanian teenagers don't rebel. It is very rare. I respect my parents. They told me to go to another school so I did. They always gave me the opportunity to discuss my situation with them. My mom, she just had a way how to convince me."

"How did she do that?"

"She's educated and thinks things through logically. She has two college degrees, one in the Albanian language, and the other in teaching. When the Communists came into power, they made education accessible to men and women. My mom also thanks the Communist system.

"After I started at the second university I took a break from school. I went into the Yugoslavian Army, and then went out of the country for three years, to Germany, Switzerland and Greece. I worked there, doing mostly labor work. After Tito died our economy began going down. It was a difficult period. The average income was $1,000 a year. So I went out of the country to get additional money. After I came back home I went back to the university but conditions, at least nationally, were getting worse. My days at school were filled with apprehension. You say I am a practical man. I had to let go of my emotions. They could otherwise drive me mad. Nationalism was growing, really spreading quickly."

"How?" I asked.

"There was a professor at the new university who was a nationalist, a Macedonian nationalist. He was against Albanians and he expressed this hatred to me. Fortunately he appreciated my knowledge. So it was a different story than the last school. This professor gave me the highest grades during the exams. He would sit with me and tell me how he disliked my people. He was really an OK guy because he didn't take his hatred out on me personally. He told me that he appreciated my knowledge. I got the highest grades concerning my knowledge about the subject, but he always asked me, 'Why don't you leave Macedonia and go live in Albania? You have your own country.'"

As we talked, Darko walked downstairs, sleepy-eyed but smiling. "I feel like I am living in a dream world. I haven't been this relaxed in years."

If I had only heard Herbi's story I would have viewed most Slavic Macedonians as discriminatory, but when Darko walked into the room

I realized that the story isn't that simple. I knew his version would be quite different. All of a sudden it seemed remarkably complicated.

Herbi hesitated for a moment. "Darko is a great man. Full of knowledge. He knows my stories are true, and it is hard for him to hear how difficult it is for Albanians. But with all his wisdom, he doesn't have answers. Except to teach children that we can co-exist."

"That's a start," I said, "but it's so hard to understand."

Herbi replied, "It's not so hard when you are discriminated against, treated as a second-class citizen. What's so hard to understand?"

"It sounds complicated," I said. Darko walked out of the room. I knew Herbi and Darko would not end up fighting with one another but I also realized that some of their differences were irreconcilable. "Should we continue the story at this point? I asked.

"I would like to finish my story," Herbi replied. Darko came from the kitchen and sat next to me on the couch. Herbi continued. "By the early nineties conditions had changed dramatically. On June 25, 1991, the parliament of the Republic of Croatia proclaimed independence. That same day, the Republic of Slovenia declared its sovereignty. The other Yugoslav Republics also expressed a desire for independence from Belgrade. In this climate of rapid change, Serbians, Croatians, and Muslims disagreed on policies for their regions. Nationalism and ethnic conflicts grew and the war between Croatia and Serbia, which also involved Bosnia-Herzegovina, began in 1992. The Bosnian War placed one friend against another, a Muslim husband against his Serb wife. Resistance movements spread across the different regions.

"By the end of 1992, Macedonia fulfilled the European Community's requirements by forming a cabinet composed of one Turk, five Albanians and the balance Macedonians. We were ready to become independent, but problems with Greece over the name Macedonia blocked acceptance by the United Nations. The Greeks claimed that the name Macedonia was of Greek origin. It wasn't until early in 1993 that this conflict was resolved and Macedonia was admitted to the UN under the name 'The Former Yugoslav Republic of Macedonia.'"

"I got married on April 26, 1995. I now lived in a new country. I married Seleste (we call her Bona), my childhood sweetheart. We met when she was fourteen and she is 24 now. I am ten years older than she is. We weren't romantically involved until she was 16. We had a huge wedding. I didn't want one, but that is the custom and I had no choice. In fact, I begged her not to make me have a huge wedding, but she said it was important and part of our tradition. What bride doesn't love to be showered with romance and gifts? It is our custom for the man to pay for the wedding and for it to be a big celebration. I had to buy all of her clothes and all the clothes for her entire family for every party and there were plenty of them. The entire ordeal lasted three days. I had to borrow large sums of money to cover the costs. I am still in debt."

"Did you borrow from a bank?"

"No. Ethnic Albanians don't do that! My uncles gave me a loan. We also had to settle on another issue, one that is cultural too. It's a tradition that when you get married a couple of males from each family get together and decide upon an amount the groom has to pay to the bride in case of divorce. This is a safety measure for the women because it is believed that she will have more difficulties in case they divorce. This tradition started a long time ago when the women were not working so they couldn't support themselves. In the Muslim culture usually the children remain with the father when there is a divorce. So there is an agreed upon amount, in gold, given to a divorced woman so she can support herself. Usually when the wedding takes place the gold is given to the bride and it remains with her. The amount of the gold varies but it can go up to even 10,000 U.S. dollars."

"Don't the courts have anything to say about custody of the children or divorce proceedings?" I asked.

"No. It is our Albanian custom for the relatives to settle the accounts, the male relatives, of course. One amount of money that the husband pays to the wife if he leaves her, and a different amount for the woman if she leaves the man. Usually it is the man who leaves the woman.

"Albanians do not register their children when they are born and even marriages are not registered. Therefore there is no legal action towards the husband or a wife. In the Albanian tradition one of the most important things is trust. We say 'Besa, besë' which in translation will mean when I say something I stand behind it. If I say that I will do it, there is no doubt that I will, especially if it is a promise. Within the Albanian community a promise is something that is stronger than any legal document, because if the person doesn't keep his promises then he will be abandoned by the entire community and his life will become very difficult, and isolated. So this contract with the men in the family is sacred. Unfortunately, that is changing with this modern way of living. For me this tradition should continue forever. When I give a promise for something I will do it no matter how much effort it takes. Only when I am dead I would not be able to fulfill what I have promised. The older generations are still following this."

"Tell me more about the wedding," Darko asked. He seemed fascinated with Herbi's traditions.

"It was extraordinary. The day of the wedding, I borrowed a black Mercedes from my cousin. My uncles and cousins came to my house in eight vehicles, all decorated, and they followed me to Bona's house. I picked her up. I was feeling mature so I wasn't nervous. We drove, in a caravan, some ten miles back until we reached my home. My father greeted us and brought us up to the door where my mother was waiting for Bona. It is a special ceremony. My mother had a plate with honey on it. Bona took the honey and touched it to the door. She also gave honey to my mother and my mother gave some to her. They used their fingers. They tasted the honey and it is believed that Bona is entering the house and that everything will be sweet. Yes, everything will be nice and perfect. Then we went back to Bona's house, with all the cars following us, and there were many people there. Everyone was celebrating and dancing but Bona had to be very serious. That's part of the custom. It was not a comfortable situation for her, but it wasn't for long.

"About an hour later everyone left to go to a restaurant where we had the wedding party, except for Bona and me. It was a custom again. We stayed at her home alone for about two hours and then we went to the restaurant. When we entered everyone applauded us and we all drank champagne and danced the tango. Almost every guest gave something to Bona. Often it was gold, which again is a custom. A golden ring, a golden nickel, money, whatever. After the party we went to my home. My mother and mother-in-law had prepared our room. We stayed in the room until the next morning. The next day we went to Greece on our honeymoon. Nine months later we had a baby, Selesta."

"And you settled into married life," I said with a smile. "Where were you working?"

"The Macedonian Center for International Cooperation. I was lucky to have such a job at the time. It was a good salary and I got twice as much money as my mom, which made her happy," Herbi said. "Susan, let me tell you about the job, but first you must understand something about Macedonia. It is an agricultural country. For several years there had been little rain and there was a problem with buying seeds so people were hungry. This organization was going into the farming communities, house to house, and checking on the people and their welfare."

"We would deliver seeds and fertilizers, things like that to the families. We did that for 2,500 families. We had 500,000 deutsche marks to spend. It was a massive effort funded by the Dutch, from Holland, to help our people. The project was good. First we started with the seeds and fertilizers, and then we went to villages to see the conditions and talk with the people. We wanted to know what services they needed and based upon that information we developed social programs. We gave the people in the villages money for their survival but then we realized that their water supply was in need of repair so we built a system to help them get water. This job gave me international experience.

"I liked the work but I was the only Albanian working there. There were 20 Macedonians employed with me and I didn't get along with some of them. They didn't treat me right. The director was great and fair to me; it was the other people. It was a USAID funded project of the World Council of Credit Unions, which was trying to establish credit unions in Macedonia. I often felt isolated and needed to create a stable position that would provide security for my family, so I looked for a job as an interpreter. Interpreters were in high demand, especially those like me 'cause I was fluent in Albanian, Turkish, Macedonian and English.

"I was very lucky. Someone from the International Red Cross heard about my skills, knowing all the languages I know, and called me to come for an interview. You can see why I got so excited. It was the autumn of 1998 and I got the job! I was now an employee of the International Red Cross and they told me to go to a workshop at Lake Ohrid, three hours from Skopje, and observe a man named Darko Jordanov. I entered Darko's workshop. I watched him and afterwards walked up to him and said, 'I want to work with you. This is my life's calling.'

"That's when we became friends; good friends, right, Darko?" Herbi said.

Darko answered, "We talked and talked for hours about our families, our cultures, our lives. Then we thought of the idea of doing a workshop together. One month later we began the workshop called 'Coexistence; A Coming Together of Cultures.' We held them every weekend in a small hotel at Lake Ohrid for students and teachers from different ethnic groups."

Herbi continued, "We built our program on acceptance and tolerance; never denying our differences but valuing them and at the same time, recognizing their similarities. We modeled healthy interpersonal behavior for students and teachers."

Since 1999 Darko and Herbi have given three-day workshops for students and teachers across Macedonia. Through different activities the ethnic Albanians, Turks, Serbs and Macedonians learn about each others' cultures. Herbi said, "We laugh together, party together and yes, even cry together. Our workshops must include different cultures because we believe that we are teaching students to value diversity. We both have our traditions as do the students who attend the workshops, but we have learned to co-exist. That is our message. We ask the group, 'Do people from different ethnic backgrounds have to like each other?' We don't give them the answer. That is something that the group decides — we do not impose our views.

"And that's where I am today. A father of two wonderful children — Selesta, who is almost four years old, and Ammar, our boy, who will be two. Being a father, that is the most important thing in my life. Professionally, I hope that Darko and I can work together and make some transformation in our country. I want us to live together, and agree on certain things — not wait until 200,000 people die and then sit down at the negotiation table." Darko nodded in agreement.

"I would say in my life that the connection with Darko and me — the cooperation is magnificent. Lots of people are amazed and ask 'how do we function?' We are a perfect team. For many things we have made the same decisions. We are almost connected telepathically. Darko, you are a very good person, very good teacher. I don't have any negative words for you," Herbi said to Darko.

Then Herbi turned toward me and said, "We have been very open to one another. We don't hide issues or say something about each other behind the other person's back. If I don't like something he does, I tell him directly. I think Darko and I are an example of how we can live together in our country. We are a model of how two people can function in our country. Sometimes I feel like I am a messenger for the Albanian population. I think that if a lot of people existed like Darko and me in Macedonia, we as a country could find a way to live together. We always find a solution when we have difficulties together.

"Darko and I work together to try to change the course of our history. We tell the story of Indiana Jones when he was hanging from the rope. If the rope is cut he will fall down and die; yet someone from the top is shooting at him, so if he doesn't jump, then he will also die. So what does he do? He has to wait. That is our motto. You know, when we are facing problems, the first thing we do is *take a deep breath and wait*. We don't make a hasty decision. Then we talk. Yes, we are an example how this country should function. If the people worked together like Darko and me, then progress would be made. We don't always agree, but we always find resolution. Yes, we make it work."

DARKO'S STORY

We sat outside on the deck of my house. It was quiet except for the chirping of the birds. The escalation of the Macedonian conflict didn't seem possible. It was an unusually warm day for April. We saw the small buds appearing on the trees, and the grass starting to have that certain look and smell of springtime. The colors of nature were reawakening, and the mountain behind our home no longer had that skeletal look of winter. We sipped espresso and Darko began.

"The situation in Macedonia is very complicated. In the past Macedonia was inhabited by many different ethnic groups. The most famous and glorious was when King Fillip ruled ancient Macedonia. His first war was against the Greeks and he conquered them. The Greek philosopher Demosthenes publicly called King Fillip 'Philippics,' a name that means that he was a non–Greek barbarian. King Fillip's son and heir, Alexander the Great, conquered half of the world and made an attempt to create a common culture. He tried to embrace east (Persia) and west (Greece). He was an admirer of Greek culture; Aristotle was his teacher.

"After the fall of Alexander's state, the Macedonian provinces fell under the Roman Empire, which split in two. The east part, Byzantium, governed the territory where there was a great influx of Slavic tribes in the sixth century. These Slavs created their own states and were in almost constant war with the Byzantium Empire. The kingdom of Samuil was the strongest of the tribes but Samuil was defeated at the end of 10th century. In the 14th century the Turkish Ottoman Empire conquered the entire Balkan Peninsula and kept parts of it until just 100 years ago.

"That brings me to the story of my ancestors," Darko said, adjusting the umbrella to keep the morning sun from his eyes. We had bought baklava, a sweet Turkish pastry from a neighborhood café, and were drinking our third espresso, promising that this one would be our last.

"It was at the beginning of the century. The Ottoman Empire ruled Macedonia. They imposed tight political and military controls and forced Islam on many of the people. Even though the Ottomans had ruled for

years, many of the Macedonians managed to preserve
their language, religion, and
tradition. It was the time of
my great-grandparents. They
were Macedonian by nationality and Orthodox by confession. My great-grandfather
was getting married in the
Orthodox Church. During
the wedding ceremony a very
well known Turkish aristocrat walked into the service.
He was asked to leave his
weapons outside and was
warned to be decent and not
crude, but he got drunk and
started to touch and disturb
the female guests at the wedding, which was considered
a great insult. He had a reputation as a womanizer and
had often started trouble and
the guests could not tolerate
him. Someone at the wed-
ding killed him; actually he
was decapitated.

Andrej, Darko, Maja and Ivan Jordanov

"Three days later two of my relatives realized that the authorities
were after them. They were also accusing my great-grandfather, the
groom, of the crime. The two relatives ran away and ended up living in
the United States. But my great-grandfather, the groom, wasn't as lucky.
He was imprisoned for several years. When he finally came home nobody
recognized him. He died silently soon after that. His bride, my great-
grandmother, lived a long time and died in the 1960s. She told my parents the story over and over again. And I must admit that she never
omitted the fact that the Turkish aristocrat who was killed was not only
violent but also very handsome. It is quite interesting that today Herbi
is my best friend and his mother is Turkish.

"My grandparents were wonderful but their story is not as colorful as that of my great-grandparents. They lived a simple life, working hard and caring for their family. My mother's father went to school to become a pilot but he was wounded on the ground at the beginning of World War II when Hitler bombed Yugoslavia. He spent two years recovering and never flew again. My grandparents were raising their family after the war, in 1948, when Tito declared an independent Macedonian Republic of Yugoslavia. It was a time of transition and their life was difficult. They, of course, struggled along with everyone else. Four families lived in my grandparents' apartment, so they had to share facilities like toilets and the kitchen. But recovering from war is never easy.

"Now about my parents. My mother and father are almost the same age. They are both Macedonian by nationality and Orthodox by confession. They were born during the Second World War in two small towns in central Macedonia; both towns were occupied by the Bulgarians (who sided with the Nazis). All of my ancestors are Orthodox and Macedonian, on both sides of the family. My father was the youngest of five children and my mother was the oldest of three. My parents met in high school and fell in love immediately. They were each other's first love.

"Before they married they never quarreled but after the wedding they started to argue and have never stopped. I believe it is because they have totally different views on the role of spouses. Traditionally in our culture, the father is the dominant authority in the house. But things changed during Communism. Women gained equal status under the Tito regime and that meant that they were equal politically and socially. Actually, in business, the women played a bigger role than the men.

"My parents had difficulties during those early marriage years because women were expected to maintain their traditional duties in the family. So cooking, cleaning and educating the children were their responsibilities, and they had to be attractive and to remain beautiful and mysterious. I don't believe that my mother was happy with all that responsibility. She was always exhausted and I think that brought a lot of conflict for my parents. And probably my father wanted the traditional role returned. Even though they fought, they loved and depended on one another.

"I was born in 1963. My brother was born five years later. I remember well the tension in our home when I was a young child. Sometimes it was hard for me to deal with because it hurt my mom. My grandmother, my father's mother, moved in with us. My father never really asked my

mother if it was okay. She just moved in. It burdened my parents' relationship. There was somebody sleeping in every room. My parents slept
in the bedroom, me and my brother in the second room, which was also
the living room, and my grandmother in the kitchen. My parents' room
was also the working space, like for ironing, and sewing. So we were
overcrowded.

"My grandmother really created anxiety in my parent's marriage.
And she wasn't close to my brother or me because we were close to my
mother and I suspect that she was jealous of our relationship. She was
never open with me."

"What was her problem?"

"I think that my grandmother didn't like that my mother was smarter
than my father. My mother graduated from university but my father
didn't. Because she had a degree, she earned more money. It wasn't twice
as much, but there was definitely more status. She is the intellect. I take
after her. She reads a lot. My father despises books, something I can't
understand. My mom would buy them and then have to hide the books
so he wouldn't see them. He didn't like her spending money on them."

"I had a similar experience growing up," I said. "My father's sister,
my aunt, came and lived with us when I was very small. My father didn't
give my mother a choice and it was an awful situation. It too made the
relationship with my parents quite difficult."

Darko continued, "So you understand how hard it is to have someone who isn't wanted by everyone in the family living with you. But one
thing was fortunate for me. I like old people very much. When I was
young, I loved to spend time with the elderly and talk with them. They
also wanted my company because I was peaceful with them. So I spent
a lot of time with my grandmother. But she was always distant to me. I
had to spend time with her when I was at home because there was no
where to go, except the toilet, to get away from everyone. Did you spend
time with your aunt?"

"As little as possible," I replied. "So that is where our stories differ."

Darko went on, "I also loved to read so I could always get myself
lost in a story. Sounds strange but I would go into the toilet, open my
book, and escape. That was the one room where I could have peace. And
I would read there for as long as I could, until someone would start banging loudly on the door.

"In high school I bought the book *For Whom the Bell Tolls* by Ernest
Hemingway and I devoured it. It influenced me a lot. Do you remember

that book? It was three days in the life of an American professor who was fighting on the side of the Republicans in the Spanish Civil War. He fell in love with a beautiful Spanish girl. And his love had no bounds. He was on the top of life. To feel that way really impressed me. I have never forgotten that story. I have felt that way only two times in my life. Both of them with my wife."

Darko continued, "Anyhow, I think I am too much philosophizing."

"Keep going," I said, intrigued by his thinking.

"My sensitivity makes my life hard. I am so sympathetic. I can sense people's emotions. If somebody is angry, furious, or even trying to hide it, I can feel that from miles away. So I felt the tension in my house. Sometimes it drove me crazy because I couldn't put up a wall and separate myself. Can you understand what I mean?"

"How well I understand what you are saying," I said to Darko. "It can be a gift or a burden, sensing someone's energy. I had an experience when my daughter Madelyn had graduated from college and decided to spend a year working in a Bosnian refugee camp outside of Budapest, Hungary. She developed programs for the refugees in the city of Debrecen. During that year I visited her. The refugees were mostly Muslim, and many had escaped from severe conditions back home. I walked into the camp with Madelyn and after forty-five minutes I was depressed and exhausted. The physical conditions were challenging and the stories heartwrenching. These were now Madelyn's friends and they were wonderful, but I had felt their frustration and their pain. Madelyn, on the other hand, gave them energy. She walked into the camp, made people laugh, and gave them hope and purpose. She had the women making slippers, sweaters, and blankets out of yarn that she brought from Croatia. She has the ability to influence her environment, rather than let it control her."

Darko likened my story to Tolstoy's well-known Russian novel *Ana Karenina*. "The brother of one of the main characters is dying. This brother is married to a very beautiful girl who was portrayed in the novel as being superficial. I mean very superficial. One day her husband goes to visit his dying brother and she insists on accompanying him. When they arrive her husband doesn't know what to say to his dying brother, but the wife, who had seemed so superficial, puts pillows around him, makes him comfortable, and takes care of him. She makes him relaxed and she really helps both of them.

"So my life, and yours, Susan, is like the brother's," he continued, "who wasn't able to be superficial. I am learning by trying to make my sensitivity available when it is helpful. And I try to go beyond myself at other times. During my childhood, I was very sensitive. I could always feel the underlying pressure in our home."

"Did the Communist government influence your family life?" I asked.

Darko answered, "Yes, of course, and in a good way. My brother is five years younger than me and our family was typical of most. Usually couples had two children. People worked, children went to school, and most people spent their holidays abroad or at the seaside, in Greece, Bulgaria, Turkey or Croatia. It was not a complicated life. The entire society seemed optimistic. We communicated with one another in the same language. The Parliament used three official languages: Macedonian, Slovenian, and Serbo-Croatian. My parents did well at the time. It was the early '70s, and there was work for everybody. People owned their own apartments and life was peaceful. No war, and no tension.

"Actually, when we speak now, I can see that there were many signs that things weren't exactly right. My parents would talk about how important connections were and that they had to depend on the will of other people all the time. So if you needed something done you had to be nice to the person. And it had to be the right person. People didn't lose their jobs. No, never. Even if you violated the rules, the government would put you back to work. It didn't matter if you did the job right. And if you did a great job, that was to your disadvantage! Everybody would like to work with you and take advantage of you because you were efficient. It was connections.

"Now, our situation was different than Russia and I presume other Eastern European countries. We have heard that it was far worse there. I know it didn't matter what your education was there; you made the same amount of money. A secretary and a doctor were paid the same amount, even a janitor and a doctor. But not in Macedonia. A doctor was paid two times the salary of a laborer. The government paid for all schooling but to get into school, just like everything else, it was based on who you knew not what you knew.

"Public services were a pain in the neck. If the elevator broke down in your building, which happened more often than not, you had to wait to get it fixed. And you waited a very long time. The electricians just wouldn't come. Why should they? If there had been competition they would have come immediately, but since they got paid whether they worked or not, only those who were very ethical would work.

"Communism never found a way to motivate people to work hard. It appears that people are lazy and inert by default, nature is maybe too strong a word. People used to say, 'Why should I work more when everybody earns the same amount of money?' It was enough for a decent life, but why not just go to work for eight hours, and do nothing, and then go home fresh? And if you wanted to work, people would not respect you for that."

Darko went on, "It happened to me when I was teaching. I used my free time for reading up on the teaching material and one colleague approached me and said, 'Are you going to earn more money because of your reading?' I had to think of a clever answer so I said reading was my hobby and it didn't have anything to do with my teaching. Another time the students had to clean the school playground. All the teachers were drinking coffee when someone realized that I was working with my students. I was helping them design a system to clean the yard. It was almost like a scandal. The teachers mocked me and I even became embarrassed that I was helping the children. And I think now, why shouldn't I help them? I still think that a teacher should not ask his students to bounce and leap if he is not ready to do the same together with them.

"At that time my girlfriend was Maja. Now she is my wife. She helped me when I was frustrated and angry. I met Maja at school when we were 13 years old, but our relationship started when we were both 19. It was a very passionate relationship. We spent most of the time together. We wanted to do everything together. We were afraid of marriage, though, and if it were not that Maja got pregnant with our son Ivan, we wouldn't have had the courage to think about marriage. But Maja's pregnancy added a family complication. My father-in-law took me aside and we had a long talk. He was a famous gynecologist, and he said, 'You are too young to have a child. You both are in school. You haven't finished your studies. You can still live together, but why do you need a child now? It can be resolved. It's still very early in the pregnancy, and I can help you.' It was very tempting to me. Of course he was saying, what do you think, Darko, about Maja getting an abortion? It was a very big pressure on me. But then Maja and I talked and we both agreed that we wanted this child. Later, my father-in-law said that he was just testing me. I guess I passed the test because after that he opened himself up to me. We had a big wedding and I was accepted into her family. And he affected my life very much. He reminds me a lot of Ron — a serious, organized man. But so opposite of me.

"When our son Ivan was born, I think my father-in-law was the happiest of all of us. Maja has one sister, so this was the first male — the one that would continue the lifeline. My relationship with my father-in-law became stronger and stronger. Branko, as we called him, continued to help me in my life. We were so close and he actually was like a bridge between my father and me. I love my father, but when I was a child, I felt that he never really accepted me. I wasn't what he wanted. I was a bit clumsy, and that drove him crazy. He was not patient with me. I couldn't enter his world because I didn't know the password. But through Branko, my relationship with my father changed. I am forever grateful to Branko for so many things."

"I know across Eastern and Central Europe when children get married, they often out of necessity have to move in with one set of parents," I said.

"Maja's parents wanted us to live with them, as did mine, after Ivan was born, but we decided to live separate from them and to continue studying. Most people would have lived with their parents, especially if they had a child. But for us, we were independent. We received our university diplomas; Maja became an agricultural engineer, examining the quality of wheat, and I majored in linguistics. But when socialism ended, life began to change dramatically for us.

"When I grew up, as you can see from what I have said, I had typical problems. But I was happy. I had friends in school. I had a good family. I had what I wanted. What more could I have asked for. Then when Maja and I married and Ivan was born, we felt blessed. And Branko, her father, added to my life. My relationship with my father improved. So life was good. But in 1991 things inside our country really began to change.

"Maja, our son, Ivan, and I went to the Netherlands on vacation in the summer of 1991. Maja's sister lives in Amsterdam and we were planning to stay for the summer. Then the Bosnian War escalated and we couldn't get back home for one year. I had mixed emotions that we couldn't leave Amsterdam. I was thankful because I didn't want to fight against people I had been raised with. I had been in the Yugoslavia Army and had gone to school in Zagreb so I had many friends, and it was unclear whether Macedonia would be part of the war. But I missed my family and friends.

"Imagine — we went to Amsterdam as tourists but we stayed for more than one year with a nondefined status. I matured there and realized how important my home is to me. I got a job as a dishwasher in a fancy French restaurant, actually the place that Maria Callas used to eat when she sang in the city. One day I was leaving work, and I had an experience that changed my way of thinking. I went to buy a loaf of bread. I was queuing in a bakery and chatting with an old lady. I spoke some Dutch. She was nice to me until the moment that I ordered the bread. The kind of bread that I wanted was hard to pronounce. It was a difficult word. She realized that I was a foreigner. She looked insulted and quit any further conversation with me. I felt as an intruder, which I guess I was. I walked out of the shop and the sweat poured down my face. I was stressed and saddened and I missed home. But the story doesn't end there.

"I stopped in a nearby bar where there was a huge video screen with a basketball match going on. I knew the players from both teams. The ones in the yellow I recognized; Kukoc, Radja and the rest. I supported them so many times. But the abbreviation under their names was no longer Yugoslavian but Croatian. I was stunned. Croatia was now a country. I was not supposed to be on their side anymore. This scene hit me so hard and unexpectedly I simply could not avoid the pain. So I admit I cried (and in my culture boys don't cry) when I realized that there is nothing left from the country I was born in. I felt so alone, but I wasn't ashamed that I cried. That was the moment that I finally understood the scene from Homer's *Iliad* when Hector explains to his crying wife that the reason he is fighting a war is because he knows that a family does not really exist without a state. So I knew what I wanted, and that was to be back in Skopje, together with my family.

"My wife understood how I felt, so we left for home several weeks later. It is funny to think that I left home with a Yugoslavian passport and came back and Yugoslavia wasn't my country any longer. But anyhow, our friends and relatives were astonished that we decided to come back when everyone else was trying to leave. But our answer was, '*Everybody should try to live as a foreigner at least once in a lifetime.*'

"Our apartment was waiting for us; my father and mother had given us theirs, and bought another for themselves. It is a rather small one-bedroom apartment (52 square meters). I find it cozy. It's the one I grew up in. First I lived in it with my parents, brother and grandmother and now with my wife and my two sons.

"I was an adult but now I was more confused than ever. I could not rely on the news because the information I heard was often not accurate. How could I, when I knew that much of what was said was not true? They would say that democracy was great, yet times were hard. The economy was not reliable and our living conditions were definitely worse than under socialism. It was a world of contradictions.

"Many of my friends were obsessed with the news. They said that they wanted to be informed. One friend, Viktor, said, quite unkindly to me, 'You are a turtle, living inside your shell, afraid to stick your head out.' But I knew a number of times when the news said one thing and I knew another. And the news did not report the whole truth."

A flashback came to me. I described it to Darko. "I remember an incident that happened to me when I was working in Croatia at the beginning of the war. I too felt that the news did not report the whole truth. It was 1991. My colleague Carol Flaherty-Zonis and I went to Zagreb, Croatia, to offer a workshop, sponsored by the Soros Foundation. We flew from New York to Frankfurt, Germany, and from there to Zagreb with UN troops and CNN correspondents. The fighting had begun, but it was 30 miles from Zagreb.

"CNN staff was staying at the Esplanade Hotel, which was not far from our hotel where Carol and I were training sixty participants in health education for four intense days. They were Croats, Serbs, Muslims. It was a successful seminar. We all bonded together and despite the fighting 30 miles away, we had a peaceful and stimulating workshop. One participant had the idea that we should all go to the CNN headquarters at the Esplanade and tell them about our workshop. A human-interest story, she said. People working together. Around twenty of us left our hotel one evening, at 10 P.M., and walked to the hotel. We asked for the lead reporter and told his assistant that we had a great story. A number of reporters came down to the lobby, and took us into an elegant restaurant for coffee and dessert. They asked us to share our information.

"A woman who happened to be Serbian began, 'We want you to film our final day at the health education workshop. Many of us are from different backgrounds and we have been working together, very well. We would like you to give some balance to the stories about the war and the killings. There are other things happening here in Croatia. Please show the world that it is not all black or white. Let the Americans see that we are human, working together to change conditions for our children. There are a lot of good things happening. Let's show something positive.'

"No one bought the idea. 'Where is the sensationalism?' they asked us. We replied, 'It isn't sensational. It is the truth and we are attempting here in Zagreb to maintain normalcy. There are people who continue to work together.' We left frustrated and incensed. CNN showed violent scenes the next day and we all watched the news with disapproval."

Darko nodded as I told him the details. "So the news sometimes doesn't tell all. Yes. I had similar experiences, especially once we returned home from Amsterdam. When we got home the news was different than Maja and I heard while we were in Amsterdam. While we were in the Netherlands, we only received news that said that the 'bloody' Serbs were wrong, 100 percent wrong, and the poor Muslims were deprived of all human rights. I unfortunately confirmed the old wisdom that you need two people to fight. There are at least two sides to each issue and the world is not black and white."

"What were the major differences?" I asked.

Darko responded, "Do you remember a bomb attack on the open market in Sarajevo after which Bosnian Serbs were bombed? Do you know that a group of people had been selected to investigate the event and to find out the truth? This group discovered that it was impossible for the Serbs to have shot the missile. Their position made it impossible. That wasn't reported on the news. Why, I ask? Why does the media only show what they want you to hear? Is there some kind of conspiracy against the truth? Who fired the bomb? We will never know. But CNN and BBC made it appear like it was all the fault of the Serbs. Serbs looked like the monsters. I don't deny that many Serbs have killed, but that isn't the entire story.

"And just like you had the situation with CNN, a similar situation occurred while we were in Amsterdam. The war in Bosnia hadn't started yet at this time. There were clashes in Croatia, those that you knew about when you were in Zagreb. There were a group of about fifty young people, both Serbs and Croats, that were demonstrating good will in the center of Amsterdam. I was there and saw them. But the Dutch media ignored it. Not a single word. From my point of view, the West does not understand us. I do not take sides. But when something bad occurs with the Serbs it is written in all the newspapers. All over the world.

"After my return from Amsterdam I did a lot of soul searching. I thought about the old socialist society and no longer put it in high esteem.

I realized the shortcoming of the Communist system. You can imagine how difficult it was for me to now feel that capitalism can't work; Communism doesn't function well, so where does my country go? To war? No. I, of course, didn't want that. I also saw that the Communists were not exclusive in their efforts to change the reality by using half-truths, one-sided facts and even obvious and shameless lies. I was a high school teacher at the time and I loved teaching but the politics in the country was always on my mind. To be honest with you, there was such propaganda. At least under Communism there was peace, and we were happy, well taken care of and we lived in an organized society. Now the situation was grave. From our side, we heard so many situations where NATO and, I must say, the American views were absolutely wrong. I am so against what NATO does."

"Why?" I asked.

Darko explained, "NATO is ready to cooperate with the devil, the KLA. The KLA, the Albanian rebel organization, was and still is a purely terrorist and racist organization. They have killed and continue to kill people, not only Serbs but Albanians as well. They started ethnic cleansing in Kosovo of the non–Albanian population a long time ago. In the future it will show that the massive exodus of the Albanian population was staged and organized by Milošević and also by the allies. There was nothing in the media about a terrorist attack on Serbians in Kosovo. Nobody reported that. And there were kidnappings and people slaughtered, massacred and burned bodies of Serbian civilians, which was started by the KLA. Two thousand Yugoslavian civilians died in the NATO bombings. Where are the bodies of the 200,000 Albanian civilians who were supposedly massacred by Milošević? Was that real?"

Darko was getting flushed as he continued, "Milošević was not the real dictator. He was placed there. The elections were monitored and approved by the European Union. Milošević did not want to join NATO. It is quite confusing so the ordinary person doesn't understand. It is meant to do that. Now there is an organization in Macedonia, part of the KLA, but called the NLA that is killing Macedonian soldiers and policemen and cleansing Macedonian villagers from the villages where Albanians are the majority. There seems to be a conspiracy against us."

"Give me an example," I asked.

"I read on a CNN Web site, 'Macedonian gunman killed an Albanian activist.' But it was not a Macedonian gunman who killed the man; I researched it. There was an omission in the title of the actual text. It should have said, 'Macedonia: Gunman killed an Albanian activist.' When I looked closely at the situation and I followed the case, it seemed that the man was murdered by the KLA in order to force an elected Albania politician to make the government include the KLA in the negotiations. The author of the article had an Albanian name.

"Another conspiracy," Darko said. "During the Kosovo war your news made it appear that Macedonia wasn't doing enough for the refugees from Kosovo who came across into our country. Do you know that we accepted 350,000 refugees from Kosovo while the U.S. accepted 2,000? And then the U.S. sent some of them to Cuba. For us to take care of an additional 350,000 people when we are so poor is too much. It put a strain on us and made life quite difficult. And then we are called nationalists if we even say that we want to protect our country.

"And then again, the news tells the public often only one side of the story, just like your incident, Susan. A man, about 58 years old, from Skopje was killed when he tried to visit his weekend house, which is about six miles out of Tetovo. There was nothing about that in the papers or on the international news. He wasn't an ethnic Albanian. If he had been, I know the papers would have told the story. The news was distorted when I was in Amsterdam, and it continues today. I don't want violence but I don't want to become a foreigner in my own country.

"Until 1989 we were taught to avoid conflict. Now we live in conflict, which is the exact opposite atmosphere of my youth. I guess part of the Communist ideology was to pretend peace. Everybody must be equal and the same. When I look back on that, I disagree. It is not realistic, even though we were happy. I compare it to a race. My ideal is that everybody starts the race at the same time, but the one who runs the fastest is the winner. In Communism everybody was supposed to reach the end of the race at the same moment. This is absurd to me now. I see that it kills the race. According to me, that is one of the reasons for the death of Communism.

"So there was much confusion in my thinking. I grew up with a socialist or Communist mentality. And life was good. But when 1989 came and I was more mature, I began to see the negative effects of Communism. Then nationalism entered the picture. We all wanted our own culture to dominate our society. It wasn't until I met you, Susan, that I was really able to change my thinking. It was 'Tribes,' yes, the group activity 'Tribes.'"

Just as Darko mentioned "Tribes," Herbi walked onto the patio and, overhearing our conversation, asked, "Darko has described Tribes so many times. Can you tell me your version, please, Susan?"

I began. "My son, Dan, and I were invited (by the Soros Foundation) to offer a mother-son workshop in your country on conflict management, based on the curriculum Dan had written. There were sixty-five participants: four ethnic-Albanians, three Turks, a Serbian woman, and the rest were Macedonians. Most participants positioned themselves by nationality. We sensed the tensions between some of the people.

"On day four of the workshop Dan and I divided the participants into four groups. We asked each group to create its own tribe; to form a government: democratic, socialist, whatever they wanted. They were to think about human rights issues and other aspects of societies.

"After one hour each group presented its tribe to the others. At the end of the fourth presentation Dan, dressed as an 'intergalactic creature,' stormed into the room. 'I have come to end the earth. I will destroy everything because you earthlings do not know how to live together. You fight with one another, and you don't treat each other with respect. You don't deserve to live. But because I am unlike you earthlings and I don't like to kill, I will give you one opportunity to save yourselves — and your planet. *But only one,*' he screamed at the groups. 'Each group must choose one of the four tribes as their own. You must decide on *one tribe only*. I will allow three negotiation sessions.'

"Each group chose one person to represent them. The first negotiation began and the four negotiators began to take ownership of their Tribe. 'Ours is the best. Yours cannot be as good as ours.' They yelled at one another; there was no conclusion. The second negotiation became noisier, with less control. Again each tribe claimed that it was the best. Again, no conclusion and the second round ended with people looking at one another, frustrated and enraged. The third negotiation began. It no longer seemed like a game. People were now irritated with one another.

"Darko had been the negotiator of his group. I rang the bell to begin, and Darko said 'It is most important to get a consensus. Our group is ready to give up our tribe and we will accept any of the others. Life is too precious to us and we don't want to die.' Vanco, the negotiator from group two said, 'We, as well, do not want to die. Yes, we will agree.' The third negotiator also agreed. But Slavica, a woman selected as the negotiator of group four, shook her head and said, 'Our tribe is the best. You must all choose our Tribe.' She said it over and over again.

"The bell rang. Time was up and earth was destroyed. Chaos broke out. Everyone was outraged at Slavica. The game had become reality; an uncontrollable half-hour of fighting before people settled down enough for us to hold a group discussion." Darko nodded at me and I looked at Herbi and said, "Men and women screamed prejudicial remarks, 'Why did you let Slavica become your leader? It is all your fault. Now you've killed us all.' People were blaming one another.

"Dan asked the group, 'If you took such possession of your beliefs in a game, what is it like in real life?' The discussion lasted hours. Slavica kept defending herself. 'Our tribe is better than yours.' Dan and I facilitated the discussion, asking many questions. 'Why do we all believe that our culture is the best? Could you accept another tribe if the world depended on it?' Unless we want to destroy earth, we must begin to change. We must listen to each other. It was the most intense Tribes activity that I had ever done!"

Darko continued, "'Tribes' is so important for us as a country to understand. I didn't understand until then how difficult it is to give up something. There are many cultures in Macedonia trying to live together. I was moved by this experience. I knew that I needed to educate my countrymen so we don't destroy our country.

"'Tribes' changed me and I changed my career, that's how it happened," Darko said. "After attending your workshop I returned to Skopje and thought constantly about how I could best help my country," he continued, again staring at the mountain behind our home. "I began to develop a program that offered similar activities to teachers in Macedonia. I worked with local and international organizations and contacted agencies that were involved in peace initiatives and volunteered my time — because I believed in the work. 'Tribes' was so powerful to me. I received funding from the International Red Cross and formulated a game plan to develop workshops on cultural diversity. And then Herbi walked into my workshop and into my life. Now we are best friends. Yes, 'Tribes' changed my life, and so have you, Herbi.

"I believe that my work, to save Macedonia from war, is just beginning. It is a lifelong task that lies before me. But I want to do it, together with Herbi."

CONCLUSION

Herbi and Darko were ready to go home. It was April 14, 2001. They were leaving the next day. We sat around our kitchen table and talked. Herbi said to Darko, "Although I am Muslim, and, Darko, you are Orthodox, our values are very similar. The Muslim faith places high priority on family. My children are the most important to me. My heart is where my children are. And Darko, you say the same." Darko nodded. "So we put much into our family. I spend a great deal of time and energy making certain that my children become good citizens; well educated. That is so important to me."

Darko nodded and continued, "But there are differences too. Because you are ethnic Albanian you had problems at the university. I didn't have such problems. Since Tito, I suspect you have been torn between being ethnic Albanian and loving our country."

"Yes, I feel that there are other even more pressing problems," Herbi said softly. "Security is zero for my people. I personally pay the lowest rent possible for my apartment which is about $80 a month. There is 40 percent unemployed now in the country, many of them Albanians. I am educated, and have worked with an international organization, but I still live a lower-class lifestyle. I worry about the ethnic Albanians who have been trapped in the battle zone, between the Albanian rebels and the Macedonian army. These are ethnic Albanians, trying to just live their life, and they are caught in a war zone. But my biggest concern is the fate of our future, both for the ethnic Albanians and the Macedonians. There are a number of rebels — they happen to be ethnic Albanians who are causing the conflict, but I am angry that some officials in the Macedonian government, and especially the media, make it appear that it is only Albanians who are creating the problems."

Darko cut in, "Yes, we agree on that, but there are times when we look at a situation in such a different way. Like Kumanovo. I believe that the population of Kumanovo reaches 90 percent Albanian. In 1961 it was 20 percent Albanian."

Herbi responded, "The statistics of Kumanovo found in 1961 were considered for the entire territory of Kumanovo, which included the surrounding villages where the majority of Albanians live. I believe that in the town of Kumanovo there are more Macedonians than Albanians."

Darko disagreed. "That is not so. The number of ethnic Albanians continues to grow and I fear that the country then will turn into an

Albanian majority. The ethnic Albanian insurgents who are attempting to take control in several villages could start a civil war."

Herbi continued, "Yes, I fear a civil war. I am of Albanian nationality with Macedonian citizenship. If you would say I'm a Macedonian citizen that means that I'm Macedonian by nationality, which I'm not. Since Tito, I have not had the same rights as you have had, Darko. Yet this is my land."

Darko didn't let Herbi end there. "But we are free today, Herbi."

"It is true that in some ways we are now free. Freer than we were under the old system," Herbi replied. "Maybe we don't appreciate some of our freedom. How do we know if we live with such fear of war and fear of death? Yet, I am not afraid to die," Herbi continued. "I know if there is war, I will die. I won't be able to kill. How could I kill a Macedonian? Darko, you are Macedonian, and if I don't kill, then either a Macedonian will kill me or an Albanian will. So I either get killed, or kill someone. So I will die." I sensed some contradiction here.

Darko looked at Herbi and said, "Oh, but I am afraid to die. I am too young. I want to see my children grow up. I want to know they are safe. I want to be a grandfather some day and know that my children are okay. I know that I have reached levels of fear that I don't want my children to experience. But in the Balkans, that is the way of life."

"You have no fear, Herbi?" I asked.

Herbi answered, "I am practical. I don't analyze; I just do. I get up, I work, I take care of my children, and I eat with my wife. I live."

"But I cannot be like that," Darko said. "If someone had told me when I was in high school that I would have to live in fear like I do, I wouldn't have understood. I think that Herbi can see both sides, which makes it very difficult for him. Right, Herbi?"

"Yes, but I know you also can see both sides," Herbi answered.

Darko went on, "I remember asking you, Herbi, 'Do you think individual human rights or collective human rights are more important?' And you said without thinking, 'individual.' That is when we became friends.

"You know, living in the Balkans is never easy," Darko said to me. "I was angry when the U.S. bombed Belgrade. How do you expect to understand the mentality of the Balkans when we can't understand our own history?" Darko went on philosophizing and I thought it was best to let him speak. "To talk about history is to talk about things one has never experienced. This in combination with the fact that the very same event is experienced in a different manner by different people. Yet we as the human race have not invented anything better to organize our presence in this world. Remnants from the past, interpreted by more or less educated, more or less well-intentioned, creative historians, philosophers, artists and politicians together with myths, legends, religious beliefs and personal wishes are the body from which we are building our attitudes toward ourselves and others. And that is all. I don't believe in 'objective' history. It is up to each of us to decide what to include in the final version."

He looked at me, his cheeks rosy, his words quick, and the tone of his voice tense. Then he stopped philosophizing. "What right did you Americans have to bomb Belgrade? It was a civil war. Would we enter your war?"

I answered quickly, "The politics that go on in your country, you are right, we do not understand. We, as Americans, don't grasp the complexity. But at least separate me, my family, and the people you have met here in the U.S. that you say you like so much. Don't stereotype all of us, please. Look at us as individuals, not as one people with one voice; just as you want us to see that you and Herbi are individuals."

Darko at that moment softened and said, "Yes, I am sorry. I don't mean to judge you." The three of us looked at each other and laughed. "Oh, how challenging and wonderful life can be!"

On April 15, 2001, Ron and I drove Darko and Herbi to the airport and bade a sad farewell to our dear friends. They were laden with packages, paraphernalia, and mixed emotions. They boarded a U.S. Airways flight to Boston, where they transferred to Swiss Air to fly to Zurich. A mere twenty-eight hours later their plane landed in Skopje.

It has been eight weeks since Darko and Herbi left Harrisburg. The situation gets more explosive each day, although it rarely appears on the news. Local papers say little; *The New York Times* usually has one or two columns, Page A6, the International News. Darko and Herbi wouldn't have come to the U.S. had the conflict escalated as it has since their return. Most of what I hear is directly from them, although I research the latest events on the Internet. Herbi is trying to get his wife and children temporarily out of the country. Darko's connections seem less complicated. Sometimes I feel that life was easier when I didn't know them. How selfish of me to even think that! But these are my friends. When I read in *The New York Times* about the fighting in the streets of Skopje, it is not strangers who flash before me but Darko and Herbi. And I get

Darko Jordanov (left) and Herbi Elmazi (right) and their families at a picnic.

very scared. What impact will these two men and their program have on the future of their beloved Macedonia? On the conflict? On the war? We are all part of history; Darko and Herbi are living their chapter.

Later I received an email from Darko (he always writes for Herbi too).

06/07/2001 4:45:48 A.M. Eastern Daylight Time

> Dear Susan,
>   Herbi, myself and our families are safe for the time being, but the sit-uation is deteriorating daily. Two days ago five soldiers were killed which resulted in violence in the town of Bitola, which is about three hours from here. Three of the soldiers were from that town. Stores owned by Albanians were put on fire. Kumanovo, a town of 120,000, has been left without water, because the terrorists held the water supply for two months.

Yesterday there were shootings in the center of Skopje. Unidentified people in a car with Bulgarian plates shot at the Parliament and Court Building. We don't know who they are. A major problem is the politics. I don't much like our Prime Minister, Ljubco Georgievski. Many Albanians and Macedonians think that he is openly trying to proclaim a state of war. When I listen to people talk in the streets, it seems like a majority of them dislike him as well but it is impossible to organize elections since parts of the territory are occupied so the election wouldn't be valid.

I was invited to participate in a teacher's workshop in Berlin but I had to cancel because I don't want to leave Maja alone. She received a letter from her sister in the Netherlands and she is trying to get a visa, possibly take the kids there, but it is very difficult to get a visa to get out of here. Herbi is trying to get a French visa for his wife and kids through a friend, but that seems even less likely. The two of us don't want to leave but we would feel much better if our families were not here, especially if violence continues in Skopje.

Yesterday a Macedonian student was almost killed; he is in a coma now. An Albanian student stabbed him in the back while the Macedonian student was drinking water at the water fountain. It was the same high school where I taught and where you visited back in 1998 — which seems many lifetimes ago. Both the kids are 16 years old. I know them. The Macedonian was my student. It all seems so futile.

For the first time since I met him Herbi tells me he is afraid. And Maja doesn't sleep at nights. She has been crying asking me what will happen to our kids. Of course I don't know what will happen with us but there have been wars before in the Balkans and some people survive. I promised her that I would try to get us out of here. To be honest with you (and I haven't told this to Maja), my plan is to try to get her and the kids out of here and I will stay. That is my plan. I will send them all the money I will earn here because I don't need much for myself. I cannot leave Skopje and Macedonia, my parents and friends, just like that. I just hope that the fighting will stop, or better yet I will wake up one morning realizing that all this was only a bad dream. (nightmare):):):).

It is a beautiful time of year. I want to feel the happiness of being alive, and I glance over at Andrej, our little baby boy, and I struggle with a sense of hopelessness and powerlessness. I feel that these two powers are pressing me to the ground so I can't turn my eyes to the sky. Sometimes it is so hard to look up. You seem to be at the end of the world, but knowing that you and your family care about us, makes life a little bit easier.

With love and respect,
Darko

On June 22, 2001, Darko emailed an update:

> Situation is as it is — difficult and unpredictable. Maja and the children are in the Netherlands; they have a valid visa until the 4th of August. Herbi took two days off— Friday and Monday. There are rumors that the real total war might start this weekend. This is not the first apocalyptic prediction. My guess is that there will be military actions. About street fighting I don't know. I am working on the English translation of the new manual for the International Red Cross. I am proud of it. Greetings for everybody there. Darko.

Would there be progress in easing tensions and quelling the possibility of civil war? We are left to wonder how and when people like Darko and Herbi will find the peace they long for in the turbulent Balkans.

Epilogue

It is now December 3, 2003. I am finishing this book while sitting on a corner couch in my favorite local café, the St. Thomas Roaster, in Harrisburg, Pennsylvania. It has been almost seventeen years since I first set foot within the borders of Eastern Europe.

Never could I have imagined that I would be an eyewitness to the historic revolutions of this region and become a participant in its subsequent political and economic transformation. In writing this book I wanted my readers to share my friends' lives before and after these changes. When the "curtain" was lifted, they had the opportunity and incentive to develop their full potential. Their enthusiasm was tempered only by the old bureaucracy clinging to its power base, a lack of democratic roots, or a rise of indigenous ethnic differences.

The transition to capitalism has not been achieved within the time period that pre-revolution leaders and intellectuals had predicted. But it takes years to build infrastructure and institutions to support such a transition. Today, despite the obstacles, my friends continue to affect and improve their societies through their vision, motivation, and creativity. Here is a brief update of the achievements of some of the people in the book:

• Dan and Simona's school in Romania has an enrollment of over 500 students. They are building a secondary school that they hope will be a model for all of Eastern Europe. The school's *Happy Kids* foundation organizes yearly fundraising campaigns for children and the elderly with health and economic problems. In 2002 it received an award for the best Romanian fundraising organization.

• Romanian artists Miki and Márta exhibit their works internationally. Although Miki prefers to be at home in front of his easel painting, Márta has recently traveled to Hungary and Western Europe showing her ceramics.

• Marius, who left Romania to attend graduate school at Illinois State University, works at Hewitt Associates in Chicago, Illinois. He is finishing his third master's degree, this one in computer science.

• Rudi is completing work on his Hungarian thesaurus and editing his son's books. Eva is still working on Hungarian environmental and women's issues. She and Rudi also enjoy being grandparents to Fanni's three young children.

• Vera, of the Czech Republic, is now sharing her program with the European Union and recently attended one of their workshops in Greece. Ivan, Vera's husband, plans to retire soon as school principal and write poetry for children.

• Zina has formed an organization dealing with child abuse and neglect, crime, health (HIV-AIDS, drugs, sexual problems), and violence in schools. Her husband, Alfredas, and my husband, Ron, still have their joint venture company, Lekrona. Alfredas continues to expand his own wholesale/retail business called Albana.

• Darko and Herbi continue to teach their conflict management program under the auspices of the International Red Cross. Their program has now spread to Bosnia, Croatia, Montenegro and Yugoslavia. Darko is also a land mine specialist and has spent the last month on special assignment in Iraq.

As for myself, I recently completed revisions to the health education curriculum I wrote ten years ago for the Soros Foundation. It will be distributed to teachers and health professionals in the countries that participated in the program. In a few months, I plan to begin oral histories of friends in Siberia, Albania, Belarus, Kyrgyzstan, and Mongolia so I can document the lives of these friends.

Appendix: Maps

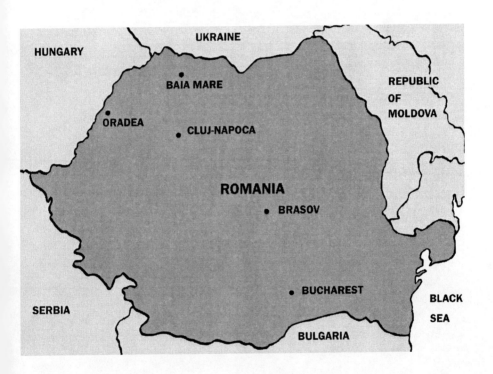

All maps by Katie Rue.

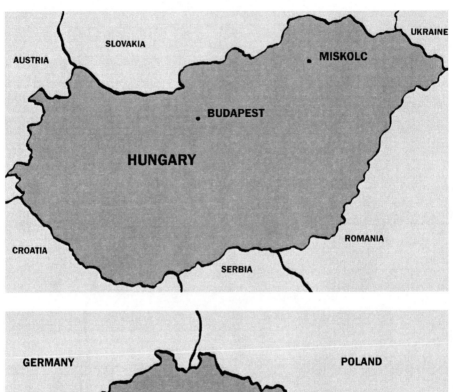

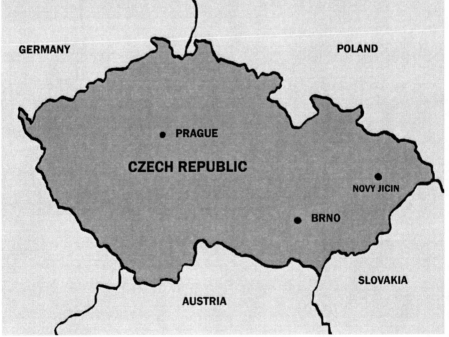

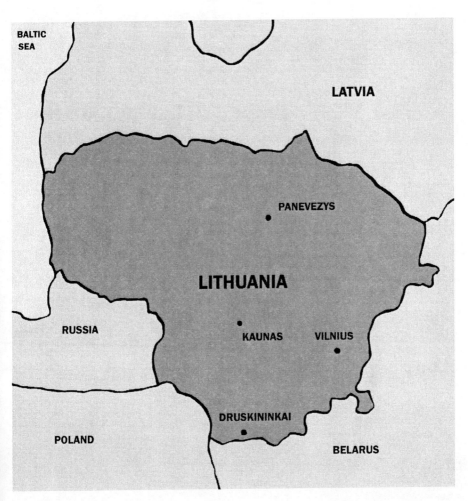

Index